PROSPERITY

by

Lynne Palmer

Prosperity

ISBN 0-9709498-0-4

Library of Congress Catalogue Number 2001 126031

Published by:

Lynne Palmer
Toll Free: 1-800-615-3352
Web Site: www.lynnepalmer.com
Email: lynnepalmer@lynnepalmer.com

Cover Design by Marcia Snow

Printed and bound in the United States of America

Books by Lynne Palmer

Astrological Almanac (Annual)

Money Magic

Gambling to Win

Your Lucky Days and Numbers

Is Your Name Lucky For You?

Astrological Compatibility

The Astrological Treasure Map

Astro-Guide to Nutrition and Vitamins

Are You Compatible With Your Boss, Partner,
Coworker, Clients, Employees?

ABC Basic Chart Reading

Do-It-Yourself Publicity Directory

ABC Chart Erection

Nixon's Horoscope

Horoscope of Billy Rose

ABC Major Progressions

Pluto Ephermeris (1900-2000)

Contents

INTRODUCTION

Astrology and Prosperity

If you are new to astrology, perhaps, you are not aware that astrological knowledge can be used as a guide to make money, get rich as well as let you know how to handle your money and how to improve your bank account. Also, astrology can be used with investments.

Just how does astrology work? What is a horoscope? What is a Sun sign? There are twelve zodiacal signs and ten planets (including the Sun and Moon, which are luminaries, but to simplify everything I will call them planets) in a horoscope. Each sign and planet represents a physical zone of the body, color, flower, gem, stone, mineral, product, profession, musical note, type of investment, material object, habitual method of thinking and behaving, and corresponds to a number and letter of the alphabet.

Your horoscope is based upon the day, month, year, time and place of your birth. There are eight planets — Mercury, Venus, Mars, Jupiter, Saturn, Uranus, Neptune, and Pluto — in our solar system as we know it. These planets, as they appear to us up in the sky, are located in one or more of the twelve signs of the zodiac, which are situated in the various constellations.

Each of these ten planets — eight planets and two luminaries — will occupy a zodiac sign. Thus you have many different signs of the zodiac in your horoscope. Your Sun sign is the sign that the Sun is in at the exact moment you were born.

There are twelve houses in a horoscope; each one represents a different department of life. The ten planets and twelve signs fall into these areas and indicate your basic characteristics depending upon the aspects (distances between two planets which may be harmonious, discordant or neutral — depending upon how many degrees these two planets are apart as to their harmony, discord or neutrality) formed by the planets.

Once a horoscope has been cast, you must also consider your Rising sign (also called Ascendant). As the earth turns on its axis, a particular sign appears to rise on the horizon at the exact hour, minute and second you were born — it is "rising" or "ascending" in view on the horizon. You may be more like your Rising sign than your Sun sign if the Rising sign is *dominant* in your horoscope — that is, if it makes many close aspects to the Sun, Moon and/or planets as they appear in your horoscope (chart) at the time you were born.

Each sign and planet radiates a particular kind of energy which corresponds to its own nature; this energy is expressed on either the positive, negative or neutral side. If the aspect is harmonious, the planets involved in the aspect are expressed on the harmonious side. If the aspect is discordant, the planets involved in the aspect are expressed discordantly (although you can alter that by changing your attitude and the way you react to the planets' discordant side). If the aspect is neutral, the planets involved in the aspect are expressed in a neutral manner — you can choose your expression of it much better than if it was harmonious or discordant.

It is all up to you, as to how you express these astrological energies that are part of your nature. You have an inner power that, when applied, allows you to control your outer environment. This inner power is represented by your Sun and/or *dominant* sign when used on the positive side. Good fortune is attracted when you use the harmonious side of the planets involved in the aspect. Thus you are inclined to attract happiness, success and financial gain — even riches.

If this inner power, which is represented by your Sun and/or *dominant* sign, is used on the negative side, misfortune, problems, losses, difficulties or poverty could be attracted. But it is up to you to tell yourself that you need to do some positive thinking and follow through with positive action. Keep in mind that *THOUGHTS PRODUCE THINGS.* Your horoscope is your attitude toward everything in life. So a change of attitude is often needed.

Most people do not change their habitual mode of thinking or behaving; thus, it's easy to determine how the abilities required to give financial success are favored or hindered according to a particular individual's horoscope. Why is one person rich and another poor? Why does an individual that was born poor suddenly go from rags to riches? This person used to his/her advantage the harmonious aspects and changed the discordant ones by being positive and ambitious and not letting anything get him/her down. However, everyone has free will which can be used to mitigate, channel, or alter these discordant habit patterns present from birth. To form a new habit one must continually persist with the new one and not go back to the old way of doing things or thinking. Remember, "Persistence is the *key* to Success."

Thus, *PROSPERITY* involves getting rid of negativity, adding in positive action and thoughts, using what I call "Magical Thinking" and "Magical Devices" which can speed up your chances to be wealthy. Plus, if you gamble, some hot tips to win can be helpful — an aid to attract lots of money. And that's what *PROSPERITY* is all about. Good luck! Let me hear from you when you've made your first million!

PART ONE

CHAPTER ONE

Prosperity and Success

What does prosperity mean to you? Is it the money you've accumulated in the bank? Or is it, perhaps, being retired and living on a fixed income? Is it because you own a mansion? Or you drive a Mercedes Benz? Is it because you live the lifestyle of the rich and famous? Is it the position you hold in life or the people you know? According to Webster's dictionary, "Prosperity is the state of being prosperous; success in any enterprise; good fortune."

What is success? Everyone has a different concept of what success is: Many view it as fame, others as wealth. Success can only truly be measured by each individual. There are varying degrees or levels of being rich. If you tell a person who doesn't have much that he/she is going to receive five thousand dollars, he/she believes that will make him/her affluent, whereas an individual in the middle-income bracket thinks that five hundred thousand dollars denotes wealth; and a genuine rich man/woman thinks in terms of billions. The investment bank firm, Goldman Sachs, has a new definition of true richness: a person who has accumulate two hundred and fifty million dollars. According to the trade paper *Investment News*, "In view of the markets in the past few years and the level of wealth in this country, two hundred and fifty million dollars seems more appropriate." There are more millionaires in the United States now, not only due to their stock market income, but also due to the many who win in casinos or the lottery and sweepstakes winners as well as gifted athletes.

There are also different degrees or levels of success: a ditch-digger believes success comes with being promoted to foreman; a secretary in a secretarial pool thinks it is reached when she becomes an executive secretary; another person believes he's made it when he owns a business; a housewife thinks it happens when she's raised her children properly and that they are all doing well.

An Aquarian client, Victoria E., once said, "Success means I don't have to "yes" someone on a job if I don't want to. I am free to do and say as I please. If I don't like a person, I don't have to work with that individual."

I know young people who consider themselves prosperous because they live off of welfare and don't have to work. Or what about the man who gets fired and believes it's his good fortune because the unemployment checks will take care of his living needs so he can attend classes without having to report to a daily job. The schooling will further his career potential when he returns to the job market, and so he considers himself successful because he's got what he wants for that moment.

Many people are rich in their achievements, whether due to an avocation or vocation, or because of their love for a spouse, child, or humanity. Thus, to be rich does not mean one has to have money. But it does help if one desires a life of ease and comfort.

THE IMPORTANCE OF MONEY

While prosperity means different things to different people, few can deny the important role money plays — on some level — in our daily lives.

Money — money — money — to get, spend, and keep from childhood we've heard the word expressed time and again. A parent earned money through work, spent it on the essentials (food, clothing, shelter); an allowance was given which was either blown away or saved. By adulthood one has established a pattern with either saving or spending. One person's habits are different from another's due to early conditioning from the family and environment, and because of the Sun sign or individual's horoscope. Money wants and needs vary from person to person. Everyone wants to live in his/her own style.

When I was in my late teens I took a trip with friends to Mexico. We hired a chauffeur-guide to drive us from Oaxaca to Veracruz. En route we passed many poverty sections where people lived in grass shacks on the hills. Smoke was coming through the grass shacks rooftops and the guide explained that the dwellers were cooking. I was shocked to know that human beings could live in such squalid conditions, especially at that time. I mentioned this to the guide and he answered, "Movies, books, magazines, and other things we take for granted in modern civilization have not yet reached these primitive areas. They don't know anything else exists; thus, they have nothing to compare their lifestyle with."

I thought about what he said and realized he spoke the truth. If you've never seen something, or don't know of its existence, you don't know what you are missing; thus, you are content to remain the same. However, from the beginning of time, there have been those who were curious, restless, and adventuresome; they took to the road, saw the sights, tasted the fruits, and desired more — once the pleasure of life was experienced, they yearned for more, ran from poverty and toward wealth. They are know as the trail-breakers and are usually found under the sign Aries, Gemini, Leo, Sagittarius, or Aquarius. However, a Taurus, Scorpio, or Capricorn will also depart for greener pastures if he/she becomes discontent with existing conditions. Such is the case of Ari Onassis, a Capricorn, who went from rags to riches. He began with a street-type-cigar business to become a shipping tycoon worth billions when he died.

Do you sacrifice everything to have a nest egg and future wealth? If so, Capricorn or the planet Saturn is *dominant* in your horoscope. Those who have Aries, Taurus, Leo, Virgo, Scorpio, the Sun, Saturn or Pluto *dominant* in their horoscopes may fall into this category. However, Aries and Leo may have difficulty saving their money because they are inclined to be spendthrifts. But if the drive to be on top is strong enough, they'll make sacrifices.

There are other people who simply work to make money, pay the bills, and live on a day-to-day basis. A single gal may bide her time until she marries and can leave the job field. A married woman may only be working to pay some of the household expenses; perhaps , she's anxiously waiting for her husband to say, "Quit the job and stay home." But there are other women who are driven toward a career and, regardless of what her spouse says, she's going to go to work and be successful. There are men who have quit their job, so they can stay home and baby sit, clean the house and cook while their wife brings home a hefty paycheck.

A person may not be interested in a career; he/she may prefer drifting through life and devoting his/her spare moments to outside interests. As long as he/she can get by with some menial job he's/she's content. Or a man may not be enthusiastic about his vocation but, because he has a family, he does his best to work, pay the rent and other bills, and save a little money — but can't wait until he's old enough to retire and live off his retirement income. (Note: all the preceding male/female types could have Cancer, Libra, Pisces, the Moon, Venus or Neptune *dominant* in their horoscopes.

In my opinion it's impossible to live a truly happy, complete, productive or successful life unless you have money. By having material possessions you impress others, move up the ladder, and feel safe and secure. You can enjoy the pleasures of life without worry. It is certainly true that "money attracts money," especially when the rich marry their own kind, or when those who have inherited wealth invest it wisely or open a business and soon amass even more dough.

Then there are those who will argue that it's not spiritual to want money or personal possessions. I have heard this statement from those who were born rich or poor.

John L., an Aries Sun sign, was in advertising and a successful account executive, materially he didn't lack anything. Suddenly, John got "in" with a group of people who were involved in mystical realms. He told me that he was going to quit his job, give up everything he had worked for, and move to the country to read New Age books. John said, "The mundane world is a sham and the real world is that of being in tune with self and nature."

I tried to persuade him not to be foolish, because John could stay on the job, be involved in humanitarian endeavors, and do the same thing (read New Age books) without creating an adverse financial condition (which I saw, when I looked at his horoscope, was going to occur within a year). But he wouldn't listen; two years later John was back and in a bad state. His clothes that once were immaculate were now shabby. He had spent almost all of his savings, and soon would be broke. However, he had finally awakened to reality and was beginning to see the light — that the mundane world was a necessity and not so bad after all.

I knew when John first came for his horoscope reading that he would not listen to reason; he had to learn the hard way — and that he did. I tried to explain to him that it is spiritual to love money as long as you keep it in circulation. When you go to a store and purchase clothing you are keeping that shop owner in business, so he is able to support himself and his family. When you buy food at the corner market or a supermarket, you are helping those who produce the food (farmers, big business), truck drivers (who bring the food to the stores), and those who work in the corner market or supermarket. It is when you hoard money that you are being unspiritual. When you give to charity, a cause, a street person, or any humanitarian endeavor you are being spiritual. When you become a recluse and tune in only to yourself you are being unspiritual — that's being selfish. To be spiritual you do your utmost to help mankind. By the time of John's second visit, he understood the full meaning of my words.

You have read or heard cases where a rich man or woman is found living in poverty with bundles of money hidden underneath the mattress. Those who do this are insecure, distrust banks, and fear poverty but, oddly enough, end their days living in poverty! In astrology such behavior is denoted by the sign Capricorn and/ or the planet Saturn when either one is *dominant* in the horoscope.

I once had a Pisces friend, Florence S., who had Capricorn and Saturn *dominant* in her horoscope. Florence was wealthy, but lived cheaply. She didn't have a refrigerator (she was seventy years old) until I talked her into going with me and buying one. She ate like a bird when she was home, but would eat heartily when someone took her out. Her clothes had holes in them. Florence was a kind and happy person in spite of her lifestyle. She was always there to help others through free tarot card readings or astrology lessons which she gave in her small one room apartment.

Florence had planned to live until she was a hundred years old; thus, she was being careful with her money so it would last that long. Florence died when she was in her late eighties, and her money was spent quickly by the relatives who inherited it. When she was alive Florence denied herself everything and worried constantly about every penny spent. She said she was content and wanted nothing. But was that attitude real, or was it a facade? It was probably real. She was into occultism (New Age books) and was very spiritual — she was not mean and never hurt a soul. It just goes to show you that every individual thinks of money differently and while to some it's important, to others it's not.

THE POT OF GOLD AT THE END OF THE RAINBOW

The majority of people dream about accumulating a fortune, but most people believe it's an impossibility. Thus they continue to wallow in their fantasy worlds. But then there's that other individual who makes his/her dreams come true by taking action in the direction of desired goals. The shiftless person says, "I really don't want money because I know I'll never get it," which of course becomes a reality. The doer says, "I want money and I know I am going to get it and be rich," and once he/she puts his/her wheels in motion, the results are exactly as he/she knew they'd be.

The old adage "birds of a feather flock together" is worth keeping in mind when money is desired. Associate with people who are well-to-do and it rubs off. Listening to their conversations about big money deals will give you ideas and keep your mind tuned to large sums; thus, you'll attract increases of those green-backs which could accumulate as you become rich. If you associate with people who are poor you will subconsciously tune in to their wave-length, thus making it difficult to attract money. This is even more noticeable if the individuals in question are negative and complain constantly about their lack of funds, debts, and other problems.

Lack of opportunities can cause wealth to be repressed, and is sometimes experienced in a small town or rural district. Those who have get-up-and-go will hold down several menial jobs and save enough money to head for the big city. Those who are inert get stuck in a rut, rarely move, and gripe; and even if they did move, they would continue to find something to complain about. Progress is change; sometimes to get really into the swing of things, it's best to let go of the old — the past — and look to the new — the future. If you don't, how will you ever find that pot of gold at the end of the rainbow?

Another way to gain those riches you've always dreamed about is to go into business for yourself. However, if you don't plan carefully, financial disasters could occur. When opening a new business the one mistake people make more than any other is not having enough capital to cover possible losses that usually occur in the beginning. You should have at least six months rent and necessary expenditures and be ready for delays, hardships, and sacrifices during slow periods. Also, the location of the business is important.

The other mistake which results in business losses is expanding when the profits are coming in; that's the time you should reap the rewards of your labor, invest the profits in municipal bonds, treasury notes, annuities, bank certificates of deposit, or some sure thing, and later expand. I am sure you all know of a small restaurant that did a terrific business. But when the owner expanded, or moved to larger quarters, the new place didn't have the same ambiance as the older restaurant and it soon had a "Closed — Out of Business" sign hanging on the door.

SPENDING HABITS

Everyone's spending habits are not the same; some spend money immediately on whatever they see and want, regardless of the price; usually Aries, Gemini, Leo, Libra, Scorpio, Sagittarius, Aquarius, and Pisces are the signs that fall into this category. Those who have one, or more, of these zodiac signs *dominant* (in their horoscope) are likely to lose money easily; it could be through gambling, the stock market, the race track, speculation in real estate, a get-rich-quick scheme, or blowing their paycheck on the lottery, numbers, or any game of chance. They'll spend on the "little" things such as cab rides, inexpensive items, and so on. These "little" things pile up, soon the money is gone, and they then wonder where it disappeared to! Money spent in this fashion is less noticeable than the enormous sums with which these zodiac signs can also splurge, so they usually don't realize the losses they accrue in this fashion. It's difficult for them to save and quite often they declare bankruptcy.

The slow spenders, those who care about the price they pay, are Taurus, Cancer, Virgo, and Capricorn. Those who have one, or more, of these zodiac signs *dominant* (in their horoscope) are likely to spend on the necessities; remaining sums will be invested in something substantial where there's little or no risk. These people are "tight" and usually make and keep a fortune. It's easy for them to save and they rarely go bankrupt.

Jack Benny, an Aquarian, was famous for portraying a thrifty character while performing on radio, television, or the stage. However, the late comedian, Joe E. Lewis, a Capricorn Sun sign and a friend of Jack's, told me, "Benny was a big spender. He was a fellow-Friar (a club) and always tipped the waiters well, helped his friends in need, and donated to charitable causes."

At the opposite extreme was billionaire Howard Hughes, a Capricorn Sun sign, and Virgo Rising (Ascendant) sign (both practical signs). Joe E. Lewis, in another true story, said, "Howard never carried a penny on him. He was a cheap-skate with almost everyone, but he liked me, so treated me fairly. Once at a plush restaurant in Miami Beach I was sitting with my friends at the bar sipping cock-tails when the maitre'd came over and asked, 'See that man over there?' I glanced at the shabbily dressed man standing at the entrance and nodded while the maitre'd continued, 'He claims to be Howard Hughes. But he's improperly dressed, doesn't have a tie, and it's against the rules to let him in. He asked if you were here be-cause, if you were, you could identify him.' I told the maitre'd to loan Howard a time and let him in.

"Soon Howard joined me at the bar. Several rounds of drinks passed and everyone bought him a drink, but he was too cheap to return the favors, except with me. Finally he was getting ready to leave and asked me to loan him some money for cab fare. So I did, as I had done on previous occasions, and, as usual, the money was never repaid. You see he never carried money on him. Usually restaurants sent him a bill."

MONEY AND BUSINESS

There are many conflicts people have regarding money. One is that of choos-ing between making money and paying high taxes or not making much and paying a minimal amount of taxes. Another conflict is that of choosing between going into debt by purchasing a home and mortgage, or by taking out a business loan. Either way money is going to be owed. It's more practical to go into business, purchase equipment, office furniture, and make steady money rather than to buy a house and decorate and furnish it. The home won't bring any bucks into a bank account until it's sold, whereas the profits made from a business could be used to buy a house and other material possessions.

When beginning a business, sacrifice is usually a necessity, especially for those who make it big. That means one has to spend less on books, food, clothes, hobbies, games, sports, movies, dinner, entertainment, and so on. But in the long run it pays off. Those signs that can make sacrifices easiest are Taurus, Virgo, Capricorn or anyone with the planet Saturn *dominant* in a horoscope.

It's important to understand the limitations of money; if you can't have everything, buy what you need, not what you want. An Aries, Gemini, Leo, Libra, Scorpio, Sagittarius, Aquarius, or Pisces usually buys what he/she wants first — his/her needs are secondary. A Taurus, Virgo, or Capricorn buys what he/she needs; his/her wants are secondary. If the planet Jupiter is *dominant* in one's horoscope, that individual buys what he/she wants first; if Saturn is *dominant* in one's horoscope, that person buys what he/she needs first.

If you have a savings account, you'll attract more money to you. Once you start to withdraw your savings, it's harder to build it back up. The withdrawal is ruled by Saturn; the planet of decrease and worry. When people get into a bind and do this, they start to worry and thus attract negative financial conditions. Most people know this, consciously or unconsciously, and that is why the majority will state, "I hate to touch my savings." By the way Jupiter is the planet of increase, thus, when you leave the money in the bank and continue to increase your savings account — you can wind up with a bundle — Jupiter is also the planet of wealth, and positive financial conditions.

If you have an idea to make money, don't wait until you have a large sum to invest before you do anything; start small and gradually expand. If you wait for big money, the day may never come and your idea will be all for naught. Excuses will be invented time and again why you couldn't get started; but if you really wanted to, nothing would stand in your way. There are various avenues to approach such as funding agencies, government agencies, lending institutions, and so forth; it's even possible you might have to start working from your home baking goods so you have enough money to open a bakery. Or you may have to start with a hot dog stand just to make enough money to open a restaurant or machinery shop. As your profits increase, you will gradually see your way clear to opening that restaurant or machinery shop by either selling the hot dog stand, or possibly keeping it as a sideline. Don't laugh! Hot dog stands make money!

I knew a Taurus man in Los Angeles, California who started with a small hot dog and hamburger stand on a corner in a neighborhood that was mostly residential, with only a few shops and stores nearby. Within a few years, Sam G. was well on his way to being rich. Ten years later I returned to the area for a visit and dropped by to see Sam. He wasn't there, but the employees told me he had amassed a fortune. However, Sam would not sell this stand because he felt it was responsible for his wealth and was lucky for him. It wasn't only his product, but Sam's location, hard work and personality that made him reach the pinnacle of success.

Those who start from scratch and became millionaires possess certain personality traits that are consistently demonstrated. They are outgoing, confident, can see the other person's view, and can sell anyone anything (these are all traits ruled by the planet Jupiter and/or the zodiac sign Sagittarius) — and they don't take no for an answer. They will persist relentlessly (when Saturn is also *dominant* and/or the zodiac signs Taurus, Cancer, Leo, Scorpio, Capricorn, or Aquarius *dominant* in their horoscopes) until they get what they want.

Friends are easily made as they climb to the top, through relentless optimism, enthusiasm, positive thinking and being aggressively cheerful, friendly and charming. They have charisma, a wonderful smile and sense of humor, a firm handshake and remember someone's name and are interested in other people's hobbies — no wonder they can sell anyone anything! They know how to uplift and encourage others with enlightening words. Through expressing the preceding traits, they get "in" with others and wind up with deals in their favor. They do not spend a lot of money, mentally or physically, before it is received. If they did, it would block the flow of dough; when those greenbacks arrive, it most often is needed to meet an emergency.

When you mentally spend money before it comes in, usually the cash that does come in goes for a necessity. Or when you physically spend dough on some lark thinking, "Oh, when I wind up this deal I will have the money I need to pay off the credit card," — that's when a deal may go sour. For example, Amy T. is a Pisces Sun sign who sells real estate. Her commission for a sale had not yet arrived and Amy was impatient. She planned to take the dough from the sale and go to Puerto Rico for a fun trip. Everyday Amy daydreamed about the fun she's having spending that money in Puerto Rico. But she didn't get the chance to use her bucks the way she had planned: her brother was in an accident and had neither money nor hospitalization insurance or health policy, so she had to lend him the dough she made on her commission. Amy's horoscope indicated that this dreaming of, and spending greenbacks, before she receive it was a pattern — as she said, "It's the story of my life."

People who criticize wealth are those who are poor; they are afraid they'll never have it and, with that type of thinking, they won't! Then there are those who idolize the rich and want to emulate them. This type of person has a good chance to be affluent if he/she pursues his/her goals and works hard.

There are many different formulas, systems, and ways to gain prosperity; each individual is unique and must find his/her own way. Some will use magic (see my chapters Magical Devices and Magical Thoughts in this book), and then there are those who pray, count their blessings daily, and praise everyone they contact, know, and don't know, as well as God or a Supreme Being. Others are lucky with investments, or with a sweepstakes contest, the lottery or a big bundle in a casino, whereas, many will become successful by pursuing their dreams. Thoughts Produce Things, therefore act, believe and think RICH. Know wealth can be yours. Mingle with those who are affluent, dress well, work hard, and be persistent. Persistence is the number one *key* to prosperity and success!

CHAPTER TWO

Investments

There are many ways to get rich quickly. Investments can bring sudden wealth; although, some have slow returns. You've read or heard about those who have made a "killing" in futures — the commodities market which is like gambling in something that could make you wealthy overnight. You probably know someone who is lucky in the stock market. When the money you invest turns into a fortune, it's a form of magic that you never want to end. Each sign of the zodiac represents different types of investments; thus, anyone has a chance to be wealthy.

"Never put all of your eggs in one basket" is something I can remember hearing all of my life. "Diversify" is what the investors cry. They believe you shouldn't put more than ten percent of the assets of your total net worth in any single investment medium.

Today there are so many investment areas that some people get confused trying to select the right one. I have noticed that people under different zodiac signs lean in different directions. For example: Aries likes short-term notes, treasury bills, municipal bonds, and no-load mutual funds; Taurus likes land (with or without structures), stocks, Eurodollars, all types of long-term bonds, collectors plates, coins, tapestries, art or antique jewelry; Gemini likes rare books and stamps; Cancer likes Series E bonds, silver, vending machines, commodities and real estate that has buildings (preferably a home) on the property; Leo likes gold and all kinds of bonds; Virgo likes land, stamps and long-term bonds; Libra likes art, jewelry, tapestry, and rare coins and Eurodollars; Scorpio likes guns, stamps, coins, plates or other treasures, mutual funds, letters of credit, mortgage investment trusts, and all kinds of bonds; Sagittarius likes short-term bonds and certificates of deposit, and will speculate with stocks; Capricorn likes mines, ores, stones, rare coins, second trust deeds, mutual funds that involve real estate, and land with or without buildings; Aquarius likes rare coins, antiques, antiquities, and short-term bonds; Pisces likes oil and gas leases, the stock market, or anything that will make a fast buck.

The Fixed zodiacal signs (Taurus, Leo, Scorpio, and Aquarius) hold on to their investments as if they were guarding Fort Knox. They become attached to everything they own; it's as if they were obsessed. The more they get, the more they want. They only sell when a profit is guaranteed.

Cancer is tenacious; like a crab, he/she won't let go of anything that gives security, and also will hold on to an investment for sentimental reasons. A Cancerian has hunches and sells if impressed to do so.

Pisces clings to an investment and worries that something dreadful will happen and result in a loss. However, if he/she listens to that psychic inner voice saying, "Now is the time to sell," the Piscean will be ahead of the game. But Pisces has to be careful not to believe or listen to the wrong people or go out on a limb by getting rid of stock at the wrong time.

Capricorn is so security conscious that he/she patiently sits on an investment, waiting for it to mature, rise in value, and become a real winner. Some call him/her greedy, others say the Capricorn is shrewd and excellent in business. All of these are true, but we can all learn from a Capricorn; he's/she's the one zodiac sign, more than any other, that never gives up even if it takes a lifetime to get what he/she wants.

A Virgo holds on to an investment only for as long as he/she deems it necessary. Facts and figures are gathered, studied, and analyzed, after which, like a chess player, the Virgo makes a slow, deliberate move. A Virgo's judgment is excellent and seldom does a loss occur.

Libra won't hesitate to get rid of an investment if a pal gives the go-ahead signal, or if quick money is needed to pay for some personal luxury. Thus losses are easily attracted through the poor judgment of others or by living too high on the hog. Libra can gain once the balance he/she seeks is attained.

Aries, Gemini, and Sagittarius leap in and out of investments so fast, they never know what they own from one moment to another. Wild chances are taken, the higher the risk, the greater the reward — so they think — until they lose. But that doesn't faze them; they are already on their way into the next exciting money-making scheme.

A Sagittarian easily attracts money, and must be careful of spending it foolishly. He/She must learn how to keep the money he/she has and accumulate wealth through wise investments. Many society and affluent people who don't work have a motto "Never touch the principal but spend, and live off, the interest of your investments."

The capital you have today should grow toward more income, or toward future education, travel, leisure, or retirement. To achieve your goal it must be continually working.

Taurus, Virgo, and Capricorn want the money to grow for more income, and education; Gemini, Libra, and Aquarius for leisure, travel and education; Aries, Leo, and Sagittarius for travel and leisure; Cancer, Scorpio, and Pisces for more income, leisure, and retirement.

OPM — OTHER PEOPLE'S MONEY

There are many ways to borrow money: bank, small business, minority, or veterans loans; finance companies; government funds; or by advertising in magazines and newspapers to attract investors. Business loans are not easily granted by banks; however, vacation loans are.

A Gemini client, Jack F., went to six different banks (not branches of the same bank) on the same day and applied for a five-thousand dollar vacation loan from each bank. Evidently the banks didn't check on one another; five of the banks approved the loans and Jack took the twenty-five dollars and invested it in some stock. The following week he sold that stock, repeated this procedure, and made a nice profit which enabled him to invest in short-term treasury bills, etc. A year later Jack was rich — all on other people's money (stemming from the original bank loans)!

Not everyone has the nerve to follow Jack's footsteps; a Sagittarian is too honest to deceive anyone, Cancer's too timid, and Virgo would rather work the hard way for it. However, Gemini (Jack's Sun sign), Aries, Taurus, Leo, Libra, Scorpio, Capricorn, Aquarius, and Pisces are clever enough to pull it off and reason that the bank does not care what anyone does with the money once the loan has been granted. The bank is only interested in getting paid back; thus, they really don't care whether or not you took your expensive vacation.

If you own a company and want to expand, sell stock in your corporation on the open or private market. The zodiacal signs that will do this the least is Scorpio and Capricorn; they like to be in control and own it all. If it's the only way for them to go into big business which they crave, they'll reconsider, but later will buy out all of the partners or shareholders. J. Paul Getty, Sr. did that with Getty Oil (he was Capricorn rising (Ascendant). Howard Hughes, a Capricorn, is a perfect example of sole ownership; while alive he refused to have partners. Another great example is Diane Von Furstenberg, a Capricorn, who bought out her partners and became chairman and the sole owner of Diane Von Furstenberg, Ltd., which was at that time a one hundred and fifty million dollar empire.

FRANCHISES

A franchise may be just the type of investment you're looking for. However, before you invest your money, it's advisable to carefully study the company's history and finances. Visit several of their other establishments that are in business, and make sure you analyze the contract by going over it with an accountant and an attorney.

If you own a small, unique and successful business, perhaps you'd want to package your method of operation, logo, and so on, and sell franchises on it. By so doing you could make yourself quite a bundle and become rich, if it's handled properly. There are special companies who package and sell franchises for a percentage, or agent's fee. Or you can advertise in magazines that cater to people interested in income opportunities. Capricornian, Conrad Hilton, became a multi-millionaire with his chain of Hilton Hotels. Libran, body builder, Jack La Lanne, was the founder of exercise salons which paid off handsomely — in the millions — for him. Since then, exercise salons are all over the world even in airports. Jack La Lanne had an idea and went for it — the act of a true entrepreneur.

OIL AND GAS LEASES

Gas and oil leases are a government sponsored program: The United States Department of the Interior (Bureau of Land Management) holds non-competitive public drawings each month for citizens over twenty-one years of age. This is, therefore, an equal opportunity to obtain oil and gas lease rights on lands owned by the federal government. These leases can then be sold to oil companies.

Gas and oil (petroleum) are ruled by the planet Neptune which, also, is the planet which governs the sign Pisces. Thus a Piscean finds gas and oil are attractive for investment purposes. However, it is risky (Pisces is a risk-taker) and could prove disappointing. Barbara L., a Piscean client, thought she was going to make a "killing" but has been unable to sell her lease to an oil company. However, another Pisces client, Jake T., made a good profit on his investment when he sold his lease to an oil company for a high price.

REAL ESTATE

The majority of people (especially the Earth signs — Taurus, Virgo, Capricorn) feel secure when they own land; they believe it will always be valuable. Yet every day there are many individuals who buy property and end up selling it at a loss. Why? If they are in a hurry an Aries, Gemini, Leo, Libra, Sagittarius, and Aquarius will get rid of something fast. They couldn't care less if a profit isn't made. These signs like freedom and really don't enjoy being tied down to a structure on a piece of land, unless it can be rented. Often, in cases of a death or divorce, the partner/mate wants to forget the memories associated with the place and, thus, will hastily jump on the first offer made.

Janet W., a Sagittarian client, divorced her husband, and sold her house against my advice. She didn't get what it was worth and two years later regretfully said, "I really should have listened to you. Now I am having all sorts of financial difficulties and could have used that profit. The house sold for what was owed on the mortgage! And I did not see a cent, not even to pay the movers! But I was anxious to get out of there and start a new life — well, I must say, I certainly did!"

A Scorpio friend, Grace M., years ago purchased farm land in northern California. She was a real estate agent and was "in" on things that were not generally known by the public. Grace is paid by the government not to farm her land because it would be competitive to the established commercial farmers in that area. Thus, Grace has land that is working for her and she does not have to do anything except deposit the government check in the bank when it arrives!

Joanna B., a Capricorn client, works for a realty firm and has made millions buying property no one else wanted. She hunts for bargains (typical of Capricorn). Joanna goes to probate court and foreclosure sales and often buys at a low price buildings that are old and rundown. She renovates them (a Capricorn trait), installs the latest kitchen equipment, and makes them so eye appealing that Joanna gets the high rent she asks for. The property appreciates in value, while she bides her time (typical of Capricorn) and then sells it for a huge profit.

A Taurus client, Mike S., worked as a common laborer for years. He deprived himself of everything, except necessities, and was able to save twenty thousand dollars in cash. He used this money as a down payment on a hundred thousand dollar property. When Mike bought the property, the annual rate of appreciation was such that his property in three years would be worth one hundred and twenty thousand dollars, which meant that Mike would make a twenty thousand dollar profit (on paper).

To convert that paper into ready money, Mike took out a second loan for the one hundred and twenty thousand dollars that it would be worth, paid off his first loan, and used the remaining twenty thousand dollars to reinvest in another piece of property. Mike still owned the first piece of property which he could sell, if he so desired. However, he was collecting rent from tenants, which paid for the monthly payments on the second loan.

He then invested in other apartment buildings and now owns a chain of them. It just goes to show what you can do if you have a dream and are persistent. Yes, he made sacrifices, but he was shrewd and, more important, he believed in himself!

Houses are more valuable than condominiums or co-ops. Farmland can be good, but is risky. Commercial and industrial property such as shopping centers (malls) can be good buys. Apartment buildings can be favorable, if the location is good you can rent them. Older buildings seem to be better than new ones in some locations.

You could get involved in what is called "Backer-Leaser" — you put up the money for a commercial building and then lease it back to the operator.

REIT'S — REAL ESTATE FUNDS

REIT's are Real Estate Investment Trusts, which are comparable to mutual funds but are traded on the stock market. They are known as Equity Trusts. The trusts typically pay out all their income in dividends after deducting a 1% management fee.

These funds are partnerships that invest in pools of income-producing property. The partnerships are free to sell and realize gains on properties that have appreciated in value. The REIT's are ongoing entities that in general are supposed to hold properties indefinitely. The REIT's shares are liquid, while an investor in a partnership may have difficulty in selling out. Investors in the fund have trouble figuring out what they are worth. Real Estate companies are the general partners. They select the properties to be acquired and arrange for their management. As the real estate companies assemble properties, they either assume the existing mortgages on the buildings or obtain new financing. REIT's are traded over-the-counter by different developers who build commercial property such as office buildings, skyscrapers, etc.

PROPERTY SYNDICATES: For a minimum investment (often $5,000, but occasionally $2,500), you can become a limited partner in a multi-million dollar real estate portfolio, whose holdings may include apartments, office buildings, hotels, shopping centers). They provide tax benefits that are not available from corporations. They usually show losses while being built-constructed (investors can deduct the losses from their taxable income) and are not charged for these losses. Investors may receive a tax sheltered cash distribution from a property syndicate in the very same year that losses are being written off. When the project is eventually liquidated (say in 20 years), you will owe tax on the difference between your investments and the final sales price plus the total tax deductions and cash distributions you have received.

SECOND TRUST DEEDS

Many people, or firms, banks and other institutions, invest their money in second trust deeds at mortgage companies. When a person owning the property can't make the monthly payments on a mortgage, the individual or institution who owns the second trust deed will foreclose, take the property, and sell it at a good price.

A second trust deed is equivalent to a second mortgage, providing a homeowner with a method of borrowing extra money on his house at high interest. The investor who buys the second deed gets high earnings, but at some risk, because the holder of the original deed, or mortgage has first claim on the property if the homeowner defaults.

Usually the person who has taken out a second trust deed is doing so because he/she is financing spending rather than an investment. If this individual suddenly becomes unemployed, the likelihood of default on the second trust deed has increased substantially.

When I first started studying astrology, I was employed as the head cashier of a mortgage company and handled the homeowners' payments. I was astounded at how much money the investors (banks, private individuals, and insurance companies) made on these second trust deeds.

Since that time I have had many clients who purchased second trust deeds; one man, a Capricorn, did very well with them. Scorpios and Capricorns are attracted to this form of investment more than the other zodiacal signs.

GNMA — GINNIE MAE

These offer investors a share in a pool of residential mortgages guaranteed by the government. The Government National Mortgage Association puts its backing behind certificates sold to investors by securities dealers to raise funds for mortgage lenders such as banks and savings and loan companies. They offer just about the highest yield of any government security. Ginnie Mae's are known as "pass throughs" because the homeowners principal and interest payments are "passed through" to the investor. The minimum purchase is $25,000 on a regular GMA, but the *Unit Trusts* make it possible for investors to get in for as little as $1,000.

CONVERTIBLE SUBORDINATE NOTES

They are backed by a second mortgage. They are the second certificate in line to be paid back. They can be converted into stocks or bonds at a set price. First Mortgage Bonds get paid off first — they are Senior bonds. Convertible Subordinate Notes are Junior security.

CONVENTIONAL MORTGAGE
PASS-THROUGH CERTIFICATES

Pass-throughs originated as a way for mortgage lenders, such as banks and thrift institutions, to generate cash by bundling together residential mortgages into pools and selling them. The issuers are able to replace the assets sold with new mortgages — often at higher rates — written with the proceeds from the sale. Minimum price is $25,000. There is no government guarantee on them. They yield a lot — usually 20 percentage points. The originator of the mortgage passes through to the investor monthly payments of principal and interest, as well as any prepayments that are received on mortgages in the pool. They are calculated on a 12 year life yield. If someone prepays the bank the money on their mortgage then when the investor received his/her monthly check the amount is increased. The investor can also profit from foreclosure. These are not very liquid and, thus, are hard to get rid of.

FEDERAL HOME LOAN MORTGAGE CORPORATION

These are also know as Freddy Mac which is a Federal Agency concerned with supporting the mortgage market (it's like Ginnie Mae). Mortgages are packaged into negotiable, bond-like instruments and sold to institutional investors, such as pension funds — "pass-through" securities and are marketed through *Ginnie Mae* and *Freddy Mac.*

MUNICIPAL BONDS

The interest paid on Municipal Bonds is exempt from Federal Income Taxes. Often, interest is also exempt from state income taxes. They are favored by those in a high income tax bracket. Because there are Municipal Bond issues with maturity dates ranging from one month to 50 years, the investor can choose the exact date on which he/she wants the capital returned. In spite of the fact that there may be interim fluctuations in its market price, the full face value of the bond is payable when it reaches maturity. However, when a city has fiscal problems and bad publicity, fear of the city defaulting keeps many would-be investors out of municipal bonds.

According to the investment firm, *Merrill Lynch,* "Municipal bonds are issued by cities, towns, villages, states, territories, and possessions of the United States, and other political subdivisions responsible for providing and maintaining such community facilities as schools, hospitals, power plants, bridges and tunnels, streets and highways, parking areas, dams, waterworks, and sewerage systems."

The attractive feature of municipal bonds is that the interest paid on them is exempt from federal income tax (IRS). The maturity dates on the bonds may range from less than one year to fifty; you can select the ones desirable for your needs.

The various kinds of Municipal Bonds are: General Obligation Bonds, Revenue Bonds, Industrial Revenue Bonds, Moral Obligation Bonds, Hospital Revenue Bonds, Trans Bonds, Special Tax Bonds, New Housing Authority Bonds. *General Obligation Bonds:* The income from them comes from whatever property tax is paid where you live (city). They are tax exempt. *Revenue Bonds:* Those issues secured by the revenues of a particular department of the municipality or of a special authority created to operate a project engineered to be self-supporting.

The authority could be: water, sewer, gas and electrical facilities, hospital facilities, housing, municipal garages and playgrounds, port facilities, ferry systems, bridges, toll roads.

Industrial Revenue Bonds: Bonds issued by cities on behalf of corporations, usually to finance pollution, control equipment. The corporation's revenues, not the city's, stand behind the bond. *Hospital Revenue Bonds:* Public and non-profit hospitals and other health care units increasingly are turning to tax exempt bonds to raise funds for their long-term expansion needs. *New Housing Authority Bonds:* They are issued by local Public Housing Authorities all over the country to finance the construction of low-rent housing projects. *Moral Obligation Bonds:* These are bonds which generally are primarily secured by project revenues and also have the moral pledge of a state or municipality to make up any deficiency in the capital reserve fund of the issue in the event that revenues are insufficient to cover debt service. *Special Tax Bonds:* These bonds are not secured by the full faith and credit of the state or municipality but are payable only from some specific source of revenue, such as a single tax or series of taxes. *Trans Bonds:* They are municipal bonds that are short term for 3, 6, 9 months or one year. They are tax exempt.

MUNICIPAL NOTES

A state municipality or authority needs money for a short period of time, usually one year, it may issue short-term municipal securities as municipal notes. Although notes offer the same tax exemption and diversity of type as municipal bonds they differ in the fact that they are issued only in short maturities. Their minimum denomination is $5,000, but they are sometimes offered in minimum amounts of $25,000.

UTILITY COMPANIES BONDS

These are issued by the utility company *not* the city nor the state. They consist of gas, electricity, power plants or the telephone. They are not tax exempt.

BIG MAC

The state-created Municipal Assistance Corporation has advanced money to the city to pay off part of its short-term debt and has assumed responsibility for overseeing the city's budget. Big Mac pays high interest rates.

BIG MAC BONDS

These are city bonds that are risky.

A Taurus client, Jim W., bought long-term municipal bonds when he inherited his parents' money after they were killed when their private plane crashed in the northern mountains of California. Ten years later he was thankful for his investment; he was in an automobile crash that left him permanently disabled. He has been able to live off the monthly interest the bonds pay, as well as some other investments he was shrewd enough to make through the years.

BONDS

Short-Term Bonds: Generally considered the safest but lowest yielding. *Long-Term Bonds:* The riskiest and highest yielding. *Corporate Bonds:* An interest-bearing certificate issued by a corporation promising payment of principal at a certain time. They can be risky. They pay an attractive rate of interest on specific dates, mature at full face value on a stated future date, have good liquidity and are backed by the credit strength of America's largest corporations.

High-Yield Bond Fund: Many bonds trade at prices substantially below their face value and offer very high interest rates because the credit strength of the company is unclear, and therefore the continuing payment of interest cannot be assured. At the same time, however, these bonds can offer speculative appreciation potential if the fortunes of the company improve and the bond rises in price to reflect this better outlook. These bonds are a class of mutual fund. The strategy they employ to generate high yields — they invest the bulk of their portfolios in low-rated or even unrated corporate bonds — generally called "junk bonds." They are risky.

CONVERTIBLE BONDS

Because they pay fixed interest instead of variable dividends, yields are more predictable than those on stocks. That helps maintain a floor under prices, yet in a Bull market convertibles appreciate in line with common stocks (though rarely dollar for dollar).

BOND FUNDS

Ginnie Mae unit-investment trusts, high-yield bond funds, option-income funds — these are fixed-income funds and are designed to give the investor a high rate of current return.

STOCK AND BOND FUNDS

Some funds are aggressive, emphasize capital gains and buy only stocks, often risky ones. Such funds, "betas," which measure how widely their values fluctuate relative to the swings in the market, are usually high — indicating that they will probably move up or down more than the general market. Funds typically charge a hefty sales commission for their services — usually about 9% of investments up to $25,000, gradually less above that. In addition they charge a management fee of about 1% a year.

CORPORATE INCOME FUNDS

This is a selection of corporate bonds assembled by a brokerage house and sold at their net asset value plus commission. Unlike some other bond funds, it consists of a fixed portfolio, although some of the bonds may be sold and the money distributed among the shareholders.

Jay (a Libran) and Marie R. (a Leo) invested in a corporate income fund. They started investing in this area at the onset of their marriage and have continued to do so, besides investing in Treasury Bills. Soon they plan to retire and live off the income of these investments.

CORPORATE INCOME TRUSTS

Since these trusts are comprised of carefully selected high quality corporate bonds and preferred stocks, they provide extra safety and high yield while also paying interest on a monthly basis.

SERIES E BONDS

These were popular during World War II and their popularity continues to grow. Many of my female clients purchase the Series E bonds at the bank. It's their secret nest egg, not even their husbands know about it. Why? Simply because they are married to men who are big spenders, gamblers, or who are wife beaters. Thus, they know they can save money without their spouses knowing the difference. In case they get a divorce, or they leave the husbands, they feel safe because they can cash them in at any time. Many of these women feel that by buying Series E bonds out of their household money, scrimping on food, and cutting down on costs, they will have security for their old age. It's easy for them to save eighteen dollars and fifty cents for a twenty five dollar bond. Of course they won't get the twenty five dollars until the bond matures, but they can get the eighteen dollars and fifty cents in case they have an emergency. Their unsuspecting husbands never will find out, because there isn't any statement coming in the mail and nothing is declared on income taxes until the bonds are cashed in. Of course, at that time if they are still married, they might have a lot of explaining to do! Dorothy M., an Aires has accumulated plenty — she keeps on buying these bonds every month. She lets a friend hold the certificate that comes with the bond. That way her husband won't see them in the house of a safe deposit box.

STOCKS

Stocks represent the subscribed capital of a company or corporation, divided into transferable shares of uniform amount. These shares are a form of investment; one can purchase and sell them whenever one desires. However, they are subject to fluctuation and a worrier (the negative side of Capricorn and Pisces), or an emotional person such as a Cancerian, will panic when the stock goes down. The stress and mental strain could cause this type of person to have an ulcer, stroke, heart attack or possibly get colitis.

A Cancerian client, David M., suffers from an ulcer. What's worse, he not only invests his money in the market, but handles other people's money as well because he is a stock broker! And his ulcer acts up every time the market flip-flops.

Years ago a broker told me, "It's best to invest in a product you always use. You'll be spending your money, but at the same time your stock in that company will pay you a nice dividend as it goes up in price. If you use *Revlon* lipstick, buy their stock; if you drive a *General Motors* car, buy stock in that company."

New Issues: The new issues of corporations going "public" for the first time and of smaller companies seeking equity financing can often prove rewarding if the performance of the corporation is positive.

Over-The-Counter Stocks: The unlisted shares of corporations which trade over-the-counter typically represent smaller, lesser known companies and offer an excellent opportunity for substantial capital gains but at commensurably greater risks.

Preferred Stocks: Preferred shares, which provide a fixed and usually generous amount of income from their dividends, are generally considered to be somewhat higher quality than the same corporation's common stock since the preferred shares have a senior position to the common.

Common Stocks: The common shares of many public utility companies and a number of industrial corporations provide income through dividends that often approaches the rates available on corporate bonds. Moreover, these shares offer appreciation potential should their dividend rates be increased or prices rise as a reflection of the company's earnings growth.

Common shares of various types can offer appreciation potential: *"blue chips"* are considered to be quality stocks and usually provide good income; *growth stocks* hold the potential for long-term appreciation; *volatile issues* can offer faster profits, but with commensurably higher risks.

Many common stocks, especially those of small companies, newer business ventures or established companies whose business prospect are unclear, carry both a higher degree of risk and the opportunity for substantial profit gains.

Trucker's Stocks: The over-the-road truckers that haul general freight between designated points for a set rate such as Roadway Express, Yellow Freight System, McLean's Trucking, Consolidated Freightways are stocks you can purchase.

Stocks in Banks: You can purchase bank stocks. Many believe, and trust, the banking system.

Stocks in Investment Brokerage Firms: You can purchase stocks in brokerage firms such as Merrill Lynch, E.F. Hutton, etc.

Stocks in Casinos: Gamblers like these stocks; they can be risky but also profitable.

SHORT SELLING

Speculating on a downward price movement of a security can be accomplished by selling short the stock and repurchasing it later when the price, hopefully, is lower. Your risk is greater, of course, since a stock's price can theoretically go up an unlimited amount.

Billy Rose was a billionaire who, at the time of his death, was the largest single-share owner of telephone company stock. Billy was a client and friend of mine who I visited frequently for three hour chats in his fifty-room townhouse in New York City. In one room was a ticker-tape machine. As he explained, "I watch the stock market constantly with this ticker tape. I gather the facts, analyze them, and once I've decided which way to go I move fast. In the last seven years I haven't lost a dime on the stock market. I learned all about investing in stocks from Bernard Baruch whom I worked for in the early part of my life." Billy's method of operating (the fact gathering, analyzing) is typical of Virgo, his Sun sign.

I know many people who would like to buy stocks, but when they called the larger well-known brokerage house, the broker said they could not handle such small amounts of money. If you want to make a small investment in stocks contact a broker from the following directory which lists brokers in the United State who handle small sums of money. Write to:

> Directory
> New York Stock Exchange
> P.O. Box 1971
> Radio City Station
> New York, New York 10010

Or you could try the Internet if you have a computer. Buy Online stocks, although you may prefer to actually talk to a broker rather than an online communication with a monitor.

The discount brokers exist for those who have their own ideas or who prefer to make their own decisions, or who simply want efficient execution at cut-rate prices to save money. Instead of getting full commission the discount broker gets half. However, when you deal with them you have to know what stock you wish to purchase and there are limitations as to the services they provide for a customer. But you might find them worthwhile.

INDEX FUNDS

These are funds designed to move along with market indicators like Standard & Poor's 500-stock index have been largely the preserve of pension funds and other large accounts. Indexing is based on the theory that matching the market averages will produce better long-run performance than the efforts of money managers.

MUTUAL FUNDS — BOND AND STOCK FUNDS

Professional invest money in real estate or an insurance company Mutual Fund. Thus their money is invested in a variety of securities selected to produce as high an income as is consistent with prudent risk. They split the same way stocks do.

Some Mutual Funds are real estate, others are insurance companies and many are oil and gas companies while some are common stock mutual funds. Numerous mutual funds are structured to provide a high level of income and also offer the benefits of professional management and the safety that arises from investment participation in a large and diversified portfolio. Many professional managed mutual funds invest their assets in diversified portfolios of common stocks, seeking to achieve long-term appreciation while offering the safety factors inherent in a large portfolio. The fact is, a fund's return in any one year is not a bankable predictor of its performance the next.

For most investors, it makes sense to play emerging markets via funds, not individual stocks. After all, funds offer the (relative) safety of broad diversification, and they offer a convenient way to invest in companies that don't trade in the United States. Emerging markets Stock Index Funds who deal with foreign countries such as Brazil, Israel, Mexico, South Africa or South Korea appeal to many investors. Or growth stocks in China. More aggressive investors want to bet a sliver of their portfolio on a single region like Asia, South America or Europe.

International Equity Index Funds or Emerging Europe and Mediterranean Funds may appeal to many investors. Bond Funds, Global Health Science Funds, Technology Funds, Bond Index Funds, that profit from liquor or gambling could be attractive to many investors. Other areas of interest to many investors are Tax Growth Funds, funds that profit from tobacco and funds who profit from firearms and military weapons.

I have many clients who invest in Mutual Funds; one in particular was Jeff H., a Scorpio. The money he made from one mutual stock fund enabled him to have extra money to satisfy his compulsive spending habits. A Cancer client, Ruth H., could never make up her mind about which stock to buy; thus, the variety of stocks involved in Mutual Funds allowed her to let others decide for her. Therefore it freed her mind so she could concentrate on other forms of investing while earning money on her Mutual Funds.

ART MUTUAL FUNDS

Knoedler-Modarco, a kind of art mutual fund, has millions of dollars in painting in vaults; its stock is traded on the Geneva Exchange. Another art consortium, Artemis, speculates mainly in old masters; it's traded in Amsterdam. The British Rail Pension Fund sunk millions of dollars in sculpture and paintings such as by artists Cezanne, Renoir and Picasso.

NO-LOAD FUNDS

These are Mutual Funds that are investments in which individual's pool their money by sending it to a fund, which in turn uses this money to buy an assorted batch of stocks and/or bonds. These funds do not have sales people or charge commission. Your entire investment is used to buy shares in the fund.

CLOSED-END FUNDS

They can usually be purchased on stock exchanges or over-the-counter for ordinary brokers' commissions. Unlike most mutual funds, they do not continually issue new shares to new investors. They buy a portfolio of securities and usually take an annual management fee of about 1% — most Closed-End Funds are stock funds, emphasizing growth or stability.

MONEY MARKET FUNDS

This type of fund requires a minimum initial investment (perhaps $5,000 or $10,000 with Brokerage account) and provides stability of principal, check writing and automatic dividend reinvestment for an even higher return. A brokerage house invests this money in large-denomination bank certificates of deposit, corporations' short-term debts (commercial paper), and government securities. Returns on these funds (also known as liquidity funds) such as their yields can move up quickly if short-term rates rise. If you need cash to pay bills on short notice you have checking privileges — this can be used to transfer funds to your checking account to pay bills or taxes.

COMMERCIAL PAPER

When a corporation wants to raise money, they put out (float) paper (a Promissory note used by major corporations such as General Motors). It is not backed up by anything. It is not guaranteed, thus is risky. You could lose everything from it if the company does not have the money to pay off its debt. Some are short-term, such as 30 days. High-grade unsecured notes sold through dealers by major corporations in multiples of $1,000 are for 30 days through 90 days.

MONEY-MARKET/OPTIONS INVESTMENTS

About 90% of the assets of this fund is invested in money-market instruments, while the other 10% is invested in options to buy stocks. Although the money used to purchase "calls" diminishes "current income" the fund retains all the upside profit potential that the call seller forfeits. It is, however a decidedly more risky kind of strategy. If, for instance, the market continues to languish, it could be a long time before the investor in this fund would be able to reap any above-average gains. If there is another big rally, however, this fund could put even the high-yield bond funds to shame.

OPTIONS

Call Options: This commits the writer to sell to the buyer 100 shares of a specified stock at a specified price (the striking price), at any time up to the specified expiration date. For this right, the buyer pays a sum of money (the premium), as soon as he/she accepts the option. Buyers of Call options profit when a stock goes up. Putting big money into buying the Calls of a single stock is the riskiest of option speculations. Writing Call options against holdings in your portfolio can provide an added source of income and a degree of downside protection, even though limiting upside potential, while speculating in the purchase of Put or Call options can offer high potential returns but at increased risks.

The hope of towering gains makes Call options irresistible to many speculators. For example, let's say a certain stock was selling just under $80 a share, a two-month option to buy the stock at $90 cost $2 a share. Seven weeks later, the stock was up 36%, to $107.75. that catapulted the option price by 850%, to $19, since the stock had soared well above the $90 exercise price of the option.

Put Options: This commits the writer to sell to the buyer 100 shares of a specified stock at a specified price (the striking price), at any time up to the specified expiration date. For this right, the option buyer pays a premium, immediately.

Note: Listed Call and Put options can magnify the percentage change in the price of the underlying common stock, but the purchaser must accept the risk of losing much or all of his/her initial investment.

Option Period: The time period for which an option is written. This can be any time between twenty-one days and thirteen months. Usually, however, an option is written for six months and ten days, ninety-five days, sixty-five days, or thirty-five days. Occasionally, options are written for one year.

Spreaders: This is an option to purchase 100 shares of stock at a price above the current market and to sell 100 shares at a price below the current market. The most common reason for short selling is the belief that a profit can be obtained if the stock will decline in price between the sale and the covering purchase. By selling and buying different Calls in the same stock, they take fullest advantage of the flexibility made possible by the new options exchanges. Spreaders rely on their ability to predict when the price of one option will rise or fall faster than the price of another option in the same stock. But they don't always come out ahead.

Short-Sale: A transaction in which the investor first sells stock, borrowed through his broker, then later buys the stock to replace what he borrowed.

Strap: The right to Call 200 shares and Put 100 shares of the stock at the same striking price for the same time period.

Strip: The right to Put 200 shares and Call 100 shares of stock at the same striking price for the same time period.

Straddle: A combination of a Put option and a Call option at the same striking price for the same time period.

Option Funds: Professionally managed option funds seek to achieve greater income return with less price volatility by writing listed Call options against an underlying portfolio of high quality securities. As in any option-related transaction, there are attendant risks that should be considered along with the greater income potential.

Consider for example, the case of a fund that holds 1,000 shares of a stock bought at $50 and currently selling at that price. The fund sells Calls on the stock with a "striking price" of $53, and receives in return roughly $5,000. As long as the price of the stock moves within a narrow range, this fund will make money. And presumably, if it pursues this kind of strategy for a long enough period, it will make enough money to protect its shareholders against those times when the price of the stock plunges.

If the price of the stock ever goes up sharply — say, to $75 — the fund forfeits most of that gain. Instead of capturing the full $25,000 increase in the market place, the fund will make only $8,000 ($5,000 on the sale of the options, plus $3,000 on the difference between the initial stock price and the price at which it sells out to fulfill the option contracts).

Money Market/Options Investments: About 90% of the assets in this fund are invested in money-market instruments, while the other 10% is invested in options to buy stocks. Although the money used to purchase Calls diminishes current income, the fund retains all the upside profit potential that the Call seller forfeits.

It is, however, a decidedly more risky kind of strategy. If, for instance, the market continues to languish, it could be a long time before the investor in this fund would be able to reap any above-average gains. If there is another big rally, however, this fund could put even the high-yield bond funds to shame.

TREASURY BILLS AND NOTES

These are in units of $10,000 to $1 million, short-term or long-term. Some are for 26 weeks, some for 90 days. They are safe.

TREASURY NOTES

These are in minimum denominations of $5,000 and may be purchased without commissions from Federal Reserve Banks and their branches. Many banks and brokerage houses also sell the securities for a small fee. These are safe; they have the full faith and credit pledge of the Treasury backing it.

GOVERNMENT GUARANTEED SECURITIES TRUST

This professionally selected portfolio of securities, such as government notes, bonds and U.S. agency issues, provides monthly income and the safety features of a diversified portfolio of securities that are guaranteed by the United States Government or its agencies.

U.S. GOVERNMENT SECURITIES AND SBA LOANS

The debt issues of the U.S. Government, its agencies and the Small Business Administration provides excellent interest income and the very highest guarantee of security.

GOVERNMENT FUNDS

Many wealthy people buy or trade government funds, which are issued by different government agencies. They usually mature in six to nine months. Bob U., a Virgo, invested in government funds which involved the raising of money for the farmers. Not only did he like the quick money earned but he felt it was good to help the farmers.

COMMODITIES

Prices fluctuate widely for all commodities. Speculators can buy commodities for a small deposit, usually about 15%, and take full advantage of the price swings. If they predict correctly, they make a profit on all of the funds invested for only the small down payment. But if the prices move opposite to the traders' predictions, they can be wiped out completely.

Note: Speculation is taking above average risks for the chance to make above average profits. You have to have the nerve — the emotional attitude — to accept rapid price fluctuations, and you should never risk money you can't afford to lose. Speculators want to buy low and sell high or if they're going "short," sell high and buy low.

COMMODITY FUTURES

Although quite risky due to rapid price fluctuation and the investment leverage that is frequently employed through the use of margin, commodity futures can provide high profits to speculators who are financially and emotionally suited to substantial risk exposure. It's pure gambling — but there are those that like the excitement of this volatile field. They are not for everyone; the temperament needed is a combination of discipline, business sense and flexibility.

They consist of foods (black pepper, soybeans), grains and feeds, fats (butter) and oils, fibers and textiles, metals, petroleum, rubber, hides (native cows), hog bellies, newspapers, sugar, coffee, precious metals (gold, platinum, silver), Treasury bills, Treasury bonds, British pounds, Canadian dollars, Japanese yen, Swiss franc and GNMA (Ginnie Mae) mortgages, frozen orange juice, FNMA, etc.

A *gold* or *silver* future is like any other commodity future. It is a contract to deliver, or take delivery of, a specific quantity at a specific price in a specific month. Prior to the delivery month, though, a buyer or seller can offset his/her contract; the buyer can sell his/her contract, and the seller can buy one.

GNMA and *FNMA* can be commodity futures either for speculative profit based on future price changes in gold. *Foreign currency* futures you buy when you speculate on U.S. dollar fluctuations. *Treasury bills* and *Treasury notes* futures are different than regular T-bills and T-notes. If interest rates go up, T-bills will go down; if interest rates go down, T-bills will go up) — the futures are commodities and speculative. *Treasury bills and Treasury notes* as futures are very risky. You buy a contract for a specific date in the future (like with Options) and if the interest rate goes down you profit. If the interest rate goes up, you have to put up more money (have to get Margin calls). You are dealing with a specific price and date and if it doesn't do what you want it to (go to the price you want), you lose.

Sugar prices soar on Commodity Futures when there is a draught in South Africa or the Dominican Republic — or wherever sugar is grown. Orange juice prices rise on Commodity Futures if Florida has bad weather or a freeze. Grain prices soar when sever floods take place where grain is grown.

A client of mine, a Cancerian, Peter E., loves the thrill of taking chances. Possibly he's attracted to Commodities because the sign Cancer rules food and silver, or because he likes to be kept on pins and needles. Cancerian's bore easily; Commodities take the monotony out of life. Peter is an emotional wreck from his dealings with Commodities. But he won't give up his favorite daily habit of trying to guess what the market will do. It is a wonder he doesn't have an ulcer or a heart attack!

INTEREST RATE FUTURES

Futures contracts on certain U.S. Government securities can be purchased as a speculation on future changes in interest rates or, by corporations, as a hedge against their upcoming borrowing needs.

MARGIN ACCOUNTS

By borrowing in a margin account part of the funds to purchase securities, speculators enhance the profit potential of their investments but also assume an equal level of increased risk. A margin account works about the same as buying a house — you put so much down and pay for it later. Your stockbroker lends you the balance for a consideration.

Chester, a Cancer client, allowed greed to interfere with his better judgment. In May 1973, Chester asked me for some good dates to sell so he could take that money and pay what he owed on his margin account. I gave him some excellent June dates to sell the stock. I told him that if he didn't sell by July 1973, he would be in a financial mess because there would not be another good selling date until 1976.

Chester did *not* sell the stock on the dates I gave him, because the price went up sky-high and he figured it would continue. I repeatedly told him it would go down, but Chester didn't believe me. He tenaciously and greedily hung on to his stock. Meanwhile he kept calling me to see if I was going to tell him it would go back up. "Perhaps," he questioned, "you made an error?" At the end of the year the stock had gone so low, and Chester was in bad shape financially he had to sell everything at a loss and place a second trust deed on his house to pay off the broker.

WARRANTS

Warrants are the right to buy a certain stock at a specified price (called the "exercise" price) within a particular time limit (usually anywhere from three to twenty years hence). Hopefully, the future price of the stock will be higher than the price offered to warrant holders. If this occurs, and it usually does in new firms, the buyer makes a good profit.

Warrants were very popular during the 1920's, before the stock market crash in 1929 and have regained a considerable amount of popularity. If you are lucky, a "killing" can be made in them. A good example is the *Hoffman Radio* Warrants in 1948: If you had a hundred dollars invested, it ballooned to fifty thousand dollars by 1950! Aries, Gemini, Cancer, Leo, Scorpio, Sagittarius, and Pisces are attracted to Warrants. If you are under any of these signs, you are attracted to taking a risk and tend to be fearless.

CERTIFICATES OF DEPOSIT

You buy these at the bank. Some banks have them with a minimum unit of $100,000; others at $10,000. They are usually six-month Savings certificates; others are 30 month institution certificates. There are some banks who have them as low as $2,000. These short-term debt instruments, issued by many banking institutions, can provide very high interest income on investments that normally mature within one year — thus, check each bank's policy until you find the one that best fits your needs.

CASH RESERVE MANAGEMENT

A professionally managed portfolio of short-term "money market" instruments, such as Treasury bills, Certificates of Deposit and commercial paper, permits excess cash balances to be invested for very brief periods, if necessary, while earning attractive interest rates and assuring excellent safety of principal.

INVESTMENT NOTES/THRIFT CERTIFICATES

These are higher-interest alternatives to Savings Certificates for investors willing to sacrifice some safety. Higher yields are available in many states on thrift certificates or investment notes issued by some finance companies. They are not insured and vary in risk.

FLOATING-RATE NOTES AND FLOATING-RATE SECURITIES

Floating-rate notes may state that the holder of the note could after two years sell the notes back (at an agreed in advance price) to the company they were purchased from, or face value.

Floating-rate securities are generally regarded as a defensive investment and in an improving bond market might not be readily saleable.

FOREIGN CURRENCY

There are many ways to hold foreign currencies. You can open up a *foreign bank account.* You can *buy the actual cash.* You can buy the cash through Deak-Perera in Washington, DC. There is, however, risk of loss. If the purchase is less than $10,000, there is no need for identification. There is the restriction of only one transaction — buy, sell, deposit or withdrawal — per day per customer. Or you can use a *bank draft,* but you need a bank account. However, questions might be raised if there's an unusual delay in redeeming drafts, like two or three years.

FOREIGN BANK ACCOUNTS

Many people invest their U.S. Dollars in foreign bank areas, such as currency, Eurobonds and Eurodollars. You don't have to live abroad to be eligible for these type of investments.

Margo M., a Libran client, is a fashion model in the United States who emigrated from Spain. She was told by a friend, who majored in economics, that the dollar would continue to devaluate for a while, so she should keep most of her money in Eurodollars. Margo, true to her Libran nature, listened and took her pal's advice. And each time the dollar went down, Margo made money. To her this was an easy way to invest, without too much effort and yet showing a substantial gain.

EURODOLLARS

The Eurodollar market is a currency market in which U.S. dollar deposits are accepted by banks in other countries, generally in Europe and Japan, and made available for lending or investing. In London they are usually on amounts of $100,000 or more.

EURODOLLAR CD'S

Certificates of Deposit in foreign bonds issued on U.S. dollars in those banks. There's no "lender of last resort," no monitoring agency. They have higher rates, but they also have a higher risk.

FOREIGN TRAVELER'S CHECKS

You can buy Foreign Traveler's Checks from American Express, Thomas Cook, the big British travel firm, or from Deak-Perera with offices in Washington, DC. Deak-Perera sells Swiss-franc Traveler's Checks. They are inexpensive, convenient and nearly as liquid as cash. Someone bought one thousand dollars worth of checks in May 1977 and cashed them in September 1977 and received one thousand two hundred and eight dollars for them; thus, a $208.00 profit was made in four months. Profits from the sale of Foreign Traveler's Checks are taxable if the transaction is over $10,000; amounts lower than this are not reported to the Internal Revenue Service by the company issuing the Traveler's Checks. They can be profitable as a hedge against the dollar when it is on the decline.

PRECIOUS METALS CERTIFICATES

A minimum of $2,500 in coins or bullion is required for silver and gold. You can have domestic storage or you can have international storage in Zurich, Switzerland. You do not take possession, therefore, there isn't any assay hassle. The Krugerrand was popular as well as the Canadian Maple Leaf or Austrian 100 corona or Austrian Ducat (four and ten ounces of gold).

GOLD

Deak and Co., in Washington, DC has a program that enables Americans to buy and store relatively small amounts of gold bullion in Switzerland. For a minimum investment of $2,500, including a 4% commission, investors receive depository certificates that can be resold through Deak & Co. at any time. A yearly 1/2% storage charge adds to the cost, but there is no sales taxes or assaying fees. Gold stocks are risky mainly due to political uncertainties in South Africa. Or a conservative approach is to buy gold stocks in two Canadian companies such as Dome Mines, Campbell Red Lake — still risky.

DIAMONDS

Diamonds are used by profit sharing, pension plans, corporate retirement plans and other fiduciary-directed investment accounts. When you invest with International Diamond Corporation (30 N. San Pedro Road, San Rafael, CA 94903; phone 415-479-6060) you obtain physical control of the diamonds. Diamonds provide reasonable liquidity — and are convertible to currency all over the world.

Market stability has provided upward price movement for over 50 years, without downturns. Customers who held their diamonds for a period of 24 months or longer averaged a return in excess of 30% capital gains. Customers who held their diamonds annually thereafter realized an average return of an additional 20% annum on their original invested capital.

COLLECTIBLES

Many people put their money in Collectibles such as coins, stamps, historical documents, art, antiques, ornate Victorian silver pieces or things that have nostalgia value. Dolls, comic books, baseball cards and so forth could turn out someday to be profitable.

Annuities

Tax-deferred annuities are popular with investors. Annuities are the Web's best source for information on tax-deferred annuities. You can discover whether you should switch annuities — is it sensible to do so? Or you can compare the benefits of an annuity versus taxable investments such as mutual funds. It depends upon how much money you have to invest in your portfolio which may consist of stocks, bonds, gold or certificates of deposit.

An annuity contract can provide regular income payments that are guaranteed by the issuing insurance company to continue at any time period selected, including your lifetime and/or that of your spouse. If you deposit principal and other income payments until a future time, interest is credited on a tax-deferred basis, permitting your funds to accumulate with taxes postponed.

TAX-DEFERRED ANNUITIES

The principal of deferred annuities, which are sold by insurance companies, usually through stockbrokers — the purchaser can let interest earning compound tax-free until the investor begins to withdraw money after retirement, when he/she may be in a lower tax bracket.

NO-LOAD TAX-DEFERRED ANNUITIES

Insurance companies, such as Washington National Life or Old Republic Life in New York City have their annuities sold through major brokerage houses. You don't have to pay commission fees on these. Interest on the principal amount of a deferred annuity accumulates under tax-deferred status, thereby permitting investors to earn interest on their principal, on their interest and on the taxes they have saved. At a stated future date, income payments can commence on a regular basis depending on the annuity option that has been selected.

DEFERRED SWISS FRANC ANNUITY

You can escape high taxes and risky investments in an Ultimate Savings Account offered by some Insurance companies, which could include tax-free income in gold, Swiss francs, or mutual funds. However, the best ultimate savings account is a Deferred Swiss Franc Annuity.

SINGLE-PAYMENT ANNUITY

This is bought with a lump sum and can produce far larger retirement benefits than a fixed-rate annuity paid for with annual contributions. *Variable-rate annuities* accumulate in an investment pool, usually a common stock fund managed by the insurance company. Variable annuities can produce a better return than typical fixed-rate annuities, but their performance depends on the stock market.

FIXED-INCOME REFUND ANNUITY

A guaranteed monthly income for life in every plan each payment is made up of both interest and principal, so a substantial portion is not included in income for Federal tax purposes. This appeals to Taurus.

KEOGH AND IRA RETIREMENT PLANS

For the self-employed or the employee not covered by a retirement plan, Keogh and IRA programs can be a systematic and profitable means of accumulating assets toward retirement. *IRA "Rollovers and Distribution Annuities"* are retirement from an existing pension plan which might generate a lump sum distribution. A "rollover" to a distribution annuity, for example, permits the recipient to avoid current tax liability and to continue building a fund for retirement security.

ENDOWMENT RETIREMENT POLICIES

These produce, as a rule, lower cash value than fixed- or variable-rate annuities. Because they included life insurance, they are able to guarantee that the face value will be paid to an individual or his/her beneficiary.

TAX SHELTERS

Since a tax shelter investment should be first and foremost a promising business venture, such investments can provide attractive capital appreciation potential over a period of time in addition to tax benefits. A reputable Tax Shelter is designed to make money, not just to generate tax losses, although profits may not come until far down the road. The Internal Revenue says you must truly expect a profit, not just shelter your income. If you are not right, you'll get audited.

Some Tax Shelters are: U.S. Savings Bonds, Tax-Exempt Mutual Funds and deferred Annuities, oil and gas exploration, cattle breeding, equipment leasing, partnership shares in real estate, coal leases, Tax-Exempt Municipal bonds, Individual Retirement Accounts, farming (field crops, livestock, vineyards, bees, nuts, fish), Unit Trusts (they hold a fixed set of long-term bonds without trading them).

Tax Shelters are not very liquid (you can't get your money out fast) and they don't start generating income for some time. *Note:* Oil and gas Tax Shelters may take up to two years before income comes from them. It is reported that about 70% of exploratory wells are dry and unprofitable.

TAX HAVENS

Ari Onassis did not pay taxes because he formed his business corporation in places that were tax havens, such as: Andorra, Antigua, Bahamas, Barbados, Bermuda, British Virgin Islands, Cayman Islands, Channel Islands, Gibraltar, Isle of Man, Liechtenstein, Luxembourg, Monaco, Montserrat, The Netherlands, Netherland Antilles, New Hebrides, Singapore, Ireland, Costa Rica, Switzerland, Turks and Caicos Islands.

INVESTMENTS IN GENERAL

Think twice before you become involved in Commodity Futures, Gold, Silver, Options, Warrants, or the Stock Market. Fluctuations occur in these areas and you've got to be a real thrill-risk-taker to play. Be as safe as possible and invest in solid things. Avoid those promises of things that are too-good-to-be-true overnight riches. Then you won't have to spend sleepless nights worrying. Instead, you'll have a good sound sleep and be ready to face the next day singing, "It's a wide, wide wonderful world I live in."

CHAPTER THREE

Magical Thoughts

Believe in magic. Magic is all around you in the atmosphere. Magic can make your dreams come true. Magic is within your soul to perform — Magical Thoughts bring magical changes and, thus, Magical Conditions into your life. You've heard the adage, "Magic is in the believing," haven't you? *Thoughts Produce Things* — it is what you are *telling yourself* as to what you will attract.

Your Mental Attitude is the *key* to prosperity. Believe in your own dreams and the power you have over them. Your mental processes stem from the conscious mind, ruled by the planet Mercury in astrology, andthe subconscious mind ruled by the luminary — the Moon — in astrology. The conscious mind operates when you *voluntarily* start to think. The subconscious mind is an *automatic* operation. In other words your daily habits (like walking) which you do without thinking. Those things you ask for in prayers and by saying affirmations are performed through the conscious mind, but they are answered through the subconscious mind.

The conscious and subconscious mind are linked to cosmic forces (God, a Supreme Being, Infinite Intelligence, etc.). Therefore if you want to attract money, love, happiness, material possessions or anything else — you must discipline your subconscious mind to think and feel strong (dominant) positive images, thoughts, emotions (such as faith) and, thus, you'll be tuned in to attract fortunate events into your life. If you continue to repeat your ideas and desires through imagery and meditation, they'll be planted deep in your subconscious mind to start acting *automatically* in your life — thus, bringing you the luck and riches you long for.

It is your habitual way of thinking that makes you what you are and what you can become. You must change your negative habits that destroy your chances to be successful and wealthy. It is best to change one bad habit at a time (thus you don't overload your mind and defeat your purpose) and one goal at a time. Once you've accomplished this, add in a new one. When you rid yourself of a destructive thought or action, replace it with a constructive thought and action. Then, go in the direction of your goal. It's important that you fill your mind with new mental patterns, thus, ridding yourself of old beliefs and actions which only serve the purpose of ruining your dreams of prosperity.

Never see yourself as a loser. Do not think of yourself as poor. Instead see yourself as an achiever, a winner, rich and happy. Do you know that wealthy people see themselves as rich. They never see themselves as being without — that's why they continue to attract plenty of money.

You've heard that "Birds of a feather, flock together," haven't you? Thus stay away from negative people and try to be in the company of those who are cheerful, outgoing, uplifting and encourage your dreams. Be sure that your friends and loved ones also believe in you. Do not surround yourself with anyone who is not 100% in your corner. Even if others scoff at your ideas or dreams, stay on course and you'll enjoy being on the winning track.

Be willing to face challenges. Think of everyday as a call for you to improve your lifestyle. Keep yourself mentally headed in the right direction toward your goals. Look at each step up the ladder as a step toward your getting to the top. Choose the path you want to take. Once you aim for your goals, it is up to you as to how fast you go — the faster you go, the closer you come to your destination.

Do not procrastinate. Realize that if you don't take action, nothing will happen. If you don't take the initiative, your life will be at a standstill and your dreams can pass you by. Always aim for the highest star in the sky, and know that there isn't any mountain too high to climb, nor any ocean too deep to explore — go all out so you can be a winner. Challenge yourself to do what seems to be impossible, then you will know just how much you need to do to achieve your goals. Never quit. Keep in mind that within your soul (horoscope) lies the seed of success — nurture it and bring it to bear fruit — then there will be nothing you can't do.

You may be a genius, have great ideas, be educated or a hard worker — but if you don't follow through with persistence than it will be difficult to attract success and great wealth. All great men, who have accomplished wonders, persisted until they reached their goals. Just don't be a quitter. Be courageous even when you think everything is unattainable. If one track proves fruitless, try another. When one door closes, another opens — just go to the door and let opportunities in.

It's important to get started and then don't stop along the way. If you come to a stumbling block, try again; find another way of getting to the top. If you get disappointed in a person, or a project falls through, don't let it get you down or hold you back from continuing. If you get discouraged, don't give up. Have faith that you will get what you want. Keep trying until you're successful. Do not back away from obstacles. Realize that you can do anything you desire. Don't be afraid to fail. Know that you'll either win or lose, but at least you will have the satisfaction that you tried. There are many challenges when you start to travel on the road to riches. So be patient, and despite all obstacles, keep your dream alive. That's what Donald Douglas did.

Are you aware that Donald Douglas was one of the world's leading aircraft builders and the head of one of the largest airplane factories in the world? While Douglas attained fame and fortune, he had numerous disappointments as well as many successes. He climbed the ladder to high achievement, but along the way was met with many obstacles, and sometimes failure. But when a person has a strong desire to reach a certain goal, and has the initiative, determination and persistence to forge ahead, obstacles and failures are a challenge to work harder toward the goal one seeks — and that's what Donald Douglas did.

Donald Douglas made use of his experiences in the unworkable projects to avoid future mistakes, and his failures gave him a better understanding of how to conduct himself and to plan ahead more successfully. He was born with three Fixed signs in his horoscope. His Sun was in the pioneering sign Aries. His sustained effort (the Fixed signs working for his benefit) led to eventual success. Aries was "DOMINANT" in his horoscope; thus, he had the courage, endurance, enthusiasm, optimism and enterprising nature which made him successful. Donald Douglas was a builder who took risks and had the desire and energy to work hard and long hours when necessary. He was able to make the most of each and every opportunity that came within his reach.

When you encounter a block, think about the many times before when obstacles were thrown in your pathway. When you are struggling, realize that you have an inner strength that can make you victorious. So apply your innermost power, and don't allow problems or frustrations to upset you. Take the difficulties one at a time, find a solution, and be proud you discovered what it was that was causing you to be perplexed. Don't get discouraged, especially if your dreams and wishes don't come through immediately. It takes time; you need patience. Beware of any negative thoughts that block success, such as anxiety, depression, resentment, blame, self-pity. Change your mental attitude and you'll be that much closer to your objectives.

Do not allow feelings of doubt, inadequacy or unworthiness to enter into your thoughts. If you become frustrated, believe in your goals. Be firm with yourself. Don't let unexpected incidents deter you — realize that challenges bring strength and courage. Know that you are strong enough to handle any problem or situation that might arise. Don't dwell on losses or imagine you're a loser. Go for the gold! Look on the bright side, and do not allow adversity to stop you from being a winner. Do not be afraid to be yourself.

Delays may seem to hinder progress. Be patient. Don't give up. Know that your dreams will bear fruit. Do not allow one doubt to creep into your consciousness. Do the best you can. Take advantage of opportunities. Concentrate on those things that, currently, make you happy and in the future will bring contentment. If you've gambled and lost in business, or in games of chance, don't fret. If various projects brought failure, don't be fearful of finding another angle — give it a fresh approach or do it when you feel lucky. Don't say, "What's the use?" Instead be like Nikola Tesla and try again.

When Nikola Tesla was twelve years of age he was a self-instructed mechanic, and built a cylinder that turned into a vacuum pump. It did not prove successful in the manner he wanted, but one day in a flash (intuition being demonstrated) came the truth as to what was wrong with it. Some years later Nikola invented the Tesla Turbine," the steam engine that broke all records for horsepower. Tesla always had new problems, but that didn't stop him from inventing new things.

By the time he was seventy-eight years of age, he had seven hundred inventions to his credit. Tesla told a reporter that people laughed at him when he told them about the cosmic ray he invented. They called him crazy when he predicted the radio, and sent the first impulse of the radio around the world. People told him,

"It can't be done." But he never gave up. No wonder! — his *dominant* sign in his horoscope was Taurus — a stubborn and persevering zodiacal sign.

By saying, "I can do it," you put a positive stamp on a thought. Your mental attitude is a key to success. If a negative thought leaps into your consciousness, say, "Out you go! You don't belong in my mind. You are not part of my life." Then divert your attention to a place you'd like to be, such as, basking in the sun while lolling by a swimming pool at some fancy resort.

Trust your intuition, like Nikola Tesla did, that inner voice that's waiting for you to stay in touch with your true self and help you solve problems. Set a time every day to meditate on your aims. If you have to make a decision, open your heart and consciousness to it by meditating. Before falling asleep, place a glass of water on a night-stand by your bed. While so doing, look at the water, caress the glass in your hands and say, "I want a solution to..., when I wake up in the morning." Choose your goals, write them down and meditate on them.

Do not allow your problems or responsibilities to weigh too heavily on your shoulders. Willingly accept responsibility. Know that the difficulties that arise are only temporary, and you'll find the answers you're seeking. If you think all of your hard effort isn't paying off — don't quit because that's when success could be just around the corner. Often when you've almost reached your objective, you fret and want to give up; perhaps, it's because nothing is happening as fast as you want. It is at that precise moment when you need to stick with it the most.

When a problem occurs, solve it and then ignore it by blessing it away just as if it never existed. Otherwise, you could put up blocks which make you confused, disoriented and make it easy to stray from your goals. Tell yourself that you are free of any negative thoughts or situations that arise. Say, "I'll be able to handle whatever happens."

Do not be led by fearful thoughts which try to convince you that your dreams are too good to be true, too wonderful to happen or too good to last. Put your best foot forward and do something definite so you'll have the effect of being successful. If fear creeps into your mind, ignore it. Review and learn from mistakes, realize it's too late to change them and move on. Apply the knowledge you learned so they won't be repeated at some future date. Do not blame anyone or yourself for bad fortune. Stop sabotaging yourself with negative thoughts; instead put a positive spin on your thoughts, thereby making them "magical."

Do not dwell in the past with regrets or, "What if I did...?" You can't cry over split milk, in other words, the past is over and done with so instead say, "What if I do...?" and then do it! Live for the future — not the past. Realize that everything happens for the best, regardless, of how much you wanted something. If you had really wanted it, or it was meant to be, it would have happened. If you cling to old ideas, you'll hinder your progress on the road to riches. Take those old thoughts and channel them in new directions. And like the song, "Eliminate the negative and accentuate the positive."

Do you know the author, Jack London, went through terrible ordeals in his youth but managed to make something of himself? He was abandoned by his father at birth, and suffered gross neglect from his mother. When he was attending public school, he sold newspapers. When Jack was fifteen years of age, he joined a gang of oyster pirates, and became a hard drinking, fighting, outlaw. He worked in a jute mill, and was a coal shoveler. Then he became a vagabond, landed in jail and decided to educate himself.

It wasn't long until Jack London went to work in the Klondike, because he heard of the gold rush there. From that experience, he returned home penniless but with an amazing fund of story material. Jack wrote about his many adventures without success, but that didn't stop him. He continued to write until, finally, he had his first book published. It became a huge success, his famous books, *Call of the Wild* and *Sea Wolf* became classics — and this man was a sailor, gold seeker and newspaperman who cleaned up his act and made something of himself. In his horoscope he had eight planets in the Fixed signs; his Sun in Capricorn gave him ambition and perseverance. In spite of setbacks he achieved goals through persistence and making use of experiences and talents.

Often you may think that your dreams have crumbled into dust in your hands. You may entertain thoughts of failure or believe that your dreams are impossible to obtain because they are beyond your reach. But they aren't! Just because you didn't win or get what you wanted the first time you gave it a try, doesn't mean that you're a loser. Your dreams could be delayed; therefore, hold on to your dreams and believe so much in yourself that you'll get everything you desire. Today may seem dismal, but tomorrow may be bright with your face lit up like the sun shining — especially if you won the lottery, hit a jackpot or received a bundle of money from a sweepstakes contest.

Avoid placing limitations on your talents with excuses and alibis. If you've dreamed about doing something — do it now! Don't wait around for people to help you or for things to just occur. Make things happen by taking action and knowing that there are no limits as to what you can accomplish. It takes time, patience, dedication and persistence to be a winner or successful in any undertaking. The world is full of all types of possibilities, thus, you have an abundant supply to choose from at your fingertips. Everything can be yours for the taking, by being honest and putting forth all of your strength and intense concentration, so you can satisfy your ambitions.

Intensity is the keyword to use when going for the brass ring. Hold the ideas you have with such intensity that you feel an exciting power going through your body as if you were inflamed. Have you ever held a pencil real tight in your hands? Or what about holding on to a steering wheel for dear life when driving a car? It is this emotional, strong and intense feeling that needs to be thrown into your consciousness. Think of it as something you crave so much that nothing else enters your mind. It is as if you're haunted by these thoughts day and night — that intense thinking, if applied with action, can put you on top of the world. Many famous giants in the industrial world took advantage of their intense non-stop drive — Bill Gates is a perfect example of this.

When Bill Gates was fourteen years of age, he experimented with a small computer and, within months, wrote three computer games. When he was fifteen years of age, he and his friend Paul Allen designed hardware and software that would analyze traffic problems. When he was nineteen years of age, he dropped out of college and moved to a cheap hotel room in Albuquerque, New Mexico. Bill was restless and driven by a single objective — to change the world. His career path was impulsive, unplanned, and full of grandiose imaginings.

Mr. Gates created markets, seized opportunities and seduced the world with his software products. He is relentless, obsessed with succeeding (typical of his Scorpio Sun sign) and driven. This multi-billionaire (he's worth around $37 billion dollars) is America's wealthiest man. He's a computer tycoon who was born with six planets in the Fixed signs in his horoscope. With that type of set up, no one, nor anything, will ever be able to stop Bill Gates from attaining his dreams. His desires are never ending — he will always be searching for new worlds to conquer.

Be like Bill Gates and have faith in your beliefs, skills and goals. Faith is a helping stone that can guide you toward reaching your aims. The stronger the faith, the better the chance you will have to be prosperous. You need to have a definite purpose in your mind — then make plans. Faith is developed through a positive mental outlook, and should be followed up by taking physical action so you can achieve your objectives. If you want a job promotion, do everything in your power to work hard. Don't stand still and let your life and dreams pass by. John L. Lewis chased his dreams at an early age, and accomplished plenty in his lifetime.

When John L. Lewis was in the seventh grade in school, he went to work. To augment his family's income, he took a job in the mines. In his spare time he earned whatever he could, which included running a debate team. When John L. Lewis was twenty-five years of age, he started to work his way up the ladder. At that time he was a delegate for the United Mine Workers and by the time he was thirty-eight years old, he was acting president.

Mr. Lewis was thirty-nine years of age when he started developing the CIO (Congress of Industrial Organization) and became its leader. His aggressive tactics led to conflict with the courts and government but was greatly beneficial for the union. John L. Lewis never gave up. He was a fighter for a cause, and had the spirit of a crusader. This great man was a self-dedicated individual that believed that he, and he alone, had the answers to the reforms needed. His horoscope indicates that he has seven planets in the Fixed signs — no wonder he stuck to his guns and fought for his beliefs which proved victorious!

Expect success! Expect riches! Walk with your head held high toward your goals. Climb to the top of the mountain. Keep going in spite of the rocky road, or falling back. Think of it as a journey; take one step at a time on your desired route.

Reach high and feel the top is near. Know that you can make it up that trail, and continue to keep your goals focused with a strong-intense-emotional and positive thought that your objectives will be achieved. Realize that within your soul is knowledge, talent and a belief you can fulfill your ambitions. Do not allow that belief to stop. Keep going, regardless, of how rough the road gets. Have faith you'll be rich. Think about how you are going to celebrate when you are victorious. Set forth the *emotion of winning,* and the *feeling* of being a winner. And let *belief* be submerged in your conscious and subconscious mind. Believe in Magical Thoughts.

Be open-minded and know that you can achieve greatness — anything is possible with the right attitude. Look for miracles — they can happen. They have occurred in the lives of others, so why can't they transpire in your life? Believe and know that you are special and have special gifts that can be utilized to bring you those things your heart desires. Perhaps, you want to win the lottery, or a jackpot at a casino, or a sweepstakes contest — be confident that it can take place. Expect changes for the better. Keep in mind that you do not make things better by fighting present unhappy living or working conditions. Take a non-resistant attitude toward the present, and know that everything is changing for the better.

Look into your heart to discover what it is you really want — then go for it! The inner most recesses of your mind will tell you which path to take. Rely on your soul to give you strength and power to do whatever you deem necessary. Make choices. Take chances. Be bold and daring. Take the initiative. Be driven to want more and more. Let your ego drive you to accomplish great tasks. Be driven like a person on fire and with this burning desire go all the way until you reach your goals. Go that extra mile — do more than what is expected of you on a job. Go out of your way to please others by doing favors for them. Plant your dreams (desires) just as if you were planting seeds. Be an over achiever and continue to want more.

Know your skills. Know that you are unique; not even Twins have the same horoscope. Know that life is what you make it. Know that you will be victorious on the battlefields of success. Know good fortune can be yours. Know that you have a potential to reach your goals because within you resides unlimited powers to be a winner. Know there isn't any reason you can't win or be successful unless you are doing something that prevents it. Know that you can make everyday better. Reach within your subconscious mind and use intellect and every resource you can to realize your ambitions. Know that the impossible dream is possible. Know that your spirit is attracting a life of Divine Order and that, somehow, you'll be helped over life's hurdles. Know that you can become the person you've always wanted to be.

Your horoscope is your attitude toward everything in life. Each planet rules a different type of thinking; thus, by changing you attitude from a negative one to a positive force — you can change your life and become prosperous or successful. Just think about how easy it is to make changes — that is all you have to do — to get what you yearn for. When your thinking is altered, changing conditions follow in hot pursuit. Look forward to new beginnings. Progress is change; change is progress. No one can help you alter your course, it has to come from within. If you want your life to be different, be serious and dedicated toward becoming a new you. At every second, life is a series of changes, so are circumstances. If you expect the worse, the worst will come. If you expect a change for the better, it will occur. Begin to act as if you expected success, happiness and wealth. Make plans; if they are altered, go down a different road. Perhaps, you'll be led down a path that will take you to your dreams. The road is paved with gold and sacrifices and is aligned with determination and patience. You may be tempted to quit just when you are almost at the end of the long ride toward your goal. Do not be afraid to take risks. Go for the top prize. Be a leader who knows how to share the spoils of victory.

If you see clouds, look for the silver lining. See the bright side of life and be inspired, zealously, with your aims. Often, you may have difficulty in believing that wonderful things are in store for you, especially when you've seen so many projects/dreams crumble in your hands. Are you aware that life is full of lessons to be learned? You can profit from them, someday, so don't let them get you down — instead, get up! Do more! Be flexible! Use self-discipline!

Every day examine your consciousness and evaluate exactly what it is that you are preparing for. Then you'll be ready to depart to greener pastures. When something strange emerges to the surface of your mind — stop! Say to yourself, "What does that signify? How can I go about attaining it? Is this a positive force to be reckoned with? Or did a negative thought creep into my mind? Am I fearful I will not have the money to pay my bills?" If you have deduced that problems are in store for you, then tell yourself, "I am going to solve my money difficulties by taking on another job." Or you could decide to quit your present one and look for work elsewhere that pays lots of money.

Energy is found on every corner and space on the globe. It is in our minds and body as well as material objects. Often people get in a rut from sameness, or negative thoughts, and bring about losses and financial straits — that's when un- happiness sets in and is noticed by everyone. Do not let opportunities drift away and be beyond your reach just because you feel sorry for yourself. Do not wallow in self-pity. Fear, envy and losses are represented by the planet Saturn on the dis- cordant side. Get out of a negative groove! Change your vibration immediately by expressing confidence, optimism and enthusiasm.

It's important that you have a mental concept of what you want. Know that thoughts are substance in matter (the ethers) which can be turned into physical things. But you must have a goal and then take action so you can fulfill your hopes and dreams. If you don't take action, ideas just hang around in substance. Mental imaging is also called daydreaming in a sense. The difference is that with mental imaging, you are making definite statements about what you want, and how to get it; daydreaming is already attaining it in your world of the imagination where no effort is required to get your heart's delight. Think of the power within you as a bright shining light that surrounds you. Bask in this light. Smile and know that as of *now* good things are coming your way.

Imagination is the name of a song. Make it your special song by imagining the things you want to happen in your life. Let your consciousness be your guide — like a compass that can direct you to go in the right direction. Picture in your mind's eye your goals, then wrap them up into reality. If you want to travel to exotic locales, imagine that you are now in the destination of your dreams. Then take action by working hard to obtain the money for your trip. Pack your suitcase ahead of time — that puts forth the notion that you are actually going on a journey. Sacrifice some fun to tend to your chores. Do not take unnecessary and expensive vacations unless you can afford it. In other words, don't spend your last dime on having a good time. Invest, put aside some money for your future.

Imagine (daydream) you are surrounded by lots of money — it's floating down from the skies and landing on you. Imagine you won the lottery or a casino jackpot. Imagine the life you are living is that of a rich person. Put lots of intense emotional feeling and energy (thinking) into everything that you're imagining. It is the power of emotion coupled with action that aids you to accomplish your dreams.

During World War II, there were many children who survived the German concentration camps. One man wrote a book about it. I saw him being interviewed on television. He said that he survived because he daydreamed every waking moment that he was somewhere else living a safe and wonderful life. In his dreams he ate well, was happy and rich. When he was released from the concentration camp, he worked hard, made money, wrote a book about his experiences in the concentration camp, appeared on the television talk circuit and became wealthy. This is an instance when a man's dream came true.

Walt Disney was a dreamer who turned his dreams into reality when he took action toward attaining his goals. This giant in the movie industry promoted his theme parks, animated films and became a financial tycoon. Disney and his brother had $45, a suitcase and extra suit when they left Kansas City for Hollywood to start a new life. Walt Disney had his struggles, but also courage and determination, and the ability to work hard for long hours at a time. He was a careful planner. This brilliant man became the brain of Disney Productions and built the Disney Empire. His enthusiasm and optimism expressed his Sagittarian Sun sign's traits. He believed in his dreams. It was easy for him to persist in his goal because he was born with two Fixed signs in his horoscope. His enormous ambition came from his three Capricorn planets.

When Frank Sinatra was young, he told himself, "Someday I am going to be rich." He held on to that belief, took action and brought it into reality when he obtained his goal. His getting on top came through a long struggle, but he saw himself as rich and famous all of the time — he never gave up hope. Frank was an optimistic Sagittarian. I knew him well because I was in his company a lot in the 1960's. He was generous to his pals — money was spent fast but by keeping it in circulation it continued to flow in.

Organize your plans, so you can manifest good things. Write down where you want to be living — in a mansion or on a yacht. State the things you want to eliminate from your life — those things (it could be character flaws) you'd like to change or get rid of. Also write down your good qualities and how you can improve yourself. Think about what you now have. Be grateful and give thanks for their now being in your possession. Review your list, cross things off when you receive things. Keep in mind that "Rome wasn't built in a day," therefore, you need patience to acquire those things you fancy.

It is up to you, and only you, to follow the low or high road of life. Map out the direction you are going to take to reach your goal. Try to stay on the smooth road. If you take a detour, don't get upset. If you're lost for a while — just think of how many successful people experienced the same thing. So, get back on the high road and keep persisting until you reach those things you hunger for. Tell yourself, "I am going to have everything I want, regardless of how long it takes." Issue commands of prosperity to yourself along the way. Tell yourself, "I am on the right road to achieve my desires and to have my wishes granted." A daily affirmation, even for a brief moment, can produce satisfying results.

It is easy to complain about hard times, lack of money, a job, lack of love or lack of fun. It's just as easy to be lazy and take the easy way out and live with indebtedness. However, by taking a few minutes a day to review your positive commands you can change all those lacks into abundance. Try to clean up your financial affairs, get out of debt, even if you pay off bills little by little. Once you start to pay the money you owe, a channel for new money opens up. Keep in mind that "what goes out, comes back." Do not be stingy or hoard those greenbacks. If you hang on to your dough, you stop the flow of those bucks coming back to you. It also implies that you doubt that you will receive any more money. One doubt could negate everything good coming your way. Just remember that when you spend cash, it is returned to you — sometimes double, especially when you donate money to a church or charity.

If you want a vivid money image in your mind, draw on your imagination by saying, "My supply of money is on the way. It's going to fill my purse/wallet. It can never be depleted." Visualize the cash in your wallet, purse or bank account — see it multiply and multiply. Think of your bank account getting larger and larger. Imagine your wallet/purse is so jammed full that you can't cram any more dough into it; thus, you'll have to hide, or spend, it. When your thoughts are concentrated on those greenbacks, believe and imagine that you are engulfed with money all over your body and house. Think of those bucks as a substance in the air — a substance that you need to tune in to through meditation, prayer, or positive thinking. Realize that your wealth is supplied by the universe — just tap your conscious and subconscious minds and soon you'll be rich. It is up to you to do your own optimistic and enthusiastic thinking. Never doubt your talents, ability to receive lots of money or possibilities to be rich. Confident thoughts are an aid to attracting prosperity. In astrology the planet Jupiter rules laughter, happiness, abundance, confidence and good fortune — it's the luckiest planet in astrology. Therefore use the self-assurance of Jupiter to bring you the wealth you crave.

Henry J. Kaiser was thirteen years of age when he quit school to go to New York City. He took a cash boy job there in a dry goods store. His salary was $1.50 a week. By the time he was seventy-nine years of age, he had amassed a $2 billion dollar Intercontinental Industrial Empire. Kaiser Aluminum and Kaiser Hospital are just a few of his accomplishments. As a youth, he had a dream and nothing stopped him from accomplishing his goals. It was easy for him to be persistent, and never give up, because he was born with seven Fixed signs in his horoscope. One alone can make a person stick-to-itive — imagine what seven did!

Kaiser loved working. Take a hint from him and do the same. If you dislike a job or situation (such as being broke, without work, etc.), do something about it. Avoid harboring resentments toward anyone or anything. If you are unhappy with the situation you are in, you will continue to attract negativity. If you dislike someone, your negative thoughts will hit them and come flying back to you on the double. It's the Law of the Universe — "What you think, you attract," "What goes around, comes around," or "Thoughts produce things." Therefore, do not allow anger or discontent to hold you back from prosperity. You have control over your thoughts and actions — there isn't anyone who can CONTROL HOW YOU THINK.

Think pleasant thoughts about others. Do not complain or be critical. Avoid lording it over someone by thinking that you are better than that individual. Give compliments. Find something about a person that you can praise. Or tell a man, "I like the color of your shirt, it looks well on you." Or tell a woman, "Your confidence is something I admire." Don't put down the ego's of others, or they will attack you by belittling you. It is their defense you attack. Be like Will Rogers who said, "I never met a man I didn't like."

If you are not happy with your job, and cannot find a way to change your mental attitude toward it, then go to work somewhere else. Or go to school, college or a special class, seminar or workshop and learn a new profession. If you want a raise or promotion, alter your bad habits and replace them with something that will attract a salary hike. In other words, be constructive. Never gossip or say bad things about others. Unhappy, discontented people who whine and complain seldom attract prosperity, unless they inherit it. If your pals or loved ones engage in negative conversations, tune them out by daydreaming. If you need to reply to what they are saying, try to change the subject to another topic.

Never pawn anything to get money. When you pawn something, you are putting out a negative thought to yourself that you *need* the cash because you don't have it or can't find another way to get money. This type of thinking defeats your purpose to attain wealth. Never think of lack or cry poverty to yourself or anyone else. If you talk about the economy in a negative manner, or the stock market or any other type of loss — you are putting forth in the other person's mind that you are poor, lack funds or are in great need. If you mention the recession or say, "Times are bad," you'll be harboring negativity. What about all the people who made a fortune during the depression when things really were bad? Those positive people became rich — they grabbed opportunities and believed they could be successful. Therefore, believe in yourself, believe in your vision of the future, believe in magic and know that your beliefs can become reality.

Rid your mind and house of clutter. Give or sell those possessions you don't use or wear. Donate them to the needy. If you are not wearing these garments, why keep them? When you give, you receive. Make room in your living quarters for new possessions. They'll come when you least expect them. If you want to own your own home, prepare for it. Start collecting linens, accessories, furniture or objects 'd art for that new abode. If you do not have the cash to spare now, go window shopping. When you look in a store window, or pass by items in a store, touch them and say, "That belongs to me and I am going to have that." Keep on noticing, and visualizing, them belonging to you. Sooner or later, you'll attract them. Never doubt that they can't be yours. If you express doubt, you'll never own them.

Ask for guidance when you meditate; thus, it'll be easier to make decisions. If you want to change your thoughts of failure and poverty to thoughts of success and prosperity, then start now. Since life and circumstances are always changing, why shouldn't you change your thoughts and become rich? Picture yourself living your dreams and achieving every desire. It doesn't cost any money to change your way of thinking, so don't make up excuses about not being able to alter things in your conscious or subconscious mind. Perhaps, you'll win a lottery, sweepstakes contest or a jackpot in a casino.

To obtain riches you mind must be conditioned (prepared) for the acceptance of wealth just as the earth's soil needs to be plowed and ready for the seeds to be planted. Can you think of a reason why you should not be prosperous? If so, that's a signal that you need to change your mental attitude. Don't make up excuses, instead, get rid of self-defeating thoughts that are useless and hold you back from the attainment of your goals. Use self-hypnosis as you lie in bed before falling asleep. Tell yourself, "When the alarm clock rings in the morning, I will wake up with lots of energy, positive thoughts and a burning drive to work hard and achieve my objectives.

Realize that the Universe wants you to have all the riches it supplies. Create your own rainbow and imagine that you've found the pot of gold at the end of the rainbow. See yourself picking up the pot of gold and spending it for those "goodies" you crave. Never see the pot of gold empty, just imagine that it refills itself every time you spend that cash. When you go on a shopping spree, tell yourself, "There's more money where that came from." It takes trust to achieve your ambitions.

You may dream of wealth, but think it's beyond your reach. Look around. You'll see, or read about, all the affluent people in magazines, the tabloids, newspapers or on television. There are more millionaires now in the United States than there ever has been at any time in history. People have prospered through winning lotteries, sweepstakes contests, in casinos (the megabucks) and through investments and hard work. If they can do it, why can't you? Don't listen to family, friends or loved ones — their negativity can block your efforts to be rich. Think big. Do not tune in to the small petty thoughts of others. Ignore them when they gripe or complain. Avoid negative people like the plague. Their discordant thoughts can be infectious.

When you expect little out of life — that's just what you'll get. Do not blame others for your bad luck. Let the past mistakes you made be a learning factor, then get on with your life and move ahead with optimism and enthusiasm. Follow your gut instincts; keep your course straight and you'll wind up a winner. Do not say, "I am doomed," or "I am jinxed," or "I am unlucky." No one is doomed or jinxed — we all make our own luck, be it bad or good, by our behavior and mental attitude — we, fortunately, have control over both.

Invest in friendships. Don't be a loner. Friends, like loved ones, are to be treasured. Look for the good in people, and in every situation, regardless of how somber it may appear. If a person does you wrong, bless that individual. Let go of bitter thoughts and wish the person good luck, love and happiness. Grudges and resentments can hold back the prosperity you desire. Think before you speak. Do not allow anyone to stop you from making your dreams come true. Choose the path you wish to travel and stay on it. Do not let anyone take you down a bumpy road — keep fixed on your chosen path and make your own decisions.

Always try to be good to others, the way Oprah Winfrey is to her family, friends and employees. Oprah struggled in her early years but she never gave up hope of becoming successful. She became the richest woman in show business through her television show, production company, magazine, acting and producing — and there isn't any end to what new big project she will undertake next. Miss Winfrey donates to many charitable educational causes; she's a true Aquarian humanitarian who spends lavishly. The more she splurges, the more she'll receive. Oprah was born with five planets in Fixed signs in her horoscope — no wonder she is determined, stays on a fixed path and will continue to be successful. This woman is master of all she surveys — a woman who has an empire — someday, she will become a billionaire.

Keep your ideas to yourself. This is something many famous people learned the hard way. When movie stars are offered a role in a film, they keep it a secret until the contract is signed. Otherwise, they believe it will be jinxed — and it often is. An artist friend of mine told everyone her fantastic ideas and projects she was going to promote to people who could invest in her future. These brainstorms were brilliant, but she was so busy talking on the telephone letting everyone know about them, that she never followed through. When she died, her ideas went with her.

Give thanks everyday for what you have, in other words, "count your blessings." Appreciate all you possess. Take inventory on your assets. Are the bills paid? Do you have money in the bank? Realize that every time you pay a bill, you'll attract money from another source. The Universe fills the void, if you stay positive in your mind. You'll be provided for. Tell yourself, "I have divine protection and will always be taken care of." Then give thanks in appreciation of your good fortune. Supply channels open up in many unexpected and unpredictable ways, so, be ready to receive them by being open minded. Always think of yourself as being blessed with friends, a roof over your head, food in your stomach and loved ones to cherish. Give thanks for all these blessings and you'll attract more. God's (the Universe's) supply is never ending.

Laugh. Smile. Play! Be happy. Have a good sense of humor. Entertain thoughts of joy, love, peace and confidence — these are Magical Thoughts. Keep your spirits up. Let your happiness reflect on everything you do. Make your life exciting. Throw gloom, sorrow and seriousness in a bucket and cover it with a lid. Sparkle. Bubble like champagne. Give circumstances a chance regardless of your living conditions. Have fun! A sunshine smile will attract people who can help you.

Dress so you appear like you're not in need. If you look wealthy, others will think you are rich, and thus, their thoughts can be an invisible tool which can help you achieve prosperity. If you tell people you are broke, the negative thoughts sent from them to you will bombard you with such negative energy that additional energy will be added to already existing conditions.

Billionaire, Donald Trump, was five billion dollars in debt due to the recession and plunging real estate values. Bankers and creditors tried to seize his real estate and casino empire. But he bailed out by working day and night to become solvent. Donald is a wheeler-dealer who is an expert negotiator. These talents led him to getting the bankers to loan him $65 million dollars to put his organization into a financial upward swing so he could create a profit and pay off his huge debt.

In various interviews, Mr. Trump, stated that to be a success, "Set your goals high. Don't underestimate yourself. Set a priority for excellence. Be at work early, stay late. Start every day with a vision of what you want from life. Visualize your dream home or that wonderful vacation and refuse to let negative thoughts stay in your mind — they lead to failure. But remember always to enjoy the game of achieving success. Keep a light heart and sense of humor as you work for your dream." Donald Trump has a total of four Fixed signs (two are angles; two are planets); thus, he could persist until he accomplished his goals. He also has a strong ego drive — the Sun (the ego) is the *dominant* planet in his horoscope.

Continue to make wishes and when they come to fruition, make more wishes. Personal success is getting what you want and continuing to want what you have. Never stop wanting something. Never be satisfied with just one thing — always want more. As your mind grows for more, so will your bank account. However, if you are content with what you have, and don't want anymore, things will stop coming your way — because your mind stopped growing for more.

When you are meditating, tell yourself, "Prosperity is around me now — it is in my mind and actions at all times. The people with whom I come into contact are going to bring good things to me. All inanimate objects such as computers, investments, collectibles, slot machines, lottery tickets, sweepstakes tickets, raffle tickets, sports betting tickets — they are NOW bringing me the prosperity I desire."

Keep in mind that one setback, or loss, cannot make your dreams crumble. So hold on to those dreams, keep searching for that pot of gold at the end of the rainbow. Look up at the sky. Wish on a star. Shine like the most brilliant star in the sky with positive thoughts radiating from your entire being. Don't be afraid of tomorrow — tomorrow may be just when your dreams are fulfilled. Know that your future is bright — brighter than it has ever been. Keep those positive thoughts flowing. Do not allow anyone to change them. Then you'll be on a magic carpet with Magical Thoughts carrying you to every corner of the Universe — that's when your dreams can come true — and that's what it's all about, isn't it?

CHAPTER FOUR

Magical Devices

According to the dictionary, "Magic" involves the belief that man can co-erce nature by the use of certain rites, formulas, actions; it can be found as an element in all primitive religions. It is an overpowering influence that proves irre-sistible or extraordinary.

Magic comes from the word *Magi;* the Magi were the three Wise Men from the East who traveled to Bethlehem to pay homage to the infant Jesus. According to St. Augustine, their names were Balthazar, Casper, and Melchior. Magi comes from the ancient Persian word *Magus* which means priest, magician. Magus also meant a sorcerer. The *Magi* were from the Zoroastrian priestly caste in ancient Media and Persia, traditionally reputed to have practiced supernatural arts and were magicians and astrologers. The Magi of Egypt and Chaldea, and even further back in antiquity, were unquestionably Masons. Astrology was studied and prac-ticed by them.

According to the dictionary the word "imagine" means: to form a mental picture or idea of something. The word "imagination" is the ability to reproduce the images of memory. The Wise Men of the East were mental builders who used "imagination" to perform "magic." In other words, Magic is the skillful use of the "imagination."

You can profit materially by combining Magic and Astrology. From antiq-uity to modern times, man has discovered that the mind is the highest type of active agent to bring you the images you want. Human actions are directed by the mind and, thus, can bring human events such as winning the lottery, or hitting the jackpot at a casino or winning a sweepstakes.

It is important to release the energy of the Magical Devices; therefore, after you have performed a ritual, do not dwell on it anymore. If you think about them continuously, you will not be letting go of the energy so your desires can manifest. Be patient. Give these Magical Devices time to work. Think of these rituals as a job in which you are there at a specific time, then you leave work and go about your daily duties.

Perform the Magical Devices at a scheduled time. Some rituals have spe-cific times when to perform them, others don't. The best time to perform some rituals (those I did not put a specific time to), can be done just before the Full Moon, the wee hours of the morning, or when the hands of a clock are going up and on the quarter hour, such as: 0h45' am (45 minutes past midnight); 1h45' am, pm (1 hour, 45 minutes); 2h45' am, pm; 3h45' am, pm; 4h45' am, pm; 5h45' am, pm; 6h45' am, pm; 7h45' am, pm; 8h45' am, pm; 9h45' am, pm; 10h45' am, pm; 11h45' am, pm; 12h45' pm (45 minutes past noon).

Once you've performed a ritual, as I said before, release, let go, let God or Universal Power, Infinite Intelligence or a Supreme Being take over. Do not be fearful of letting go of this positive Magical energy. Nothing is lost once it is released into the atmosphere (the ethers), it then becomes part of Divine Substance which is in return your Divine Supply of Abundance. Are you aware that every word you think or speak is released into the atmosphere and will bounce back at you for good or bad depending upon what type of vibration you put into it? Mentally say, at the end of a ritual, "I fully and freely release this positive energy into the ethers so it can work in my behalf. So shall it be!" Isn't it wonderful to know that your MAGICAL THOUGHTS AND MAGICAL DEVICES CAN HELP MAKE YOU RICH?

OLD WIVES TALES — MAGICAL DEVICES

These old wives tales have been handed down from generation to generation; they were employed by housewives who believed in them and received satisfactory results. After all, "Magic is in the believing." Some of these are still practiced today by people who are superstitious. So, you might have heard of them — but here they are:

For good luck, carry a rabbit foot in your pocket.

When salt is spilled, throw salt over your left shoulder for good luck.

*The noise of clinking glass when you give a "toast"
scares away evil spirits and brings good luck.*

*Place a horseshoe over your door. Hang the horseshoe with the open end up
(so luck won't spill out) over your door.*

*Always enter your apartment, home or a room
with your right foot first — this brings luck.*

Bubbles in your coffee mean you're going to get money.

Look at a New Moon over your left shoulder — for luck.

Sing while you bathe — for luck.

When your left hand itches, you are going to get money.

When your right hand itches, you are going to spend money.

The Druids in ancient England, cut down Mistletoe from the oak and let the mistletoe fall on a piece of clean, fresh cloth — mistletoe brings wealth.

Buy cinnamon in the spice section of a grocery store. Put a little cinnamon in your morning coffee or hot tea. Think thoughts of winning and great wealth when you drink your coffee.

Buy Mustard Seed in the spice section of a grocery store. Or buy Mustard Seed in the herb section of a health store. Sprinkle it in the corners of every room, and watch your money increase. Carry the Mustard Seed with you by sprinkling a few of them in your wallet or purse. If you are in your own business, place some Mustard Seeds in the cash register or accounting books — accounts receivable. Or take the seed, plant it in dirt and visualize your money growing as the seed sprouts. Every time you look at it, say, "I am rich and getting richer." Or say, "I am a winner." Give thanks ahead of time (after you make your statement) for your wealth even if you don't as yet have it.

The Chinese celebrate their New Year with many traditional symbols which bring good luck, such as:

The home filled with narcissus (good fortune and prosperity).

Bright red "Lucky Money" envelopes with a small amount of money in it and is exchanged with a child, loved one.

Red (Chinese people believe the color red symbolizes LUCK) diamond shaped paper; use as stationery.

Crab and fish encourage prosperity and abundance.

Fish shaped ornaments, tiny Buddha statues, red rearview mirror charms, jade pendants.

"THE LUCKY BOX" MAGICAL DEVICE

You need a small box (4x2, 4x4, or a little larger). On the outside top lid of the box, print or write. "This box contains the key to many hopes and wishes untried; to goals and plans and dreams; to courage, strength and pride. For it you will just believe in all the dreams you want to come true, BELIEF will be the very KEY that opens up the door."

Open the box and on the inside top lid, write or print, "And every time you look in here to find your precious key... please know I wish you all you need to live a happy, successful and prosperous life."

On the inside bottom of the box, place a gold key (cement or glue it on).

In this box, put pictures of the things you want or write on separate papers things you want. When your wishes are granted, take them out. Put new wishes in anytime you want.

Each time you put something in your "Lucky Box," when alone, close your eyes and repeat out loud, listening to your words such as the sum of the money desired, or happiness for you or another, a good job, a raise, promotion, to win the lottery, etc. Read it upon rising and just before retiring. See yourself going through the actions which will bring you your desires (money, promotion, etc.) FEEL the money in your HANDS. You must express an INTENSE EMOTIONAL CHARGE OF DESIRE when you say or feel the preceding. Hide your Lucky Box. Do not tell anyone what you wrote in it. Once you've got what you wanted, then it is okay to tell others about it.

"THE LUCKY PENDULUM" MAGICAL DEVICE

The Pendulum has been known to be in use by Emperor Yu in 2200 BC, and almost every country in the world has used it for some purpose or another. The Pendulum is a modern outgrowth of the ancient art of divination (also called "dowsing"). It has been used to determine health, disease, freshness and quality of food, to locate underground water, minerals, and oil. Also it has been used for its magical powers in rituals (religious, etc.), and by ordinary people who want answers to their problems or who want to know about the future.

We live in an energy universe. And every organism is surrounded by all kinds of energy — beneficial or destructive. The Pendulum measures both your inner and outer energies and force fields. Your inner higher intelligence communicates through the nervous system which gives signals. Thus, the Pendulum is an instrument that amplifies and interprets signals through the codes set up between YOUR conscious and subconscious minds. So, when you hold the Pendulum over an object, such as the diagram below, you are measuring the interaction of a given force with YOUR OWN nervous energy.

Make your own Pendulum, if you can't find one in a New Age book store. You can use a bead, crystal, small ring (such as a wedding ring), locket, pendant, small fishing weight or any small pointed object. Attach one of these objects to a chain, cord, white hemp, nylon fishing line, twine, black silk thread or a heavy thread (do not use sewing thread; it lacks the strength needed). You need something flexible, pliant and strong. Make the object symmetrical (it's less affected by the wind this way). You might find a button easy to make into a Pendulum because it has a hole (or holes) which the twine (etc.) can be looped through — an eight-inch length of twine is good. Thus, you hold the Pendulum with your fingers at the top part of the twine; then the Pendulum (button) is down about an inch away from the diagram.

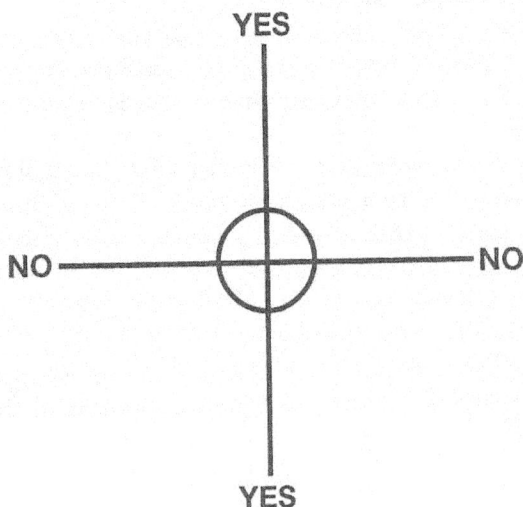

YES

NO———————NO

YES

Be in a quiet place, stay away from electric or electronic devices. Sit down with your feet firmly planted on the floor. Do not touch your hands or legs with each other. If you are right-handed, hold the Pendulum in your right hand; if you are left-handed, hold the Pendulum in your left hand. Keep your other hand down at your side.

You can only ask a "Yes," or "No," question. Phrasing is important — don't ask, "Is it raining cats or dogs?" as no such thing exists. Be realistic and concrete in your questions. If you are upset, or elated, or in any kind of emotional tizzy the Pendulum may not give you the correct answers. Your emotions must be calm and stable; otherwise, the Pendulum will pick up your feelings and move erratically (jump, wobble), and give you the wrong answers — strong emotions shock the nervous system, remember the Pendulum obeys your subconscious mind.

If, after you ask a question, the Pendulum moves up and down (your arrows on the diagram), the answer is "Yes." If, after you ask a question, the Pendulum moves from right to left, or from left to right, the answer is "No." If the Pendulum moves in a clockwise or counterclockwise motion, it could mean that at that moment the subconscious mind does not know the answer or that the subconscious mind does not wish to answer. Try the same question at a later date; perhaps, you'll get your answer at that time. If the Pendulum does not move within a few minutes, it is a sign of resistance and the subconscious does not wish to respond at all.

When asking the Pendulum the amount of money you should wager on gambling, do as follows: "Is $_____ (dollars) what I should put into a slot machine?" or "Is $_____ (dollars) the amount I should buy lotto or lottery tickets with?" or "Should I spend $_____ (dollars) on a sports bet — the fight between _____ and _____?" or "Should I spend $_____ (dollars) on such and such a horse at such and such a race track?" or "With Blackjack, should I bet $_____ (dollars)?" and "With roulette, should I bet $_____ (dollars)?" Note: Mention dates of bets you want to make; be specific and name players you want to bet on, such as with Sports Betting; mention casinos you are going to play in; mention which State's lottery you are playing; mention amounts you want to bet in Craps.

You can start with $1.00 and continue upward, or do it in your usual manner of betting. If all answers are "No" on the dates you ask about, do not bet on that date.

You can also ask about Numbers you should play. Make sure you mention the date you want to play, type of game and where. Numbers go in cycles; during certain times a number, or numbers, come up more than at other times. For example: with Keno (there are 80 numbers) and often in the course of one hour the cycle you keep seeing is 12, 14, 22, 32, 17, 41, 72 (one or more of these numbers appear in consecutive games) then later, it's another cycle of numbers appear. In Craps, the same thing. Often you see Craps (on the dice a two, three, or twelve) thrown a lot; then there are times when you seldom see these numbers. Often nine is thrown continually for about 30 minutes then 5 may become the next cycle-number thrown most often. So, when you are going to a casino to play, ask your Pendulum for a number (or numbers) to play at the specific TIME when you will be playing.

"THE LUCKY ANGELS" MAGICAL DEVICE

Angels are the guardian of hope and wonder, the keepers of magic and dreams. You are never alone; there's always an angel watching over you. Angels help you even though you may not be aware of their presence. Whenever you hear music, an Angel is speaking to you. Whenever you believe in Angels they help you believe in yourself — in your dreams — and to win. Angels are constantly finding ways to make your wishes and dreams come true. Angels can give you hope, strength, comfort and courage. Angels inspire you to find happiness and bring rainbows after the storm.

The next step is to call on your Angels to help you win the millions you dream about. The mystics through the ages taught people that everyone has an Angel (or higher self), and that when you want to reach an Angel that you should "WRITE" to the Angel. Everyone has read, or heard that they have a Guardian Angel. But there are other Angels around you at all times. You can call on these Angels for various things. For example, on a minor scale, you are looking for a parking place in a parking lot, just say, "Parking Angels, find me a parking place." It is amazing that a parking place is suddenly available. Call on Angels for various things, and after your request has been met, say, "Thank You."

How about writing to an Angel? Just how do you go about this Angel-writing method? You could write, "To my Angel, I bless you and give thanks that you are bringing me money that will help me and others and we all will be blessed by it." Or you could write, "To my Angel, make me win the lottery." Write the statement to your Angel fifteen times (the Ancients believed in using the number fifteen to break up and dissolve hard conditions). Then seal the note in an envelope and place it in your Bible or away from the eyes of others.

Now suppose you are going to a casino to do some gambling, what do you do with Angel-writing? Write fifteen times, "To my Angel, I bless you and give thanks that you are making me a big jackpot winner." It's best to do this ahead of time and seal the envelope, put it in the Bible. Then, the day you go to the casino take it with you. Select the slot machine that (from a distance) stands out — that your eyes are drawn to. If you like, you can ask the Angels to direct you to the right slot machine. When you win, don't forget to give thanks.

When you go to the race track or do Off Track Betting, write your note to the Angels saying, "To my special Angel, I bless you and give thanks that you are beside me and helping me win some big money today at the race track." Write your note fifteen times, put it in the Bible for fifteen minutes, retrieve it and take it with you to either the race track or the Off Track Betting location. Do not open it at the race track, but rub your hand from right to left over the envelope and say, "Thank you Angel."

Do you need to get the bills paid? When the bills begin to arrive in the mail, do not resent their coming — that puts a negative thought on your bills, and thus, on your money. Instead put positive vibrations on those bills. Write on the outside of the envelope (that the bill came in), "I GIVE THANKS FOR YOUR IMMEDI-ATE AND COMPLETE PAYMENT. YOU ARE IMMEDIATELY AND COM-PLETELY PAID THROUGH THE RICH AVENUES OF DIVINE SUBSTANCE." Also, if your bills have piled up, make a list of the amount owed and to whom and beneath (or beside) each person's name (and amount owed) write out, "I GIVE THANKS FOR AN IMMEDIATE PAYMENT IN FULL. YOU ARE IMMEDI-ATELY PAID IN FULL THROUGH THE RICH AVENUES OF DIVINE POWER." And say, "THANK YOU ANGELS FOR EVERYTHING. YOU ARE TRULY BLESSED AND LOVED."

"THE LUCKY WATER" MAGICAL DEVICE

Do you know what it means if you dream about water or that water is in your dreams? If the water is muddy, it implies that you will be spending money, probably on bills. If you dream of clear water, it means that you will be getting money. How much money will you get? It depends upon how much water is in your dream. If you dream of a trickle, it will be a small amount of money. If you dream of a pond, creek — small amounts of money. If it's a river or an ocean (the ocean is the biggest amount of money), then it is substantially more money than the water in a swimming pool.

When you dream of CLEAR WATER, as a rule, you will receive money. You could win it in a lottery or in a gambling casino. Or those greenbacks could come from any game of chance: betting on the races or sports, table games (craps, blackjack), poker, betting when you play golf with others, or you could get a raise from a job, win a court settlement, inherit a fortune, find it in the streets, etc.

The "Lucky Water" Magical Device has to do with water flowing in your place of business or home. Have you ever noticed places of business that do a thriving business have water flowing in or outside their establishment? For example: A restaurant may have a water fountain inside or outside. In Geneva, Switzerland there are hotels and many places of business that are along the lake. Lake Geneva, in Geneva has a large water fountain that skirts water up in the air. This is an example of flowing water — all the establishments around this area are booming. In Rome, those places that have fountains do a thriving business, especially around the famous Trevi Fountain. In Las Vegas, the casinos that make the most money have flowing water, such as water that squirts up from a lake in front of the casino, or water that flows over rocks, or a pond or lagoon inside or outside of a casino.

This constant flowing water is one of the things used in the ancient art of FENG SHUI, which is based on Chinese folk wisdom, Chinese Astrology and I Ching (the book of Changes). China is a big country with varying beliefs and traditions. The Chinese people all have some type of flowing water in their homes to bring MONEY TO THEM, a continual flow of water means a continual flow of money. Most of the Chinese in their home and business' use small outdoor scenes (with trees, etc.) and water flows over them in a huge dish (bowl). The department stores sell these in the United States as this form of Magical Device has become very popular in the United States. They come in various sizes: large water fountains or mini-flowing water bowls. They are battery operated in some cases. Most of them are plugged into an electrical socket. They are kept on at all times because you don't want your money to stop flowing. You can set them on top of a table, desk, entertainment center or where ever you like. Once you set it up (they come with instructions), fill it with water everyday — add new water in. Do not throw out the old water. That could suggest you were "throwing away money." Look at it, concentrate your mind on LOTS OF MONEY or WINNING THE LOTTERY, etc. and know and believe from that moment on your money is going to increase. Do not let the vessel become empty of water. If you like you can have them in every room of your house.

Or you can have a small water fountain flowing (with a water pump) in your abode. Flowing water symbolizes money coming (flowing) to you. You can purchase them in department stores, psychic book shops and in Chinatown. Try making your own. Buy a water pump, plug it in and you're on the way to attract continual money flowing in.

A simple and inexpensive "Lucky Water" Magical Device is to simply place a knife in a jar of water and put it behind a door for luck.

"THE LUCKY TAROT CARD" MAGICAL DEVICE

Although the tarot may be new to you, it is almost as old as man himself. According to Hermetic traditions the Tarot cards are known to be 35,000 years old. The Book of Thoth, otherwise known as the Tarot, was known all over and even stretched to the remotest sections of antiquity. They were used and researched by the ancient Magi (wise men, magicians, astrologers). Also gypsies and the ancient Masons relied upon these Tarot cards. The language of universal symbolism is painted on the Tarot cards. They were marked with their appropriate symbols by the ancient people of Chaldea and Egypt. These Tarot cards were marked with these occult (means hidden) symbols so those giving the readings from them could tune in to various forces. The Tarot card pictures could be found painted and engraved in the walls of the ancient temples of initiation in Chaldea and Egypt. The Tarot is recognized as one of the mysteries of the Kabala. Every symbol on the cards are there for a significant reason only known to a few in ancient times. The Tarot represents The Silver Key (in life); The Golden Key represents Astrology.

The Tarot card shown here is the Five of Coins. Coins in the Tarot cards represent MONEY. On the upper left hand corner of the card, you will see the number 5. In astrology, 5 corresponds to the planet Jupiter. Jupiter is the planet of abundant wealth (millions, billions or to what you think is wealth), enthusiasm, confidence, happiness and positive thinking. On the bottom left of the card is the symbol of the planet Mercury. Mercury represents YOUR CONSCIOUS

THOUGHTS. Thus, the ancients knew that if your conscious thoughts were positive you could attract ABUNDANT WEALTH.

The upper right corner contains the symbols for the signs Aquarius and Gemini. It would take pages to explain the significance these two planets represent, therefore I will only tell you the meanings that contain to your ATTRACTING WEALTH. Gemini is the zodiac sign that is known as 'THE THINKER." (Thus positive thinking can attract abundant wealth.) Aquarius is the zodiac sign that represents, sudden changes, shocks, wonderful surprises and unpredictability. Thus through positive thinking (Jupiter and Gemini) your entire life can be unexpectedly altered (Aquarius), and it could come through your attracting ABUNDANT WEALTH.

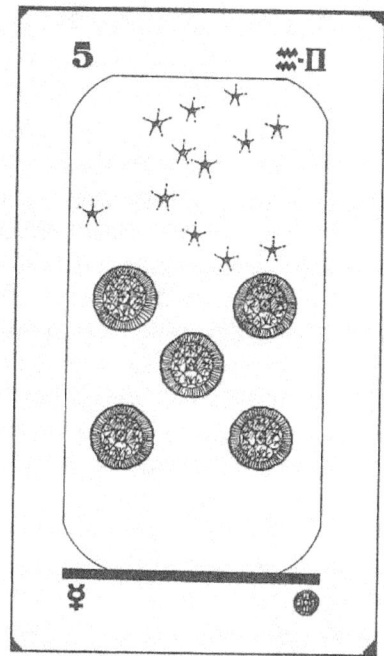

The 12 stars pictured on the Five of Coins Tarot card represent the 12 signs of the zodiac which can denote that abundant wealth is coming from the sky (Stars, using the positive side of the 12 zodiac signs, or the positive side of your zodiac sign). If we but analyze our dreams we shall find that symbolism is the common language of the unconscious mind. And the successful use of the Five of Coins Tarot card is an instrument in which you could get what you want — dependent upon the response you receive through training your mind to think positive thoughts AT ALL TIMES. Think of it as a visual aid to ABUNDANT WEALTH.

To use the Five of Coins Tarot card to your advantage, cut out the card, mount it on sturdy paper or cardboard. Use it for meditation. Before you go to sleep, look at the card and visualize all the things that the card represents and what it is you want. Picture the money coming from the stars (on the card), out of the blue just as lightening strikes (represented by the sign Aquarius). Touch the corners, the stars, the coins as your mind is thinking positive thoughts. When you are picking lottery numbers, follow the same routine. If you go to a casino or race track, take the card with you and follow the same procedure.

The Tarot card used is by permission of the publisher, The Church Of Light. If you wish to own a deck of these Egyptian Tarot cards, and/or study the Tarot with deeper meaning than given here then purchase the book *The Sacred Tarot by C. C. Zain,* by contacting The Church Of Light at 111 South Kraemer Boulevard, Suite A, Brea, California 92821; or go to their Web Site at www.light.org; or call their Toll Free phone number 1 (800) 500-0453.

"THE LUCKY HERBAL" MAGICAL DEVICE

Jupiter is the luckiest planet in astrology; it represents great wealth — millions, and even, billions of dollars. Jupiter is the planet that governs positive and optimistic thinking. Everything in life is ruled by a planet, or planets. For example, Jupiter rules the color purple, jade and garnet gems, the number 7, tin, Thursday, certain flowers, perfumes, herbs, and cell salts. Thus, you can enhance your luck by wearing the colors, gems or perfumes ruled by Jupiter.

Are you aware that certain herbs ruled by Jupiter can attract money and prosperity? Cloves and cinnamon can be added to the food you eat; they can be mentally charged with positive energy that as they enter your body, you will attract riches. Or you can carry skullcap and tonka beans in a purple bag to bring luck, money and affluence. Valerian root is known to attract money. If you're in business, try having red counter tops; they attract customers. Mistletoe can bring success, gold and good fortune — so, it's not just used for kissing during the holiday season!

Now how do you go about using these herbs? Cinnamon, cloves, sandalwood, mustard seeds, and tonka beans can be crushed into a powder. Sprinkle the powder anywhere money is kept, such as in a purse, wallet, cash register drawer, safety deposit box, check book (behind it), or a money belt. Or carry the powder in a purple bag to sprinkle when you gamble.

When you are crushing these herbs into powder, think positive thoughts, such as: "These herbs (this powder) is going to attract prosperity to me." Then when you sprinkle it around, say the same thing. You can continue to make this powder and use it for as long as you like. Keep in mind that things, sometimes, don't come right away — that is especially true if you have one doubt — you must BELIEVE and KNOW that this will work.

After you buy your lottery ticket, sprinkle the powder on it and repeat the affirmation "Luck and great wealth is coming my way. I give thanks in advance." Try to do MAGICAL DEVICES in private; you don't want anyone's negative thoughts to work against you.

If you go to the race track, sprinkle this powder on the racing form entries you have selected to Win, Place or Show. Repeat the affirmation; try to do it silently and without drawing attention to yourself. Once you've bought your ticket, or tickets, sprinkle the powder on them repeating the same affirmation, silently.

When you go to a casino and gamble, take your powder and sprinkle it on a keno ticket; repeat the affirmation given above. If you are going to a slot machine, sprinkle it on the area where the money comes out. Keep in mind that you do not want to draw attention to yourself, so be as quiet and discreet as possible. All casinos have cameras on every slot machine. People (some) smoke and put ashes into the places where the money comes out — so what's a few sprinkles of magic powder going to do? Once you've won, or change slot machines, wipe up the powder. Do not throw the powder away, use it on another slot machine — it is then reinforced with more energy. Always say the affirmations before playing (while sprin-kling the powder). Don't think that if others see you doing this that they'll think you are crazy. I have seen many weird practices performed at slot machines, with arms waving and affirmations being said — and these strangers were winning lots of jackpots. This Magical Device may sound strange, but the results may amaze you.

"THE LUCKY HEXAGRAM" MAGICAL DEVICE

Hexagrams were used in the century before Confucius. Chinese scholars were well versed in their usage and the good that they could bring. Usually it was the aristocracy in China who were familiar with them. Hexagrams are used in many ways. The Hexagram represents power or energy. It is the power of time and the energy to bring money into your life that I will be telling you about. Thus you will note on the Hexagram the positions of the seasons (spring, summer, autumn and winter). See diagram that follows.

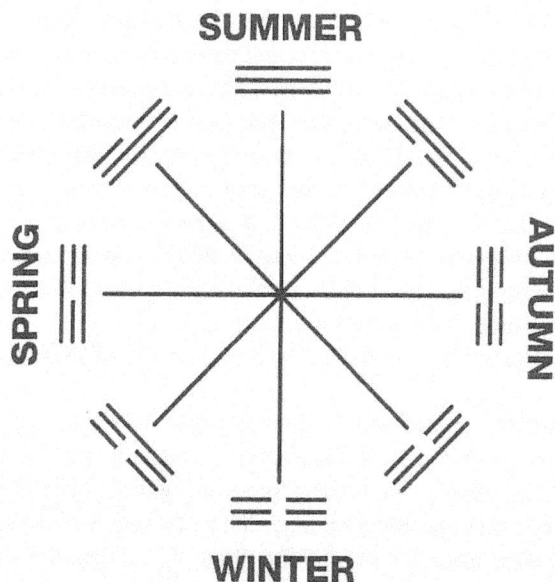

SUMMER

SPRING

AUTUMN

WINTER

The seasons on the Hexagram represent the planting of seeds, and the ger-mination (sprouting) growth of the seeds. Seeds can be planted in the ground or in the mind. When you want to be a winner, it is best to plant seeds in your thoughts — and those seeds (thoughts) sprout, grow and end up being fruitful. This is a visual and mental aid toward winning the lottery, or a jackpot in a casino. The seasons also represent the time when you could be a BIG WINNER.

You will notice on the Hexagram solid and broken lines in each of the sea-son areas as well as four areas that are unnamed. On the solid lines write in your desires (repeat them on each of the season areas. In other words, there are two solid lines for Spring, three solid lines for Summer, and one solid line for Autumn. On these lines you could write: "Win the lottery as a multimillion dollar winner," or "Great wealth," or "Millions of dollars," or "I am rich," etc. There are no solid lines on Winter — on the Winter section, do not write on the broken lines but on the space between the lines and the word "Winter," write something positive such as "I AM RICH," or "I WON THE BIG LOTTERY."

On the solid lines in the areas that are unnamed, write the other things you want in life. The most important things you desire should be written on the solid lines where the seasons are given; less important things are in the other unnamed solid lines.

Visualize your desires on the screen of your mind, by looking at the Hexagram. Then close your eyes and count to ten. Visualize the sky and the cosmos. See the Light of the Universe. See White Light coming to you and surrounding you. With your eyes still closed, see your desires given to you. In other words picture the attendant in a gambling casino giving you cash for winning the jackpot, or see your picture being taken while you are holding a large check that says you've won millions of dollars — this check could be from a casino or the state lottery check. Then picture the White Light around you, count to ten and open your eyes.

You may wonder what the unbroken lines represent on the Hexagram. They represent IDEAS of YOUR DESIRES that need to be LINKED UP to the solid lines of thought. In other words, you may have an idea to invent something, write a book, song or play or to open a business. But these ideas need to be linked up to MONEY. Money to open the business, money that comes in the form of royalties if you write a book, song or play. Money that comes from something you invented and let someone market for you. Your solid lines (or at least one) should have written in the word MONEY or RICHES or GREAT WEALTH or MILLIONS OF DOLLARS.

The best time to meditate on your Hexagram is in the wee hours of the morning when everyone in your household is asleep. If you live alone, the wee hours are still preferable — that is the best time to work MAGIC. Also, look at your Hexagram before you buy your lottery ticket or take it with you to the casino and look at it before playing a slot machine. But the image on the screen of your mind may be so strong from your deep meditation that you need only to bring it up again mentally — in that case, you don't need to continue to look at the Hexagram. If you feel more secure by looking at it physically, then do so.

"THE LUCKY STONE" MAGICAL DEVICE

In Bodrum, Turkey you can buy Good Luck Stones in stores, shops and at open markets; you ask for a "nazar boncugu." But you are not in Turkey; therefore, you can get your own Lucky Stone in a store that sells stones, or go down the street and look for a stone that catches your eye. A friend of mine found her Lucky Stone in the Palm Springs desert. Others find them in vacant lots. A small stone is preferable over a large one because you may need to carry it with you on certain occasions. By the way, when I refer to "Stone" I also mean "Rock."

Once you have the stone, bathe it in sea salt (or regular salt is okay but not as good as sea salt) and spring water — this will cleanse the stone and neutralize all unwanted vibrations and energies. Paint your Lucky Stone your favorite color. Use watercolor, actual paint, crayons. If you take a marker pen in your favorite color that will do fine; highlight pens are good too. If you want to go one step further, sprinkle dried Dill or Fern, Irish Moss or Honeysuckle on your stone — or better yet, surround the stone by any one of these items. (Note: fresh Dill can be used too.) Dill and Irish Moss, according to ancient magical rituals, attract Money and Luck; Fern attracts Riches and Luck; Honeysuckle attracts Money.

Wrap the stone in a white (for purity) cloth until you are ready to perform the magical ceremony. Hold the stone, charge it with intense emotional energy with thoughts of wealth and winning. Visualize yourself winning. Visualize yourself receiving the money. Visualize yourself spending the money you won. Visualize yourself living the life you've dreamed about. Do this once a day; whenever the urge (your intuition) strikes, do it. Then forget about it for a while. Keep your Lucky Stone out of the reach and sight of others. Do not tell anyone about this as you do not want their negative vibrations sent to you. Also keep your Lucky Stone surrounded by the Irish Moss, Dill, Honeysuckle or Fern.

When you go out of your abode with your Lucky Stone, carry it in a yellow or green cloth bag. Instead of a bag you can cut a square of green or yellow cloth, place your Lucky Stone in it, and tie the corners together with a string of the same color (or substitute a ribbon for the string).

You may wonder, "When do I carry my Lucky Stone with me?" If you play scratch off Lotto, or when you buy a Lottery ticket and fill out the numbers you are going to play, rub your Lucky Stone while you are doing these things. If you go to the race track, rub your Lucky Stone when you are trying to decide which horse you should play. When you rub your Lucky Stone, say, "Bring me Good Luck with the right choices that which will be for my divine good." If you go to a casino, rub your Lucky Stone while sitting at the slot machine and say the preceding to yourself. If you are playing table games (poker, craps, blackjack, roulette), try holding your Lucky Stone and rubbing it; if that is difficult to do (because you need your hands to play), then rub it before the table is approached. Mentally say, "Bring me Good Luck. Let me play the right number and make the right decisions to be a winner."

When you gamble and do the Lucky Stone Magical Device, keep in mind that everything (like winning) comes from within — self-directed energy. When it comes to winning, you must PROJECT POWERFULLY. You can be happy, fulfilled and truly thankful when you win. You may feel that the world and everything in it is yours. Think (Project) those powerful thoughts when you are visualizing various things. Sense that everything is working together in harmony for you. You can be happy, feel connected and engaged with what is around you. You can experience accomplishment — know that you have goals and are moving toward them successfully. Realize that you are in a position to receive your heart's desires. Feel that you are holding the world (when you are holding your Lucky Stone) in your hands — give of yourself to the world with positive thoughts. And bless the rewards returned to you.

"THE LUCKY CANDLE" MAGICAL DEVICE

In Astrology, Venus represents "ready cash," cash such as comes from winning the lottery or a jackpot, or a contest, sweepstakes. Venus also represents the color yellow. Therefore, you need to use Yellow candles for the following magical devices. Etch (with a pencil, knife or needle) the word "WEALTH" on the side of a yellow candle. When you feel the urge — follow your strong desires and: (1) Light the candle, hold it for five minutes over money such as a dollar bill or a bill which you received for goods bought. Repeat this every day for a week. (2) Place the yellow candle in a candle holder and pile money around it. When you finish, dab a piece of the candle wax on your wrists, forehead and behind your ears. Wipe it clean after thirty minutes. If you want to dab the wax on jewelry as the candle burns, do so — afterwards — wipe it clean and wear the jewelry. The jewelry is charged with the wax and in turn is infused with the energy of your Lucky Candle. This will help attract prosperity.

Or another effective "Lucky Candle" Magical Device can be used. On a yellow (rather large) candle, etch (write) your name and the words "MONEY, WEALTH, RICHES." Then light the candle and grasp it firmly in your hands (don't burn yourself, go to the bottom section to hold it). Hold it until you feel your pulse throbbing beneath your fingers — a sign that your subconscious mind is mingling with the spirit of the candles and the things you want — think, "My intentions are now firmly grounded in the candle." Use lots of emotion and say, "This candle brings me wealth and riches." When finished, put the candle down and extinguish the flame with a spoon, candle snuffer or your fingers. DO NOT BLOW THE CANDLE FLAME OUT — YOUR BREATH CAN CHANGE THE MAGICAL DEVICE AND TAKE AWAY FROM YOUR OBTAINING YOUR HEART'S DESIRES. Begin this Magical Device on Sunday (for the day ruled by the Sun — which represents "Power"), or Thursday (for the day ruled by Jupiter - which represents "Wealth"), or on Friday (for the day ruled by Venus — which represents "Ready Cash"). When you relight the candle (after having first done it) on another day (other than the first time), be sure that the candle burns out completely by itself. Daily repetition for a month will increase the energy of the Candle for this Prosperity Magical Device. It becomes more effective when, thus, energized and is entered into your subconscious mind as prosperity.

If you want to save some wax from any of these "Lucky Candle" Magical Devices, put the wax (a very small portion) on your lottery ticket. Or take the wax with you to the race track or a casino. In the latter cases, place it on a paper next to your money, seal (cover) it with saran or any wax-type of paper so it doesn't rub off. This also seals the magic in.

When you are in the casino, at the race track, at a Bingo game or buying your lottery ticket, repeat to yourself silently the affirmations said when you were performing your "Lucky Candle" Magical Device — picture the candle (and great wealth) in your mind. Say, "This candle wax from my Lucky Candle brings me wealth and riches."

You can also draw a picture of a candle, or cut one out from a magazine or newspaper — put the wax on it and take that with you to the casino, bingo game, race track or lottery ticket place.

"THE LUCKY CRYSTAL" MAGICAL DEVICE

Do you know that crystals can help you win a fortune? Wouldn't you like to boost your chances of becoming a big winner by tapping into the power of these common and inexpensive crystals? Are you aware that crystals have rare powers and have had a long history in Western culture? Since the times of the Greeks and Romans, crystals have been known to contribute good fortune to the owner who uses them properly.

The most important thing to remember is a POSITIVE ATTITUDE. Crystals are capable of transmitting and absorbing energy. Each stone has a different vibration that channels bioelectricity from your mind and body, thus helping you develop luck and your highest potential. Crystals can become extensions of your being; they can aid you to amplify, focus and release energy in harmonious and powerful ways.

Now for the magic part. Hold a crystal in one hand and slowly let it go over your body — without touching your body. Start with your toes and work your way up to the head. This will draw out the negative energy that holds back success. While you are moving it over your body, say, "Out all negative energy goes."

Next, relax your mind and let your thoughts flow freely over the material things you desire. Visualize yourself as already owning them. Then, write them down on a piece of paper and call it your "Lucky Crystal List." Let the crystal slowly touch all of the items you wrote down. And while so doing, see them in your possession. Meditate. Pray. Be positive you'll have the objects of your desire.

When you meditate, take slow, deep breaths and concentrate your mind on money, possessions, travel — or whatever it is you wish to obtain. You must put FEELINGS and EMOTIONS into your thoughts. Feel as if you have the money in your hand and that it is falling all over you and every space in your living quarters. Devote about ten minutes a day to your "magic act." After three days, cease the "magic act" until three months go by. It is necessary to release the energy so it can work for you. By constantly thinking about it, you are not releasing the thought energy for your desires. Once you get what you want do the "magic act" with other things you desire. It is best to concentrate on ONE thing at a time.

Once you've finished your "magic act" with the crystal, put the crystal in a container and cover it completely with salt (salt destroys negative energy). Do not let anyone touch your crystal. Hide the container. Do not tell anyone about the material things you desire. Often others, innocently, do not see you obtaining the things you want. The next time you are ready to do the "magic act" with your crystal it will be ready.

You may ask, "Where do I buy a crystal?" Perhaps, you own a ring, necklace or earrings made of crystal. If not, try a gem store or New Age Bookstore. When you buy a crystal, purchase the one that first catches your eye. Crystals are inexpensive. For the purposes of Money Magic, a plain white crystal may be best suited for your purpose.

"THE LUCKY ELEPHANT" MAGICAL DEVICE

Do you know there are many affluent people who collect statues (miniature to large) of elephants with their trunks raised? Years ago, I remember visiting the homes of many movie stars and producers who had elephants in all sizes (with the trunks raised) displayed in various rooms of their mansions. Some were in special glass display cases, others were sitting on tables, some were life size — they were in ivory, porcelain, marble, ceramic and various types of stone.

In Poland, and other countries, an elephant with trunk raised high is a symbol of Good Luck. In Poland, and Asian countries, people collect images of elephants — it may be in a drawing, a charm, talismanic charm, jewelry, ceramic, stone, wooden (painted white), ivory and may be in miniature or life size. Many are made in fine china. You can wear them as a charm, necklace or keep them in a pocket. Most people set them out on special collectors tables; however, a bookshelf or any type of stand will still bring you luck, according to what I have seen with the hundreds of people I know who collect elephants. Photos of elephants with their trunk raised high can also be as effective as a statue.

If you are unable to buy your mini-elephant with the trunk raised high, then the following drawing can be cut out and used.

IT IS VERY IMPORTANT THAT THE ELEPHANT IS WHITE OR GREEN JADE. THE IVORY OR GREEN JADE ELEPHANTS ARE THE TYPE THAT EVERY SERIOUS COLLECTOR POSSESSES. You can cut out the above elephant drawing and paste it to a piece of cardboard to keep it sturdy. Make a cardboard stand to put it on, or lean it against a wall on a shelf. You can make a collage of these elephants (paste many of these same drawings together).

The next step is to meditate. You can touch your elephant, or just look at it — the choice is yours: both methods are effective. When you are meditating: believe that you can make your dreams come true and that patience and determination will make them happen. Let your dreams (thoughts) take you to those special places your heart desires to be. Look to every day as a day of new beginnings, opening your mind to positive action and unlimited sums of money.

"THE LUCKY ASTROLOGICAL GAMBLING MAP" MAGICAL DEVICE

You must use mental effort, consciously or unconsciously to attain your desires. Thus once your mind has set a wish in motion, it can be more easily and quickly granted than if you left it purely to chance. Your horoscope indicates your secret desires, and attitude toward everything in life. Thus your Lucky Astrological Gambling Map is a mental and visual aid to attract luck with gambling. Use the following horoscope wheel as your very own Gambling Map. Be sure to write your name, day, month, year, time (if known) and place of birth as on the example below:

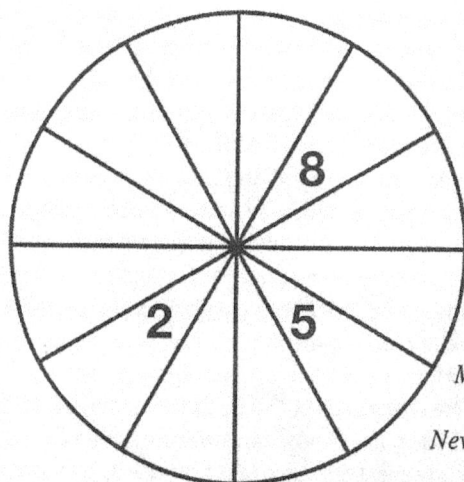

Jane Doe
March 17, 1941
9:00 a.m.
New York, New York

You will notice that on this horoscope wheel, there are 12 segments with the numbers 2, 5 and 8 written in three of these segments. These are called Houses in astrology; they represent different departments of life. The Number 2 House represents Your Money — income coming to you. The Number 5 House represents Gambling. The Number 8 House represents Other People's Money — money that a casino pays you when you win; money the state pays you when you win the lottery. Make copies of this blank horoscope wheel so you can use it over and over again.

Write the money you desire to win in the 2nd or 8th House (or both Houses of this horoscope wheel). In the 5th House, write the type of gambling you are engaged in, i.e., Lotto, the Lottery, Keno, Craps, Roulette, Blackjack, Race Track,

Sports Game (name of fighters, name of football, baseball or basketball team). To go even further write the date of the Sports Game or horse race, or the date you are going to the casino or that the lottery winners will be announced.

How does it work? When you've written your wishes in the proper Houses, those departments of life are enhanced with extra kinetic energy to bring them into manifestation. To understand it easier — think of your horoscope as the blueprint of your soul and your Lucky Astrological Gambling Map coincides with it; thus it enhances everything which then becomes a clear and visible print for you to see. Thus, every time you look at your filled in Lucky Astrological Gambling Map, you set forth certain kinetic powers that can help move and bring into being the money you desire. It is the Law of Nature (a Universal Law and Principle) working just for you! Energy is being reinforced in the direction you indicate on your Lucky Astrological Gambling Map.

Set aside a time each day, so you can concentrate all your mental energies on what you want. Meditate. Visualize yourself already winning the money. It has been said, and proven, that "What the mind can conceive can happen." Thoughts produce things and writing them on your Lucky Astrological Gambling Map speeds up matters and helps ensure success. You are tuning in to a high force such as God (the Supreme Being, Infinite Intelligence) tapping your subconscious mind and using your conscious mind to bring it closer into being. These are secret rituals used for centuries by the ancients and handed down orally to a chosen few who were initiated in the mysteries of the occult.

Hide your Lucky Astrological Gambling Map, once it's been completed. Do NOT tell anyone about it, especially what you requested. You never know when someone may put out a negative thought against your wishes being granted. This discordant energy could work against you, or just take longer for your desires to manifest. Others may be skeptical, even though you don't believe they are. Therefore, don't take the risk of confiding to anyone. Be secretive.

Once you've hidden your Lucky Astrological Gambling Map, try to forget about it... until it's time to meditate. The best time to meditate is in the wee hours of the morning. Go about your usual chores during the day. The more your mind dwells on your written requests, the more difficult it is to attract them — it may delay matters. Release the thought-energy to a higher-than-human power (God) which can help bring these things into reality.

Once you've been granted your wish, blank out the old one, and write a new one. Or take a new horoscope gambling wheel and write it in fresh. When you meditate, or buy a lottery ticket, go to the races, or a casino — wear clothing, or an accessory, in the color yellow. Yellow in Astrology, is the color for Venus — the planet which represents READY CASH.

Save this Lucky Astrological Gambling Map and use it over and over again. Be patient. Often it takes time to win; depending upon how intense your emotional energy is at the time you meditate. The stronger, the better. The more you visualize yourself winning, the easier it is to win.

"THE LUCKY FOUR-LEAF CLOVER" MAGICAL DEVICE

The clover plant which has four leaflets, is known to be an omen of, and brings, GOOD LUCK. You have heard an old cliché, "To be in clover," which refers to be in most enjoyable circumstances — to live luxuriously or in abundance. Isn't that the way you want to live? It's not impossible to live the lifestyle of the rich.

A hundred years ago it was customary for the French to send greeting cards on April 1st. The cards featured fish as their central motif, accompanied by OTHER GOOD LUCK SYMBOLS such as horseshoes, pansies or the four-leafed clover. This custom was believed to spring from when the Sun changed from the sign Pisces (Fish) to Aries (the Ram) — Aries, the Ram, symbolizes the beginning of spring, new life. And years before this custom, the Four-Leaf Clover symbolized Good Luck to those who picked one. Thus, various cultures all over the globe have used the Four-Leaf Clover for luck.

If you are in a locale where there are Four-Leaf Clovers growing, try looking for one and pick it. If this can't be done, then there are other alternatives. The first option is to use this diagram of a Four-Leaf Clover.

The second option is the following recipe for money, so you can attract wealth and all the material goods you want. You will need to buy these items in the spice section of a grocery store or in a health store that sells herbs: Mustard Seeds, Mistletoe, Cloves. Take one tablespoon of each and put in a bowl. Go to a Botanica, grocery stores or health food shops who might carry the following: Safflower oil, Sandalwood oil, Jasmine oil, Myrrh, Frankincense. If you cannot find all of these ingredients then use as many as you can. Once you have gathered these ingredients, mix them together, and while so doing, focus your complete attention on the purpose of why you are mixing them together. For example, your thoughts may be: "Make me win lots of money," or "Make me be the big lottery winner — winning millions," or "Let me win the jackpot at the casino," or "Make me rich through winning a sweepstakes," or "Make me wealthy by winning a contest," etc.

Take the ingredients out of the bowl, place on a clean cloth. Cup your hands around the ingredients and continue repeating (charging the energy into the ingredients) by stating all of the things you want to accomplish. Say out loud (when you are alone), "I charge these herbs to bring (state what you desire). This incantation is to bring changes into my life which will bring me gains beyond my wildest imagination. All of these changes are for my benefit and, thus, once I have them will help others. I ask that this wish of mine is correct and for the good of many people, including myself. So shall it be." You can do the preceding any time you wish, but for the best results the day or night of the Full Moon is best.

Once you have finished the incantation, place the ingredients back in a bowl and hide it where it cannot be seen by anyone. The reason the Mustard Seeds, Mistletoe and Cloves are used is because these are all lucky herbs. The cloves represent the Four-Leaf Clover, if you are unable to find a real Four-Leaf Clover. However, if you cannot find the real Four-Leaf Clover and you want to use my diagram then perform the preceding ritual.

If you have a real Four-Leaf Clover: touch the four leaves of the real Four-Leaf Clover; as you touch each leaf, meditate on it's lucky power to bring you the prosperity you want. As you touch each leaf, then wave your hand over all four leaves and you can say various things such as: "Make me a millionaire," or "Make me win the lottery," or "Make me rich," or "Bring me millions of dollars," or "Make me the big jackpot winner at the casino," or "Let me be the big winner of a sweepstakes contest," etc. You should visualize yourself receiving a check with the money desired. Visualize yourself living this life that you yearn for. Take the real Lucky Four-Leaf Clover with you to the casino or when you buy a lottery ticket or go to the race track or any other place. If you own a business, take it to work. Try to have more than one real Lucky Four-Leaf Clover and hide them in a wallet, purse, cash register (if you own a business), or a checkbook.

"THE LUCKY MOON LIST" MAGICAL DEVICE

Changes in the earth's magnetic field explain why the Stars, Sun, and Moon really do affect us. The magnetic field is like an invisible ocean enveloping the whole planet. Gravity from nearby planets affects the magnetic field the same way the Moon's gravitational pull affects ocean tides. It's predictable the same way tides around a coast are predicted in a tide table. Cosmic magnetism shapes our destiny because it generates tiny electrical impulses — and the human brain is influenced by those impulses. Therefore, "The Lucky Moon List" is based on the phases of the Moon: New Moon, Full Moon, First and Last Quarter of the Moon. And, thus, since the Moon is involved (The Moon is the subconscious mind of the individual, according to astrology), your subconscious thoughts are important as to the success of using this Magical Device.

Sit back and think about the material things that you want and need. Evaluate these desires for about fifteen minutes. Discard those things which are not really necessary. Select those things you have a strong urge that you MUST HAVE. Write out the list of those things you desire. Do this on the Moon's phases, such the day of the New Moon; the day of the Moon's First Quarter; the day of the Full Moon; the day of the Moon's Last Quarter. Look in the newspaper for the phases of the Moon, or call the library for this information.

Write out your affirmation, such as: "During the phase of this Moon is the time for Divine action. God's (the Supreme Being's, Infinite Intelligence's) Love and Power will bring me the things I request. I will not allow any negative thoughts to enter my mind. The Spirit of Prosperity is now with and keeps me animated and positive, thus the substance that surrounds me is my money supply that will sustain me, and bring me everything that is for my better good. I am now attracting wealth and happiness. So shall it be!"

When you are alone, take a few minutes to repeat this affirmation. Then repeat it just before you go to sleep at night, so it will be fresh on your subconscious mind while you are sleeping. This is to be done only on the phases of the Moon. By reciting your desires out loud, you are charging the atmosphere with intense vocalization; thus, the projection is fortified with magical energy to bring your dreams to fruition. While you are repeating your affirmation, touch and look at your "Lucky Moon List." Then give thanks in advance to God, or the Higher Intelligence of the Universe, to grant your requests. Do this four times in one month (if all of the Moon's phases are in that one month), then burn the list.

When you buy your lottery ticket, on one of the phases of the Moon, take your list with you, repeat it mentally — pick a time of day or evening when you feel most relaxed to buy the ticket. You need time to meditate silently — if you're in a rush and stressed out, it is difficult to meditate. You need to be positive in your thoughts and visualize yourself as a winner.

If you go to the race track, get there early enough to look over the racing form — and meditate on each horse — hold your list in your hand at the same time. Do some handicapping of your own (rating the horse yourself) as to the horse's past performance, type of track, etc. Go to the betting window with a positive thought as you meditate along the way. It's best to go to the track, also, on the phases of the Moon — if one is handy in your area.

When you go to a casino and gamble (slot machine, craps, blackjack, roulette, bingo etc.), go on the phases of the Moon with your list in your hand. Try to silently meditate on your winning. If you are playing Keno, apply the same principle as you do when buying a lottery ticket. Visualize the balls with your numbers rolling out and those same numbers appearing on the Keno board.

The most important thing to remember is to RELEASE THE ENERGY so it can work in your behalf. For example: If you continue to think about winning, or the numbers you want, you are holding on to those numbers and thus making it difficult to win. You've already put your needs (thoughts) into the ethers with your affirmation — so, let go — forget about winning, forget about the numbers — relax your mind. Play. Have fun. Let go and let God (or the Higher Intelligence) help you. That is not your job — you've done your necessary part — so, let go and be calm and know that you are a winner!

NOTE: A University in Las Vegas, Nevada did research on gambling and winning to see when most of the winnings occurred. They discovered on the Full Moon dates there were more lucky winners than at any other time. This was followed by the dates when the other three phases of the Moon occurred.

"THE LUCKY MIRROR" MAGICAL DEVICE

The mirror is like a magnet, and can be utilized as such when you are doing magic. You, and everyone around you, is a magnet — a magnet to attract good or bad. It's up to you to be positive and radiate those harmonious vibes that will make you a magnet to attract everything your heart desires. The physical body is composed of electromagnetic energy; thus, it is through this electromagnetic energy that you are a magnet to attract what you think. Thus, when your thoughts are positive, you're a magnet to attract prosperity — be expectant of success and it will knock on your door. If you are depressed, unforgiving, and express self-pity or other negative thoughts, you are then a magnet to attract unfortunate events into your life such as loss, indebtedness, loneliness, or poverty.

Use a hand-held mirror and look into the mirror saying good things to the image of you in the mirror, such as: "Everyone likes you." Or "You are a good person." Or "You are lucky." Or you can say, "The boss likes you and is going to give you a raise." "The boss thinks so highly of you, you are going to get a promotion." "You are going to get a better job." "You are going to have an increase in your income." "You are going to do well with bonds." "You are going to do well with your stocks, they are going up." "You are going to sell property and make a good profit." "_____ (name of person) loves you." "You are good looking." "You are losing weight and getting thinner and thinner."

The Lucky Mirror and Gambling: Hold a hand-held mirror and say: "You are going to win at lotto." "You are going to win a jackpot on a slot machine." "You are going to win at the race track." "You are going to win on _____ sports game bet." "You are going to win _____ contest." "You are going to win (tonight) in Bingo."

If you go to a casino, race track or sports game; after you have made a bet (or before), go to the restroom and stand in front of the mirror and make your affirmations. Or, use a hand-held mirror, while you are sitting at a sports game, race track or slot machine — mentally say your affirmation, such as: "This machine I am sitting at is lucky for me." "This horse I just bet on for _____ race, is going to be lucky for me." "This fight _____ (name of person fighting) is going to be lucky for me." Or say whatever positive thought pops into your mind. Your image is reflected in the mirror — and, thus, so are the things you say while looking in a mirror — your words bounce back from the mirror to you! Thus, how can you not be a winner?

"THE LUCKY TRINE" MAGICAL DEVICE

In astrology we have aspects which are the distances between two planets. Some of these aspects bring struggles and problems, whereas others bring favorable events. The "Trine" is considered the luckiest aspect in astrology. It expresses LUCK and is also called "Lady Luck." You've heard the expression, "Lady Luck is smiling at you."

The ancients who were well versed in astrology found that rays of planetary force when meeting at a 120 degree angle (the Trine aspect distance between two planets) produces whirls in the ethers (air) that are constructive in nature. They discovered that a Trine brings luck to the individual. The good that comes through the Trine comes easily and spontaneously. Favors come with little effort. Things grow naturally and opportunities are forced upon you without being asked for. A Trine signifies good qualities that bring you LUCK.

You may wonder how a Trine as a Magical Device can work for you. It works the same way as the other Magical Devices — it is dependent upon your ability to use imagery and DIRECT YOUR MIND to be positive and mentally build those things you yearn for, such as being rich, successful, happy or finding a mate.

Cut out or copy the following diagram of the LUCKY TRINE. Or you can draw your own LUCKY TRINE. Bless the Trine to bring you LUCK and a FORTUNE. If you want, you can color the LUCKY TRINE in the color yellow — yellow is representative of the planet Venus — the planet that rules "ready cash," which is available by divine substance, the Universe. But you must tap divine substance harmoniously so that you can attract the money desired. By tuning in to "The Lucky Trine" Magical Device, you will be one step further toward finding that pot of gold at the end of the rainbow.

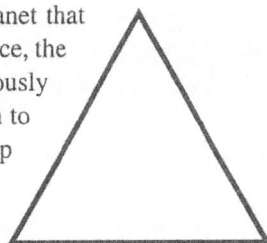

Touch the LUCKY TRINE at all three points. While touching each point meditate that you are NOW RICH, or that you want to win the lottery or whatever your heart desires. At the same time you are touching and meditating, visualize your thoughts (using IMAGERY - the IMAGINATION) to the point that you can actually see yourself rich, winning a lottery, jackpot, having a dream house or dream vacation or whatever it is you want. Take this LUCKY TRINE with you to a casino and touch all three points before playing a slot machine. Take this to the race track and touch it before each race. Take this LUCKY TRINE out when you are writing your numbers on a lotto or lottery ticket or Scratch ticket. Touch this LUCKY TRINE when you enter a sweepstakes contest. Or use it in other ways. Perhaps, you want a raise. Touch it before asking the boss for a hike in salary. Or maybe you want to get married, touch it and meditate on your being wed. Use it for anything your heart desires. Remember the key word, in astrology, for a TRINE is LUCK.

"THE LUCKY MIND (MENTAL)" MAGICAL DEVICE

Decide what it is you want: a home, car, furs, jewelry, designer clothes, to travel or win the lottery or hit a jackpot in a casino. Then visualize the things you want, and in your mind see the results as you want them to happen in your life. The time to do your visualization is in the wee hours of the morning or just before midnight. If there is a drawing (lotto, lottery, sweepstakes, raffle ticket, etc.) then do your visualization the night before the drawing. If you are going to a casino or race track, do your visualization the night before you plan to go; repeat it the moment you wake up, and repeat it on the trip to the casino or race track. Repeat it thirty minutes before the races start or before you start to play the slot machines or table games in a casino.

For In-person Drawings Or Gambling: If this is a ticket drawing such as takes place in casinos, or raffle ticket, etc. then mentally look into the eyes of the person who is drawing the ticket and visualize your ticket as the winner, and mentally say (when looking in the eyes of the person selecting the ticket), "Draw my ticket!"

If you are playing Roulette, visualize the ball rolling on the number or numbers you have wagered, or if you wagered on a column, black or red, or even or odd, or numbers from ___ to ___, then visualize the roulette ball hitting one of these things. Mentally say, "Let the ball roll on ___(whatever you wagered)."

If you are playing Blackjack, visualize the cards you need. Look in the dealer's eyes and mentally say, "Bring me a card I need to win." If you are playing Craps, visualize the dice rolling the number you want and mentally, and verbally, repeat this number as if you were casting a spell on that number — strong and intense thought is needed. Or you can also look into the eyes of the shooter and mentally say, "Roll my numbers," or "Roll me number ___."

If you are playing a Slot Machine, look the room over — and the slot machine that catches your eye (stands out in your mind), go to that Slot Machine and play. As you put your money into the slot machine, visualize, and mentally say, "Make me a winner."

If you go to the race track, and you get a chance to go to the paddock and look in the eyes of the horse — mentally say, "Run fast! Win the race!" or while the horse is running, visualize the horse (you bet on) running faster and passing all the other horses. Visualize the horse winning the race. Mentally, look (from a distance or with binoculars) at the horse you bet on, and say, "Come on! Run faster, faster, faster!" Repeat this until the horse is at the finish line.

For Distance Apart Drawings: Often you do not know the time of a Sweepstakes or Contest drawing, but you have the date of the drawing. Therefore, during various morning hours visualize your ticket being drawn and repeatedly say, "Draw my ticket! Make me a winner!" If you are watching television at the time of a Lottery drawing, mentally look at the ball and say, "Let my numbers be drawn. Make me a winner." Repeatedly say this and visualize your numbers being drawn.

"THE LUCKY JAR" MAGICAL DEVICE

Perhaps you are the type of person who puts your extra change in a jar. Or perhaps, you just save pennies, nickels, dimes, quarters or silver dollars. Therefore, the Lucky Jar Magical Device is similar.

Take an empty jar (the larger the better) and after you've magnetized the money to be put in it, you can fill it with any denomination desired. To magnetize the money: place it on a table (while you are alone) — do one coin or bill at a time. Touch it, visualize it multiplying to 50 times that amount (50 is the number Jupiter vibrates to — Jupiter, the planet of wealth), or 5 times that amount (still a Jupiter vibration). Put the coin or bill in the jar. See (visualize) the money in the jar multiplying so much that you need extra jars to fill because what you have is over-flowing.

Have you ever been short of cash? Have you always been broke because you live from one paycheck to another? If this is the case, go ahead (before your Lucky Money Jar is filled) and dip into the jar — it will keep you in an endless flow of cash. Because the Law of the Universe will supply you with more when you spend it; however, don't ever let your jar get empty — always keep something in it to attract more money. Hopefully, you won't have to dip into your jar because money may be showering upon you from all different directions.

"THE LUCKY KEY" MAGICAL DEVICE

Buy an unused key from a locksmith, hardware store, or any place where keys are sold. When you get home, and are alone, magnetize the key by putting the thought that "This key is going to open the door of riches for me," or "This key is going to open the door of opportunity, thus attracting me good jobs, money, invest-ments and so forth." (Name those things desired, but always see the key as OPEN-ING DOORS FOR YOU — it could be just to meet the right people who can help you get to the top (or the ideal spouse). Repeat your desires for several minutes then hide the key in a place where it will be away from the physical touch (vibra-tion) of others. You can take the key to the casino and while you are at a slot machine, see (visualize) the key as opening up the money inside the machine (just as if an attendant in the casino has to come with a key to open up, and put more money in the machine — especially to pay off your big winnings).

"THE LUCKY MONEY-SUGAR" MAGICAL DEVICE

Take a photograph of money or a phony bill of money (the larger the de-nomination the better), place it on a table (while you are alone) and sprinkle white sugar on it. While you are doing this, mentally say, "You are sweetening this money so I can attract more cash into my life." Then take a small mirror and hold it (or stand it) next to the money with the sugar on it and say, "This sugar is enhancing this money so it will bounce back (through the mirror's reflection) and multiply to enormous sums. So shall it be." (NOTE: Venus rules sugar and "ready cash," thus enhancing your chances to attract money — but keep positive at all times. Hide the money with the sugar in a closed jar or stone box so the ants won't be drawn to it. You can continue to add more money with sugar sprinkled on the money — each time you add more money and sugar, repeat the same ritual. Or you can take the money and sugar on one you already did, and reenergize it with more sugar, posi-tive thoughts, and visualization that the money, like sugar cane, grows and grows.

"THE LUCKY LETTER" MAGICAL DEVICE

The letter you write to yourself should be done two days after a New Moon (call the library or look in the newspaper for New Moon dates), if quick results are desired. Do not date this letter. Sign the letter — The Law of Abundance.

The following is a sample of how the letter should be written:

Dear _____, (your first name and last name)

You have just won $500.00! It will be paid to you sometime in the near future. Congratulations for being a winner!

The Law of Abundance

After you write the letter, touch it, meditate on it. Visualize the money you won being paid to you. Then say to yourself (be alone when you do this ritual), "So shall it be!" Take an envelope and address it to yourself. For the return address write:

The Law of Abundance
Universal Substance
The World

When you finish, put a stamp on it, mail it. When you receive the envelope, open it, meditate on it. Burn it, and the envelope. Thus the words will go into the astral substance (the ethers).

The following month, two days after the New Moon, repeat this ritual only write in $1,000, instead of $500. Then the next month, repeat the ritual and write in $5,000. Then the fourth letter, a month later, two days after the New Moon, write in $500,000. And the fifth letter, a month after the fourth letter, and two days after the New Moon, write your last letter for One Million Dollars. Each time you write the letter, perform the ritual, meditate, etc., put the stamp on, mail, open, read, burn. And then wait for The Law of Abundance to make you a winner, that is, if you didn't win anything before the 2nd, 3rd, 4th or 5th letter arrives. NOTE: If you want the letter to have extra power, put a hair from your head or body in the letter; the hair also gets burned.

◆ ◆ ◆

You can also use a scientific formula to turn a game of luck into a game of skill. It worked like magic for the 74 first prize Lotto jackpot winners who won $97 million dollars using Gail Howard's amazing Lottery formula. Try it yourself FREE by visiting her Web Site at www.gailhoward.com, or call Toll Free 1-800-945-4245 for information about her books and software.

CHAPTER FIVE

Gambling

This chapter is mainly some tips and hints about various forms of gambling. If you want details on how to play Craps, Roulette, Blackjack, Video Poker Machines or Sports Betting you need to purchase my book *Gambling To Win*. You can write, fax or call Star Bright Publishers for *Gambling To Win*. The book will then be shipped to you immediately upon receipt of your check, money order or when your Visa or MasterCard Credit Card information is given.

Star Bright Publishers
2235 East Flamingo Road, Suite 300-D
Las Vegas, Nevada 89119
Toll Free: 1-800 615-3352
Fax: (702) 894-9918
E-mail: starbrite@softcom.net
Web Site: www.lynnepalmer.com

CRAPS — TIPS AND HINTS

The game of Craps is probably the most fascinating of all the table games. It is the best game with the best odds and the best chance to win. Large sums of money can be made or lost on the single roll of the dice. One night I saw someone win $30,000 on the High Low (a 1-1 and 6-6 — which is 2, the low number and 12, the high number).

There are eleven numbers in the game of Craps: 2, 3, 4, 5, 6, 7, 8, 9, 10, 11, 12. You can play your lucky numbers, follow your intuition or go the way of the seasoned Craps player. The number 7 comes up the most. Then 6's and 8's (they can be made 5 ways); 9 and 5 can be made in 4 ways; 4 and 10 can be made in 3 ways; 3 and 11 can be made in 2 ways; 2 and 12 can be made in 1 way.

The best numbers to bet are 6 and 8 (but not the corner Big 6 or 8, instead bet the 6 and 8 above the Come Line on diagram). Then every time a 6 or 8 are rolled on the dice, you make money (you do not have to play the Pass Line or anything else — some people just play 6 and 9). It is smart to play 6 and 8 when you first start playing Craps because you can build up a bankroll then if the table is hot, you can play the Pass Line, Craps, and other things desired.

When you play the Pass Line, play the odds, back it up with money — ask the dealer how much you can back it up with). It is not good to play the Don't Pass Line, although there are people who play it and win — I have seen people lose plenty by playing it. It is not good to play the Field (sometimes you win, but most often people lose — you put money on the Field that one of those numbers will come up on the next roll of dice — usually beginners are Field players. Many people bet on the Hard Numbers, meaning these numbers are hard to make. They

DON'T COME BAR · 4 5 6 8 9 10 · COME · 5 for 1 · 7 · 5 for 1 · COME · 4 5 6 8 9 10 · DON'T COME BAR

PASS LINE · DON'T PASS BAR · DON'T PASS BAR · PASS LINE

PAYS DOUBLE · PAYS TRIPLE · 10 for 1 · 8 for 1 · PAYS DOUBLE · PAYS TRIPLE

(2) 3-4-9-10-11 (12) · 10 for 1 · 8 for 1 · (2) 3-4-9-10-11 (12)

FIELD · 15 for 1 · 30 for 1 · FIELD

DON'T PASS BAR · 15 for 1 · 30 for 1 · DON'T PASS BAR

PASS LINE · PASS LINE

BIG 6 · BIG 8 · BIG 6 · BIG 8

ANY CRAPS 8 for 1

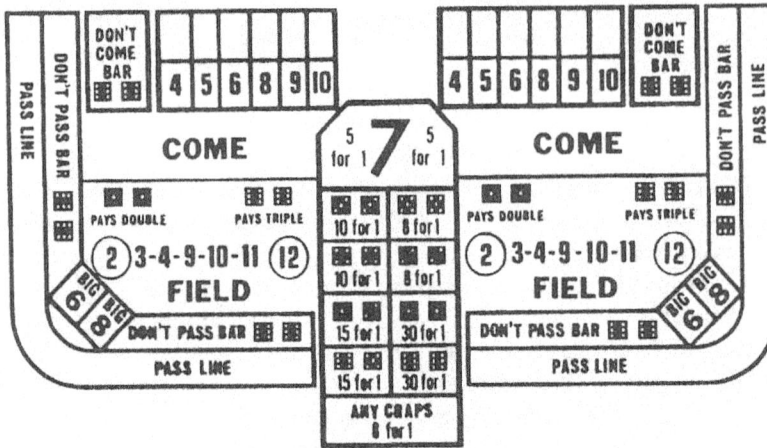

are 2-2, 3-3, 4-4, and 5-5 (that's 4, 6, 8 and 10 but the die have to be as mentioned — a two on one die and a two on the other die).

When the Shooter (the person rolling the dice) first starts to roll the dice, (before the Shooter has made a point) the Shooter is trying to roll a 7 or 11 (the Shooter wins when either of them come up on the first "come-out" roll), bet a certain sum on the Pass Line and for insurance, in case the Shooter throws a Crap (1-1, 1-2 or 6-6 (2, 3 or 12) also make a bet on Three-Way Craps. If the Shooter rolls a 7 or 11 you win on the Pass Line and lose on the Craps. However, if the Shooter throws a crap, you lose on the Pass Line but win on the Craps. Let's say, you had $5 on the Pass Line and lose it; however, on Three-Way Craps, you had $3 and if the Shooter threw a 1-2 (3), you would receive odds 15-1, or if the Shooter threw a 1-1 or 6-6 (2 or 12) the odds would be 30-1. You could also play the Horn (which would be a minimum of $4) when the Shooter first comes out (starts to shoot the dice) then if the Shooter throws a Crap or an 11 you win. If you had money on the Pass Line, you would also win on the 11 the Shooter threw.

If you won on a crap throw (before the Shooter has made a point) then double up your bet (say you had $1 and won, now add another $1 and make it a $2 bet, and if the Shooter throws another Crap you will win twice as much. And if you feel the Shooter can throw a Crap for the third time in row, bet it by adding another $1 making it a total of $3 riding on the Crap bet. You can do it for the fourth time too, if you feel it will happen again. I have seen people throw a 6-6 (12), four times in a row — one person who was just betting on the 6-6 (12) won thousands of dollars on Craps.

If you intuitively feel a certain number is going to come up, you can bet on just that number, for example: the Shooter has made a point but you feel a 9 will come up on the next roll of the dice: make a wager with the dealer of a 2-way nine (that means a 5-4 or 6-3 is going to come up next); if it does, you win 15 to 1; if it doesn't you lose your bet at that instance. This is called a Proposition bet and also called "on the hop."

A seasoned player gets a gut feeling and realizes that certain numbers often fall on the dice after a specific number. For example: when a 6-3 is thrown, often a Crap follows — this is on the come-out roll as well as during the course of the game. Thus, if you bet a Crap would be thrown, and it is, you win; otherwise, you lose on this one-time roll of the dice.

SLOT MACHINES — REGULAR AND VIDEO POKER

Keep in mind that a desperate person (someone who feels pressured to make money, because it is desperately needed) usually winds up a loser. Therefore, play with a positive attitude (use Magical Thoughts and Magical Devices) and think of gambling as Entertainment. It is best to be disciplined. When you get obsessed with winning, and try to make up for the money you lost, you could continue to lose. Often you are on a losing streak and should quit for a few hours, or wait until another day to try your luck again. The longer you play at a machine, the more money you'll put back into the slot machine. The casino owners make money off of addicted gamblers, they lose money with disciplined gamblers.

Play according to your budget. Don't spend more than you can afford to lose. Most people put aside a set amount of money and call it entertainment expense. Once that is gone, they quit. Figure out how much your total amount to lose is, then call it quits. If you win, and are satisfied — don't go for more — more people lose from greed than anything else. Be thankful you won and quit. Keep in mind that you can not win every single day — winning goes in cycles, which is indicated by your horoscope and whether you have lucky or unlucky aspects on a specific day.

If you do not have much money to start gambling with, then play the nickel slot machines; if you win then you can change to the quarter slot machines; if you win on the quarter machines, move to the dollar machines — that is if you feel you are on a winning streak.

Regular slot machines and Video Poker slot machines are computer based. They have a random number generator and a computer chip that selects the number, or card, or what it pays. Slot machines all over the world pay differently; thus, always look at the machines and see what each one pays off. Compare machine pay offs, and get the best pay off for your money. Often a dollar machine pays off better than a nickel slot machine. Certain casinos have machines that pay off better than other casino's machines. The casinos in downtown Las Vegas pay off better than those on The Strip. But the residential area casinos, where mostly locals play, usually have the loosest slots (paying the most and more frequently). Most machines are tight, some are set to pay off in small amounts from time to time — they never make it to the larger amounts. Other machines are loose and pay off most of the time. The loosest slot machines are located at the end of aisles or where there is heavy traffic — the casino owners want customers walking by to see that a machine is paying off great and, thus, will induce the customer to start playing slot machines in their casino.

It is best to always play the maximum coins (if you can afford it) for that slot machine — maximum amounts vary from 3 to 50 coins. If you play a small amount, let's say one quarter on a quarter Video Poker slot machine — and you get a Royal Flush (the best you can get), you would win 250 quarters which equals $62.50. However, if you play the maximum coins of five quarters, and you get a Royal Flush — you would win $1,000. It would be a real heartbreaker, if you didn't have the maximum coins in — Royal Flush's don't show up that often.

When you put the maximum amount of coins in a slot machine, you have a better chance to win big. It is best to play jackpot machines that have smaller pay offs because they pay off more frequently than the slot machines with larger pay offs. If you want to play a Progressive slot machine, look above the machine and see how much the money is up to (every second the amounts change). When the money is at a large figure, then you can play them, hoping to get a big payoff. They pay off better than other jackpot machines, but less frequently. If you notice that the Progressive machine has accumulated a small amount that implies that it paid off recently; therefore, it is unlikely it will pay off again. Usually it pays off big, then goes down to a small sum — and as players put money in — the machine starts to increase the amount it pays until it gets up to an enormous sum. If you go to a specific casino most of the time, keep your eyes on the amount it pays off when it is big, and when it is down; then you can judge when you should give it a try.

Regular Slot Machines

Slot machines with 777 and fruits (like cherries) are usually good slot machines. If you play quarter slot machines, you may want to give Quartermania a try — but your chances to win the enormous sum it pays is slim. Dollar machines can be good, but you may have to invest $50 to $100 before you win big — and then, you still may not win, especially if there was a recent winner on that machine. Megabucks are dollar slot machines that you can win small sums (like $300 or more), but to be the big winner of a million dollars or more — you have to be really lucky. When it comes to gambling: the person with the best aspects (astrologically) is going to win the big jackpot money.

You could start playing a slot machine with a small amount of money invested in it to see how the machine is paying (either slow or fast), then either put more money in it, or change machines. If after two plays on a slot machine, you get only small amounts — you could stay with that machine or move to another slot machine. If you've made ten plays and nothing has happened, you should definitely move to another slot machine. In fact, I have noticed that most slot machines start on a downward escalation scale when for four plays, nothing is won. That will eventually take you out (make you lose everything you poured into it) — that is a cold machine that has been computerized to pay off very little or infrequently.

If you have small returns on your money, after playing a slot machine for a long time, move on to another machine; perhaps, that is all that machine will ever do. Play less coins when you are losing (the slot machine is on its downward escalation — that's when you are not winning anything on a play), if you want to stay at that slot machine. Often, when you are down to one coin left to play, you'll lose it. If the slot machine lets you win once with your last coin — it is likely to make you lose the next time. It is best to leave a machine when it is on its downward escalation — don't put emotion into playing, use logic and analyze what the machine is doing — take your time with each play to make sure you realize just what the machine is doing.

When a machine is hot (you are winning on almost every play), stay with that machine. That is when you can play more coins because the slot machine is escalating upward — this machine could have been set up to pay off frequently — especially the jackpot.

Single lines on Multiple coin slot machines cost more to play; you'll only get a small return if you play a small amount. Therefore, if you are only going to play a Single Line, it's best not to play a Multiple coin slot machine. If you play the maximum amount of coins, your chances to win are improved because you can hit many lines in various ways at one time. That's when you can win big bucks. But keep in mind, you can also lose. There are many people who play fifty nickels at a time on the Multiple lines machines — some of them have won big, others lose. But it all sums up to gambling — which is risky.

Video Poker Slot Machines

The Video Poker slot machine is very popular and a good slot machine to play (you win more frequently on them than you do regular slot machines). The Video Poker slot machine is for any person who has a desire to win some money along with entertainment, regardless of whether a person is twenty-five or eighty years of age, poor or well-to-do.

There are several types of Video Poker slot machines: Draw Poker, Bonus Poker, Joker Poker, Deuces Wild Poker, Double Bonus Poker, Double Double Bonus Poker, and Kings or Better Poker. Draw Poker pays the least of all the slot machines, although it pays off more frequently. Bonus Poker pays off more often than Draw Poker. Joker Poker, in which the Joker card is the Wild card, is more or less on a level with Draw Poker when it comes to paying off.

Always look on the various Video Poker slot machines to see what each one pays off — compare them before playing. The Double Bonus Video Poker machine is a good machine to play. It derives it name (Double Bonus) because it will pay more than the regular Bonus machines, or many other Video Poker slot machines when it comes to the higher bracket of pay offs such as a Flush, Full House, Four of a Kind or Straight Flush. The Double Up Machines, once you've hit the button "Yes" for doubling up, do not double up again for a while (as a rule) because you may lose the smaller amount you won by not doubling up. Often, I have seen the Double Up machine pay off many times in a row, before it stopped doubling up. Use your intuition when Doubling up.

A good Video Poker slot machine to play is the Deuces Wild. It pays on a semi-regular basis more frequently than other types of slot machines. Also you play longer (get more play for your money) than any other type of regular or Video Poker slot machine. The Deuces Wild slot machine pays with consistency, in fact, I have seen people win over and over again on this type of machine. Because they pay off frequently, many times they are put "out of service" for days at a time, or they are moved to another location. Therefore, get the serial number of the machine you like, in case it is moved elsewhere — you could win on it one night and the next night it could be moved to another part of the casino.

Pay Offs: The best pay offs are in the following order with the first one listed as the most money it pays off, and the last one listed is the least amount of money it pays off: The Royal Flush, Four Aces, Straight Flush, Four of a Kind, Full House, Flush, Three of a Kind, Straight, Two Pair, Jacks or Better.

The high cards are the Jack, Queen, King, Ace. The low cards are 2, 3, 4, 5, 6, 7, 8, 9, 10. Look at the screen on the Video Poker machine because it will tell you whether you have a Royal Flush, Four Aces, Straight Flush, Four of a Kind, Full House, Flush, Three of a Kind, Straight, Two Pair, or the Jacks or Better cards. Do not keep the kicker (one Jack, one Queen, one King or one Ace) if your other cards are all low cards. When playing Video Poker, the idea is to try to get something (a combination) that will pay off — such as any of the combinations listed under the above PAY OFFS section.

Straight: A straight is five cards in sequence; they do not have to be of the same suit (suit implies — diamonds, hearts, clubs, spades). If you have four of the five cards needed (to make a straight), and the one card missing is in the middle of the sequence, it is best *not* to draw for that card. It is harder to catch a card in the middle than it is to catch a card on either end. To go for the middle card, you only have four chances to draw. If you draw (go) for the Straight at either end, you have eight chances to draw the card you need; therefore, it is smart to draw a new hand and discard all of the other cards (do not put the Hold button down on any of the cards).

However, if you have four of the five cards in sequence (in order) such as, 4, 5, 6, 7 or say 9, 10, Jack or Queen — it is advisable to hold the cards in sequence and then draw for the one card you need for the Straight — because it is open on both ends of the sequence, then your chances to get a Straight are vastly improved.

Straight Flush: A straight flush is when you have five cards in sequence (consecutive numbers) and in the same suit, such as all Diamonds and 6, 7, 8, 9 and 10. A Straight Flush on most machines pays 50 to 1; if you bet the maximum of five coins, you get back 250 coins.

Flush: A Flush is when you have five cards of the same suit, regardless of their sequence. If you have a Flush with say, 6, 10, Queen, King, Ace of Hearts — you should definitely disregard the Flush you have in your hand. You should discard the 6 of Hearts and go for the Royal Flush. A Flush will only pay 8 to 1, whereas if you discard the 6 and you draw the Jack of Hearts, you would collect

250 to 1. If you had in the maximum amount of coins (5) with such a bet on a quarter machine, you would win $1,000. If a dollar machine, you would win $4,000. That's not bad, is it?

Two Pairs: When holding Two Pairs, such as card numbers below the Jack (2, 3, 4, 5, 6, 7, 8, 9, 10), there is a possibility you will draw a third card to match the pair. This will produce a better pay off because it is Three of a Kind. When you hold Two Pairs and draw one card there is a possibility that it could match the Two Pair which you hold. This would give you a Full House, which is a much better pay off. If you get Three of a Kind, discard the other cards and go for Four of a Kind which is a very good pay off.

NOTE: Once you get a Royal Flush, Straight Flush, Four of a Kind or Full House, the Video Poker machine starts to escalate on a downward trend. If it goes four or more times down, you could lose everything you won, if you stay with the machine. However, if it is a hot machine and escalates down once after you've gotten any of the above, and goes back up again, then down, then up — you could continue to win. But once it starts to go down more than four times without winning anything that would be a sign to quit that machine. I have seen people get Four of a Kind five times within ten minutes — thus, that was a hot machine. And the next night the machine did the same thing; after a few days it was moved to another location.

Usually Video Poker slot machines (with the exception of the Deuce machine) will take you out on a gradual basis once nothing comes up for four times in a row. These slot machines have teasers to keep you playing. Therefore, you could go back up, only to be taken gradually down and out. Often, when you are on your last coin (or coins) the machine may tease you with a Straight or a Full House — but then it will still most likely take you down and out on a gradual decline. In other words, you'll win a little, lose — win a little then lose and finally start losing more — remember they are computerized. Once a Video Poker machine has gone down four times in a row, it's advisable to go to another machine. The Deuce machine may go down seven or eight times, before it starts to escalate on a downward basis. Thus you have a better chance for it to go up than you do when the other type of Video Poker machines are played. Many people cash out when the Video Poker machine goes down to a Full House, or if you were taken back up (after a gradual decline to one or five coins) and get a Full House. Usually, after a Full House Video Poker machines go down.

Deuce's Wild: This is played almost the same as a regular Video Poker slot machine. The exception is the Deuce (two) card is Wild and can be substituted for whatever you need to get a winning hand. When playing the Deuce's Wild Video Poker slot machine, anytime you get three Deuces, discard all the cards (except the three Deuces) and go for the fourth Deuce. On the Deuces Wild machine the four Deuces will pay 250 to 1, which if you have five coins in, and it is a quarter machine, you will be paid $250.00. If it is a dollar machine, and you have five coins in (playing at one time), you will be paid $2,500.

There are also times when only two deuces show up on the machine, then you should discard the other three cards as long as it is not a big pay off — and go for the Four Deuces (it's a chance you are taking, but that's what gambling is all about, isn't it?).

On the Deuce's Wild machine, you may get a "Wild Royal Flush" which will pay 25 to 1, you will see on the screen a Royal Flush with Deuces. If you get a Royal Flush *without the deuces,* and you have five coins (quarters) in, you will win $1,000. If you are playing the dollar Deuce's Wild machine, and have five coins in, you will win $4,000.

I wish you lots of good luck with gambling, and don't forget to use Magical Thoughts and Magical Devices to enhance your chances to be a big winner.

PART TWO

CHAPTER ONE

Aries — Money and Investments

Those born from March 21 through April 19 have the Sun in the sign Aries. Every sign of the zodiac corresponds to a particular type of prosperity; it's what you do and how you use it that determines whether you'll be successful or not.

Do you want to wind up in a mess because of your careless spending habits? Instead, wouldn't it be better if you could prevent losses, shortages, headaches, and banish worrisome thoughts from your mind? By knowing your faults and how to correct them you can enjoy life more, save money, and, be in tip-top shape. And that's well worth the effort, isn't it?

YOUR MONEY

Money goes through your hands like water. Your sign is known as the "Spendthrift of the Zodiac." You burn the candle at both ends, squandering every cent you have like there's no tomorrow. It's possible you originated that old adage, "Money burns a hole in your pocket." (Aries is a Fire sign, hence has rulership over burns.)

You move fast in a store, immediately buying what you like. Sometimes you are so carried away with your purchase you don't realize how much you've spent until you receive the bill, or until you find yourself without the cash to pay for something else.

You spoil your loved ones, children, and friends. You buy them gifts on the spur of the moment if something attracts your eye, especially if it reminds you of the person. If it's something you want, you purchase it without blinking at the price.

Both you female and male Ariens cheerfully part with your dough, without counting the cost. You gals are known as clotheshorses; when garments are bought your buoyant personality comes to life. And when you guys spend money quickly on your numerous hobbies, your sunny dispositions light up even more. Aries, you sure like to keep money in circulation, don't you?

You jump into the fire whether you can afford it or not. Those closest to you know that you'll help them out if they are in a pinch. Time and again you've come to their rescue, haven't you? Your bank account could suffer the strains of your spendthrift ways, but you just don't care, do you?

Because you take such great delight in mixing and mingling with others, you'll spend your last cent on fun and pleasure. The restaurants you go to can vary from inexpensive to expensive; it's the good food, drink, atmosphere, and company that's important to you.

It's easy for you to amass wealth. You are not lazy and enjoy being kept busy with a career. The female Aries has been a woman's libber from the very beginning of time. It's interesting that Gloria Steinem, who pioneered in the women's movement, is an Aries.

You gals want your own money; it's your ticket to an independent life. And you must handle it yourself. Your greatest success comes from doing it alone. You want to stand on your own two feet at all times. To rely upon others is a real no-no with you.

It doesn't matter whether you spend those greenbacks on your personal interests or in business; either way they are gone the moment they touch your hand. And after you fret and fume for having gone on another one of your mad sprees, you swear never to do that again. But that's a big laugh because generally you never learn from your mistakes. However, there's a positive and a negative side of Aries, and if the positive side is expressed you have a better chance of not winding up behind the eight ball financially.

Your Positive Side

Do you take the initiative in financial matters? Does a money challenge spur you on to excel beyond your own wildest dreams? Do you earn income through being involved in many enterprises, or through creativity, or by being a pioneer, executive or competitive? Does money come in fast? Do you want to make a buck so you can be self-reliant? If you answered the preceding questions with a "yes," you are using the harmonious traits you are known for, and as a result, wealth can be more easily attracted.

Do you know that you have the capacity to improvise and seize the opportunity of the moment? Money is gained by quickness of decision and action. It's exhilarating for you to take a risk, especially when the stakes, or odds, are high.

You are the first to try something new — it's all in the aim of greater accomplishment. True to your Aries nature, you are never content to sit still. And your ideas never cease; they seem to overflow.

Those dollars may be gained through strife; you may have to fight for any advantages earned, but you usually are triumphant. The desire for dough makes you forceful and energetic. You're not afraid to tackle the most gigantic tasks regardless of the sums involved.

Your impulsiveness takes you down many interesting and varied paths; money is made on all of them. If the road is too smooth you become bored — it's thrilling for you to take chances, and you worry about the outcome later. And why not? You know where you are going and what you want. It's all or nothing. And you know you're going to reach the top. You're nervy enough to compete with the best of them.

You don't get down in the dumps for very long over financial problems. Seldom do you follow the counsel of others, although you'll listen to advice and if it makes sense you'll try it out. You are always seeking to improve yourself.

Your worthy ideas are constantly pushed into action. To develop projects on a large scale and spend money freely on an enterprise is a necessity; partners who would oppose such action are frowned upon quite heavily. You lead others onto dangerous paths and expect them to follow. And they do, mainly because your enthusiasm is so overpowering. You need gutsy people with you in business ventures. The go-ahead signal for each activity is governed by you; if someone tries to buck you, he can expect a battle. You are a fierce competitor and are out to win everything — your way or not at all.

You delight in calling the shots and tightening or loosening the purse strings as you deem necessary. It's important for you to prove yourself right at all times.

Like Arien V. I. Lenin, the Russian leader and revolutionist, you tear down the past to build the future. If asked, "Did you ever suffer a defeat?" the reply is, "No, only setbacks." And yet an outsider would consider your setback a defeat. What makes you reply in this manner? Simply because you have forgotten and put completely out of your mind the bitter past experience. Your eye is only on new, present, and future enterprises.

With your great physical strength, incessant activity, and busy brain, you endure the bumps and hardships, rise to your feet, and present an amazing display of second wind that leaves others breathless — but you're in the chips!

When a creative project captures your interest, you spend money without thinking twice. If it doesn't earn the sums expected, the satisfaction of having accomplished it is just as important as the financial prospects. It's the love of adventure and excitement, rather than the actual cash, that makes you want to succeed. However, those greenbacks give you freedom and independence that you find ever so enjoyable. And the way you spend dough, you need lots of money!

Because you put a lot of energy and activity into earning and acquiring legal tender, it pays off. You have the drive and fearlessness to attempt the unusual. Your courage and aggression are great assets. You are the "go-getter" who comes up with a profitable gimmick.

You can gain money through having a gambling spirit with finances, winning an objective in spite of opposition, daredevil enterprises, entering into tournaments in competitive sports, and from being able to conceive and give life to an idea, invention, or music, etc. Anything connected with finances — deals, banks, actual labor — must be done in a hurry. Whatever project you become involved in must be developed into something monumental; otherwise boredom sets in.

Greater efficiency is desired — that's why money is spent readily on computers, machinery and the latest in office equipment. However, with your heavy expenditures you have to restrain yourself from spending too much money needlessly; to do this you have to muster up and utilize all the willpower you can. The rewards are reaped when capital is accumulated, profits come pouring in, and expansion occurs.

Your Negative Side

Do you spend money as fast as it comes in? Are you overly generous? Do you always seem to have the urge to spend every dime you have? Is it difficult for you to restrain yourself from shelling out those greenbacks? Do you spend money foolishly on sports? Do you throw away dough on gambling? If so, are you a big loser? Does your temper cost you financially? Do you put a lot of energy and activity into earning and acquiring money? If so, does it backfire because you're too impetuous? Do you have heavy expenditures because of the way you handle your funds? If you answered the preceding questions with a "yes," you are using the inharmonious traits you are known for, and, as a result, it's difficult to attract wealth.

Have you noticed that you rush head first into deals, without thinking through propositions thoroughly? Are details regarded as if they were of no consequence? If so, you attract liability to loss through being too quick, or as a result of not applying the proper safeguards.

It's difficult for you to say no to a risk because the gambler in you comes to the fore and wants that one big stake. You feel compelled to prove something to yourself and others. If you find you're not getting ahead in one area, you'll quit that and go leaping into something new. If you don't stick with anything long enough to see it prosper, success will be difficult to obtain. The Aries impatience is your downfall.

You lose money through strife. Your emotional explosions rub others the wrong way. You irritate those you deal with by your lack of tact and diplomacy, even though you are only telling someone what you think is best for him or her. You demand of people more than they are willing to give. When the results you want aren't immediate, your hot-headedness takes over and you destroy the best of deals and friendships.

You have to guard against being defiant or insulting a few bigwigs or those you work or deal with. If you don't mind your P's and Q's, don't be surprised if you are ousted not only from the project, but the job. And then where will you be financially? Up the creek, especially if you're in debt (and you probably are) when this occurs. But as usual you'll rally forth and be back on your feet in no time.

It's not easy for you to regulate your monetary habits and build up a reserve. There is always something to buy, a bill to be met, or a new venture to invest in. This urge to spend money will put you into a hole if it is not under strong control. Your buying on impulse something you don't need is one of your greatest faults.

You want what you want regardless of the practicality of the matter. Your hobbies could cost you a fortune, especially if you tire of one and take up another equally expensive one. One of your bad habits is to purchase an item just because you want it to be at your fingertips if you need it. You may never use it, tire of seeing it, and end up throwing it out.

You attract immense obligations and liabilities because of your extravagance. When you're pressured to pay those you owe, headaches occur. The stress and strain involved could easily make you fly into one of your temper tantrums.

Disagreements over money are mainly due to your own carelessness, rather than that of other people. But debts are paid because you dislike owing.

You spend — and spend — and spend! Money is squandered on projects that are started and abandoned. The chances you take are really wild; in fact, too much so. Your ideas are hard to harness because your mind is running in many directions. But when you tell others about these notions, they turn away. You dislike being ignored; if you are, that's when you could fly into a monetary rage.

Some of your financial difficulties are attracted as a result of your not seeing the total picture clearly. Your opportunities to make money are enormous, but your impulsiveness ruins all your hard work. You are headstrong and can easily lead yourself, and others, to the edge of the cliff.

It's a great thrill to take chances, isn't it? You believe it's a boon in business. However, when you goof, it isn't fun, is it? But you're not sorry you tried, and if you had it to do all over again, you'd go the same route.

Temporary financial setbacks occur when you jump into buying computers or equipment without investigating whether it's economically sound to do so. Because you are so carried away with the new — the latest — computer or machinery, you can easily overextend yourself to the point of finding yourself in a real bind. You pay cash for it or get a loan; either way it takes you a long time to reap the rewards of the new computer or equipment. Usually before you do, you're ready to buy another computer or machine that is supposed to be an improved version over the last one you are still in debt with. And there you go, leaping in again to buy more computers or equipment. But you *must have* the best, fastest, and most productive computer or machinery available. As a result it's going to cost you each time around. But you don't care!

Money is lost through competitive, creative enterprises, fires, haste, an undue expenditure of energy, destructive action, and willfulness. It also is lost through indulging in those sprees on office equipment.

Spending more than you make is your biggest problem. You should learn how to handle money so you don't wind up behind the eight ball.

HOW TO HANDLE YOUR MONEY

Have you ever wondered how to get the most out of your money? Wouldn't it be nice to avoid financial pinches? Have you ever tried to dig deep within to see why you are such a big spender? Have you noticed that when you have a flare-up with someone who is close to you, you will, to compensate for your anger, go on a spree? The next time this occurs, stop! Think for a moment! Don't let the other person get the best of you by putting you in debt just because you quarreled.

Are you spending too much on a luxury apartment or home? If you're without a car, and a city dweller, do you take cabs rather than use the city transportation system? Do you buy new clothes when you don't wear half of what's in your closet, even though your present clothes are in style and in good condition? Do you eat out most of the time?

If you answered "yes" to the preceding questions these are some of the areas you've got to work with and change. Habits are difficult to break, but not impossible. It's best to try one step at a time, but if you want to get ahead quickly (and you do), try working on them all. Rather than spend money you don't have, you should save until you can afford the item desired. It's a difficult request to ask of an Aries, but a necessary one. Of course, impulse buying is a real no-no; to curb it, don't carry charge cards or much cash with you.

You have to learn to live within your means. Yes, I admit it's not easy for you to do, but it's a must if you don't want to be behind the eight ball. You can still enjoy your money and spend it, but if you have a little (or big) nest egg on the side that's not so bad, is it? Of course this is not an area that someone born under your sign is that taken with, but it would be wise for you to think about it, and better yet, act upon it Aries style — fast!

Gamble only what you can afford to lose. Review expenditures before spending. Buy what you need; think about what you can do without. When shopping ask yourself, "Am I getting value for my money?" Look for bargains. Try comparison shopping. It'll drive you berserk because you don't have the patience for it; but in the long run, you'll be ahead if you compare prices before purchasing goods.

You splurge for genuine jewelry. Why not buy something less expensive? Some simulated diamonds are made so exquisitely perfect that only an expert using a magnifying glass can tell they're fake. However, if would bother you to own, or wear, fake jewelry. If you must buy that precious gem you've got your eye on, first make sure you can afford it before going head over heels in debt.

Avoid being generous to a fault. Your loved ones will still care for you; in fact they'll appreciate surprises every now and then a lot more than if they get accustomed to your spoiling them on a weekly or monthly basis.

Think about the mortgage payments before you sign your years of labor away on a home. Don't buy the most expensive house around; be realistic and realize that you're not Rockefeller. Be practical and ask yourself, "Do I need this house? Will it be easy to sell later? Is the neighborhood good? Do I really know what I am getting myself into?" Talk to the people who live in the vicinity. Think about all the pros and cons before you shell out any money on a piece of property. Keep in mind that if you go into debt with a home, you'll have to spend on furnishing it, plus you'll have to curb some of your *other* high-living expenditures. Is that what you want?

Watch taking risks in business. Avoid recklessness. Try to recall past experiences when you've gotten yourself into a jam because you leaped into spending enormous sums on some project you were carried away with.

When buying new equipment in a business, avoid jumping in first and looking second. Check it out, see if you really need and can afford it. If necessary, ask an accountant whether your financial status will allow you to purchase it.

You have to be confident you can save money. The first step is to write down every cent you spend regardless of whether it's an ice cream cone, new shoes, or bus fare. By keeping a record of your expenditures you'll be shocked to see how those "little things" added up to large sums of money.

Keep your eyes and ears open; pay attention to how others save. Take your lunch to work; go out every now and then if you must. Go potluck or Dutch treat with friends, instead of being the big spender in the crowd. If you go to the movies or theater several times a week, cut down to once a week or every two weeks; you'll enjoy it that much more when you do go out. Do the same with sporting events; you can save a buck by watching your TV set.

You like to have a nice home, clothes, and fun and you like to travel; this is more important to you than money in the bank idling away or earning interest. But you need a reserve to fall back on. Remember when you were caught short and worried yourself sick while you paced the floor thinking how to solve your dilemma? Why not avoid a recurrence of those sleepless nights? "How?" you may ask.

Start a financial plan that will both let you enjoy yourself now, and when you are older, or retired, still give you something to fall back on. Because you don't like to be told what to do, tell yourself, *"I am* (the key word, for Aries) going to save for me."

To start with a budget is essential. The details of it are a drag to you. In fact the very idea of a restriction placed on your pocketbook turns you off. But you can make yourself believe anything you want, so tell yourself that you need this security for your old age.

Write down how much you make, how much you need for the basic necessities (rent, utilities, telephone), food, transportation to and from work (including car insurance if you drive a car — don't include car payments), medical, and dental. Figure out how much is spent on clothing, eating out, entertainment, recreation, and gifts bought at Christmas and throughout the year — these are the areas you can cut down on in order to save money and/or invest it wisely. When you are figuring your budget put aside seven percent of your earnings, or more, in savings or investments.

Now what about the money you pay out in loans, credit cards, or charge accounts? List them and pay them off as fast as possible; you'll save interest. Add up the interest you've been paying and think about what you could have purchased with that money in cash. Eventually cut the cards up, throw them out, and pay cash for all future purchases.

Don't go overboard with entertainment expense. Keep your allowance down to a minimum. Go to inexpensive or free concerts, theater plays, or musicals. Perhaps in one of those out-of-the-way spots, like a church, school, or off-Broadway show, you'll see some future star performing!

Go to the museums, playgrounds, jog, get involved in competitive sports, but don't splurge on an expensive tennis or ski outfit. Keep your hobby expenditures down to a minimum. Rent whenever applicable. Don't go overboard on some new interest that could be given up as soon as you tire of it.

Outline your desires to save money in red ink. Look them over every day, and when you start to spend do it only according to your budget. If you run into a snag when trying to get a balanced budget, seek professional help in the way of an accountant or write to: National Foundation for Consumer Credit, 1819 H Street NW, Washington, DC 20006 or consult your telephone book for the number of the local consumer credit counseling service. Usually there is no charge for their services; they can even help you get new, lower monthly payments on the debts you owe to the banks, finance company, department stores, etc.

Now the next step is the hardest for an Aries and that is to stick with your budget. If you attack it as if it's one of those adventuresome games you delight in, then you should be able to come through with flying colors. Ask your pals if they are on a money-saving program. If they are, be competitive with them. Try to outdo them by saving more, and saving more quickly, than they do. Because you must always be the winner, this is your chance to enter something that has high stakes for your future years. As a result you'll be on a real high. If you want wealth — vividly imagine it, ardently desire it, sincerely believe it will come to you and enthusiastically act upon your desire, and watch it come to pass!

YOUR INVESTMENTS

You can benefit by setting aside money now so your future will be secure. Or perhaps you prefer investing in something other than a business. However, before you go leaping into any undertaking, it would be to your advantage to understand your assets and shortcomings, thereby avoiding pitfalls.

Your Positive Side

A "yes" answer to any of the following questions indicates that you are expressing harmonious Aries traits, thus enhancing your chances to gain wealth. Do you seize the opportunity of the moment to make a buck? Are quick gains more desirable than slow ones? Do you like to gamble with investments; if so, do you win as a result? Is money gained by quickness of decision and action? Do you rush enthusiastically into investing? If so, is the outcome always favorable? Do risks pay off? Are you an impulsive investor? If so, do you come out ahead every time?

Are you aware that you're a born speculator? Quick profit is your bag. The greater the risk, the greater the adventure. Everything has to be short term because you're too impatient to deal with long-term maturation. You are a nervous wreck if you have to wait around for profits to come pouring in. It's the immediate gains that appeal to your zealous nature. Action is desired with investments; if they don't move the way you like, you'll go out or find a means to make things move faster.

If a new stock or development in real estate springs up, you're the first one on the scene to seize it. Once you've gone gung-ho on it, you tell all your friends about it so they'll invest in it also. If you get a hot idea you act on impulse to bring it to fruition. When the dollar is devalued, you don't hesitate to invest in Eurodollars or any other foreign currency.

You push yourself, the broker, a pal, and anyone else you can if your object is to get fast results. Your temper is easily aroused and if you think your broker or real estate agent is wrong, you'll argue vehemently to prove a point. Caution is sometimes thrown to the wind. The gambling spirit within you has to let the world know that you'll be successful if no one interferes with your method of operation.

An auction excites you because it is competitive, spurs you on, and livens all of your senses. If you are carried away with a painting, you outbid your opponent. Luckily, the moment you see a work of art you can size it up quickly; you know its value.

If a friend dares you to take a chance on options, you jump in as if you were going to attack some beast of prey. But the real game and hunt is on when you and a pal compete with each other in the stock market by selling short. You make quick decisions and speculate on selling the stock short and repurchasing it later when the price, hopefully, is lower. It's neck and neck with your buddy to see who is going to be the winner. The greater the challenge, the greater the thrill. You speculate just for the excitement of it, and when you come out ahead you tell yourself, "It's all worth the effort."

Your Negative Side

A "yes" answer to the following questions indicates that you are expressing the inharmonious Aries traits, thus lessening your chances to gain wealth. Is it difficult for you to resist taking a risk, in the hope that you'll make big money? Do you lose when speculating? Will you leap into investing in the first pioneering project that comes along?

Do you take chances now and worry about the outcome later? Is money lost by quickness of decisions and action? Do you invest just to be competing with someone you know? Are you an impulsive buyer? If so, does it cause a loss? Is your main reason for investing due to the excitement and peril involved? Do you lose money because you don't check out the details?

Are you aware that you never learn from your past errors? The gambler in you won't look back or cry over spilt milk; instead, you live for the moment. You feel an overwhelming surge of excitement when you plunge in head first (Aries rules the head). Risks are taken for the sheer love of actual danger to your wallet or pocketbook. It's as if you are a destructive kick so you'll lose money on purpose. And maybe you are!

Sufficient thought is *not* given to the practicality of the areas you invest in; therefore losses are attracted. Usually your mind is busily engaged on a dozen other subjects; thus, you're not paying enough attention to your transactions. Later you may regret some of your foolhardy commitments and maneuvers.

It's when you're bored or in a rut that you are most likely to make wild and crazy investments. It is as if you were playing a game of Russian roulette and the gun is about to go off at any moment. Your worst losses occur when you run your fingers over the stock listings in the newspaper and then invest in the stock that your big thumb has landed on. This so-called ESP system keeps you in debt and makes it difficult for your head to rise above the water.

When someone gets you all hopped up with investment notes, bonds, gold, and no-load mutual funds, you manage to leap onto the bandwagon, afraid it'll get away before you have an opportunity to do your "thing." However, the music you hear isn't so sweet when your money goes down the drain!

A margin account is comparable to a roller coaster ride — a daring thrill every moment. No wonder, it's your "bag." You thrive as the roller coaster goes up just like the gold you bought. And then when it takes a downward plunge you get that butterfly feeling in the pit of your stomach. Your mind and body hunger for the hazards involved; however, you may believe you've got an ulcer or are about to get one. This margin method of operating is too costly to your health and the financial benefits aren't worth it in the long run. But you don't care. You'd be better off purchasing gold bullion outright as a hedge for part of your financial assets against a recession.

WHAT SHOULD YOU INVEST IN?

Risky ventures are preferred; however, if you want to profit you should stay clear of taking too many chances. To compensate and keep you happy in constant anticipation of a quick return, your best bet is to follow a short-term policy in the investment field. In other words be in and out of everything with ninety days, six months, or a year. You've got to see instant returns on your money.

Purchase a house, make improvements on it, and sell it a year later. Buy six-month Treasury bills. Invest in municipal or corporate bonds that are payable in a year. Purchase certificates of deposit from your bank, but make sure they are due to end in a year's time.

Go to an auction, buy a contemporary print made from a woodcut, or an object d'art, and sell it to the highest bidder within a year. You're a player from the word "go" when it comes to stock-market speculation (that's your favorite way of handling stock). You are keen about, and have some measure of success; when you buy stock, it goes up a few points, and you sell it immediately.

Short selling is your "thing," which means, of course, that your risk is greater since a stock's price theoretically goes up to an unlimited amount and it's the downward price movement you are speculating on; that is accomplished by selling short the stock and repurchasing it later when the price, hopefully, is lower. This type of action keeps you keyed up to the point that you feel like you're walking on pins and needles. You may swear you're going to have a stroke or heart attack. But you love every hectic and heart-rendering moment of it.

If in the past you've gained through speculation, then continue along these lines; however, if the reverse holds true, stay away from this because you are expressing the Aries traits on their negative side and are likely to get a repeat performance. Abide by this rule with margin accounts or any area that is known to be risky (commodity futures, options, commercial paper, and Big Mac — Municipal Assistance Corporation — bonds, etc.).

Your enthusiasm when dealing with a margin account is amazing when the stock goes up. But what happens to your bundle of nerves when it goes down and you have to meet the deadline with the money that was borrowed? Pure havoc takes place as you run around selling an antique to pay the broker. However, if you've expressed the harmonious side of Aries in the past and profited by having a margin account, perhaps you'll do so again.

And what about commodity futures? That's an area that really appeals to your sportive nature. The greater the hazard, the greater the thrill. You will plunge in, but your emotions may never be the same if you take a beating. But if high profits are gained, Lady Luck is on your side because you're attracting the harmonious side of Aries. Beware of being so carried away by success that you take chances by doubling up the amount because you want to play for higher stakes. Your motto is "Nothing ventured, nothing gained" — regardless of whether you win or lose.

You should stay as far away from options as you can because you won't devote the necessary time to studying them carefully. And once involved you must accept the risk of losing much or all of your initial investment. Because of your tendency to pounce in for the big kill, the caper could prove too costly, especially if your timing is off. However, if you've been successful with them in the past it could happen again.

In the foreign-bond market your sign is attracted to the Aries-ruled countries of Andorra, Luxembourg, Spain and Japan. If you have enough cash to make it worthwhile you may find Eurodollars a sound investment. Foreign currency — Euras, English pounds, and the Japanese yen — appeal to your sign; invest in them.

A regular savings account is useless for you to gain by. If you needed a buck in a hurry, regardless of whether it was for paying a bill or living it up, you'd withdraw the sum needed before the interest became due and payable.

To offset your chances of being in a poor position as prices rise, and due to your speculative nature, you need to invest in a financial program designed to provide future security. The one that might appeal to you the most is annuities, which is a guarantee of your principal, the tax-deferred compounding of interest, and the future stream of income that is assured to last for a stated period. Or perhaps, *deferred annuities* are desirable because you want the opportunity to realize attractive appreciation potential without the burden of immediate taxation.

You do keep abreast of the trends and what's happening in the world; therefore, you are one step ahead when it comes to investing wisely. However, the small details bore you, and that's when you need to seek the advice of an expert.

A broker who thinks along the same line as you may be desirable. Therefore deal with another Aries, Gemini, Leo, Scorpio, Sagittarius, Aquarius, or Pisces. These signs will encourage those calculated risks that you must beware of, but not necessarily act on. They, like you, take chances. So from a strictly financial standpoint they may not be the best signs for you to listen to or be involved with.

You really need a broker who is practical and able to provide the balance you so sorely need. For this consider Taurus, Virgo, and Capricorn. They are the best suited for safe and sound investments. But expect daily disagreements with them. And their slowness to action, as well as in speech, might bug you. By the way, Cancer and Libra are too indecisive for you.

If you are lucky you might find a broker who is an Aries, Gemini, Leo, Scorpio, Sagittarius, Aquarius, or Pisces Sun sign and this individual *may also have* Taurus, Virgo, or Capricorn as a *dominant* sign in his/her horoscope. If this occurs you'll have the best of two worlds: one who is inclined to speculate but who uses sound judgment.

Astrology can guide you in the type of bonds your sign should consider investing in. Therefore be on the alert for the Aries Mars-ruled bonds that deal with the military, police, or fire department, or engineering projects. Also firms that specialize in road, bridge, and large structural building. Iron and steel companies are likewise attractive to you.

Because everything in life has an astrological correspondence, each type of corporate bond, stock, or commodity has a sign/planet that rules it. Under the Aries/Mars influence, you should invest in manufacturing corporations that produce iron, steel, machinery, and sharp instruments: razors, scissors, knives, swords, spears, needles, nails, and thumb tacks.

If these areas don't capture your interest, why not try companies that produce tools, dies, casts, molds, surgical instruments, cooking utensils, and stimulants: hard liquor, wine, beer, as well as coffee, tea, tobacco, and other caffeine-related items? Or what about pepper or heating products? Perhaps in the commodity futures poultry, broilers (dressed), beef, pork loins, hams, hogs, pork bellies, or steers appeal to you.

Because you love sports, become part owner of a team. Or, perhaps, sports equipment (weight lifts, balls, racquets, paddles, arrows, darts, sling shots, skies, etc.) might appeal to you. If that doesn't turn you on, what about war equipment: bombs (other than atomic), torpedoes, and other munitions?

Also, as an Aries, you'd be intrigued with investing in explosives, fireworks, guns, pistols, revolvers, rifles, and other instruments of destruction. Equally interesting are those manufacturing companies which produce implements used in construction work: tractors, bulldozers, and jackhammers. Or shops that sell coffee might appeal to you. Or what about dealing with redwood or mahogany?

Perhaps you'd like to invest in the gem your sign rules — the amethyst? Buy shares in this jewel, purchase your own mine, or go into amethysts as a business.

HOW TO HANDLE YOUR INVESTMENTS

Safe and sure areas should be sought rather than the risky ventures you favor. You can still make big money from sure things, and in the process your health won't suffer, or your pocketbook. Be leery of new projects. Sure they appeal to your pioneering spirit, but have them checked out thoroughly by a lawyer or an accountant. Rather than worry later, think about what the possible outcome may be if a loss occurs. Perhaps that type of thought may make you think first rather than second when investing.

Your sign is not psychic, although if Pisces/Neptune is *dominant* and harmonious in your horoscope, you could lean in this direction. Therefore, if the preceding fits you go ahead and use your ESP; otherwise, avoid trying to pick a stock by letting your thumb fall on the name of a corporation listed on the stock exchange.

Stop, think, and analyze the pros and cons of every step you wish to take. Never leap into an investment when you're angry. Wait until you are in a relaxed and calm mood before you take action (if that ever occurs). If you can't sit still long enough to make a controlled decision, ask a qualified person.

Find out how much you can afford to lose. An accountant can guide you in this matter. Perhaps you'll invest most of your money in blue chips and put aside a small amount to satisfy your gambling nature. Listen to the accountant or investment counselor because you could not only learn something valuable, but could wind up making a neat profit.

Avoid investing just because you want to compete with a pal. Your buddy may not always fare so well. If you are indulging in a whim to outdo your friend, you'd better be well informed of the risks involved; so ask a broker, investment counselor, accountant, or lawyer before going that competitive route.

Try to stay clear of margin accounts. Don't buy something unless you can afford to pay for it. Curb your impatience in all investment areas. Consistent effort should be sought if you wish to reap financial rewards.

You need to invest in something you can't immediately convert into cash when those sudden spending urges strike. A saving account is too tempting and allows you to indulge in those wild expenditures you go on more often than you should.

Are you a winner or loser? It not only depends upon your Sun sign and how you use it, but also on the influence of Jupiter and Saturn. Jupiter attracts a gain, whereas Saturn attracts a loss. Everyone has these planets in his/her horoscope. But their influence depends upon whether their harmonious or inharmonious side is expressed at the moment a decision is made.

Under the influence of the positive side of Saturn, you are practical, conservative, cautious, serious, contemplative, and make a move only when you are sure the time is ripe. Long-range investments are favored. You use sound judgment, and thus can buy to advantage.

Under the influence of the negative side of Saturn you are pessimistic and cry poverty; you worry, gripe, complain, and have the blues. You are slow because you are afraid of making the wrong move, and thus can attract losses. You lack confidence and chances are if you purchase anything, it could be a real downer.

Whenever you are depressed and feel the Saturn negative traits, avoid investing in anything, because your Saturn is being stimulated in your horoscope at that moment (this could last an hour, a day, a week, a month, a year, or more). If you do invest when this inharmonious energy is being expressed, you are likely to attract a loss.

Under the influence of the positive side of Jupiter you are confident, optimistic, cheerful, easygoing, honest, understanding, happy, and generous. Speculation is favored and brings success. You use sound judgment and can sell to an advantage, take options, buy on margin, and do well all around.

Under the influence of the negative side of Jupiter you are overly confident, too optimistic, wasteful, ostentatious, extravagant, and refuse to take into account prices, expenditures, or the views of others. You are in the mood to do everything to excess. At a party you'd be on center stage making everyone laugh. If you sell an investment when you are in this frame of mind you won't get the price it's worth; your judgment will be off.

Whenever you discover you are using the negative side of Jupiter, don't take a chance with the stock market or any other form of investment. Lie low and wait until the positive side of Jupiter is being expressed, then sell. It'll be worth the wait.

In astrology *buying* is ruled by Saturn and *selling* by Jupiter. Every time you buy under a harmonious Saturn aspect your purchase will be a bargain, a good deal, or investment. Every time you sell under a harmonious Jupiter aspect your sale will be considerable gain. The moment these planets are activated in your horoscope are determined by your time, place, day, month, and year of birth. But you don't need a horoscope to know when you are in a depressed state or happy mood. By being aware of your frame of mind, you'll know how to invest wisely. The moment the negative side of Jupiter, Saturn, or Aries is expressed, that's the time to watch out for losses; the reverse if true when their positive side is expressed.

Now that you are armed with this information you can invest wisely and be ready for whatever the world economy brings. However, you are one step further ahead than the majority of people because by using this positive energy you can improve your chances to be wealthy.

CHAPTER TWO

Taurus — Money and Investments

Those born from April 20 through May 20 have the Sun in the sign Taurus. Every sign of the zodiac corresponds to a particular type of prosperity; it's what you do and how you use it that determines whether you'll be successful or not.

Do you want to wind up ahead of the game? Your resistance to changing certain habits could cause problems along the way. Wouldn't it be better if you could prevent loss, worry, and constant denial? By knowing your faults and how to correct them you can enjoy life more, save money, and, be in tip-top shape. And that's well worth the effort, isn't it?

YOUR MONEY

You are extremely money-conscious. Most of your waking moments are centered on how you can make a buck. That familiar phrase "You have to spend money to make money" is something you believe in and follow. Your associates are amazed at the results. But you're not; you expect it. If it's not a sure thing, you won't have anything to do with it.

Have you ever heard anyone call you Mister Moneybags? The astrological symbol for your sign looks like a bag of money with the drawstrings pulled tight. Ironically that's how you keep your purse strings! Your friends or loved ones may say you're cheap, but to you it's just being practical.

Money is spent only when deemed necessary. Your conservative approach is used regardless of whether it's for personal or business reasons. Inwardly you have a fear of losing money and going into financial debt. Therefore, you must make sure this never happens. You seldom make a mistake, but when you do you learn your lessons well — they are never repeated.

Comparison shopping must have been started by you. Before a purchase is made you make the rounds slowly from store to store. Once you've figured where the best deal is, you'll return and purchase the desired item. With all transactions you are calm, cool, and collected. You do not live above your means — whatever is bought is because you can afford it.

Once at a lecture on decorating, Shirley Temple (a licensed decorator) remarked, "Well, what I'd do is try Sears ready-mades, then probably sew on an extra row of fluffy ball fringe." Her answer about kitchen curtains was typical of her Taurus Sun sign — use your head and hands; spend where it counts and don't waste money on expensive frills.

The necessities are purchased first; then you buy items that have a good investment return, like fine jewelry, art objects, tapestries, Oriental rugs. Your home is comfortable and is elegantly furnished, if you are in an upper-income bracket. No one is spoiled in your family, but all members are well provided for.

It's important that you get value for your money. Good meals at reasonable prices are a must. A diner which advertises and serves "All you can eat for $5.00" is perfect for your wallet and stomach, if the food meets with your approval — though you are a gourmet and do overindulge sometimes in gastronomic delights, your only weak spot as far as spending money goes. However, to save a buck you may go to a late supper at a fancy restaurant because the prices are cheaper. To hobnob with the elite gratifies your desire to be in the company of those who are well off.

Wealth impresses you so much that you attach yourself to those who already have it or are on their way to acquiring it — be it friend or potential spouse. You have a sound sense of material values. If you're married to a big spender you prefer to handle the finances. However, you can become overly cautious, thus attracting difficulties in all phases of your life. There's a positive and negative side of Taurus, and if the positive side is expressed you have a better chance of achieving your aims.

Your Positive Side

Has your steadfastness with money decisions been to your advantage? Is it necessary for you to set aside a good portion of cash for a rainy day? Are you willing to wait a long time for money deals to jell? Do you like to accumulate money and land more than anything else? If you answered the preceding questions with a "yes," you are using the harmonious traits you are known for, and as a result, prosperity can be more easily attracted.

Do you know that your patience is one of your greatest assets? Money is gained through applying logic, perfecting details, and taking action when you are sure it's the right time to do so.

Common sense also helps bring those dollars in. Your plans to make a buck involve long-term projects; you don't trust anything that smells of overnight riches. You can see through the exaggerations of others; phony schemes are spotted immediately. Your judgment is good although it takes you considerable time to take action. True to your Taurus nature you are capable of making silent decisions and pursuing them with a steady perseverance that would tire most people. You plug along being ever faithful to your goals.

Your ability to handle large sums of money carefully is an asset. People trust you with their possessions and in business deals. You are tactful and know how to carry your ideas and plans into actual materialization. The financial rewards drive you to greater accomplishments.

It's important for you to know in advance how much money is going to be gained from a job or project. You know how to bide your time if something doesn't work out as scheduled. When the appropriate moment comes, you forge ahead, clinching all deals. Money is easily gained through banking, wholesale associations, trading societies, and your charming personality. Regardless of the type of career market you enter, you will ultimately earn your share of material wealth.

You are noncompetitive, believing that diligence will bring you the gains desired. Your love of routine cannot be tampered with. A smooth road is a must; it keeps you gentle and kind. Your methodical tactics and painstaking efforts show where it counts the most — your bank account.

You must be certain of the ground you stand on; therefore your path is carefully laid out before you tread on it. Once you've made up your mind to go in a certain direction, no one can force you to change. You believe you are right. Financial problems seldom occur because you are prepared for all contingencies. If they do arise, they are approached calmly and solved slowly.

No one can rush you or ruffle your feathers. You are disciplined in thought and action and mentally block out the exasperation of others, especially when they comment on your snail-like pace. Generally your plodding ways pay off in the end.

New ideas and modern equipment do not appeal to you at first; usually you are the last one to try them. You prefer to stick with the old and familiar. Before purchasing or renting, you must know how others have benefited from their use. If a colleague or salesman is subtle enough in the presentation, you will be more open to it. However, a lengthy deliberation follows before you give your consent. If the profits are high, and the expense affordable, you are then ready to give the go-ahead signal. Once you've accepted something as reliable, you excel at improving upon it and, as a result, money comes flowing in.

You can't stand to scatter your energies in several directions. A new project is not undertaken until you've accomplished the one initiated. Also, everything you tackle must be thoroughly scrutinized for its net worth. The esthetic value is not important; it must pay off in dollars or you won't touch it.

The desire for security and solidity results in your becoming a workaholic. Your loved ones won't see much of you as you busily engage yourself in hard labor. You resist anyone or anything that tries to interfere or stop you from attaining your material ambitions.

Your desire to make a fortune is deep rooted. It's not for a power or showy effect, although it may appear that way. It's the love of money and what it can do for you that's important — a sizable bank account, multiple investments, personal possessions including jewelry, land, and a home.

You know how to earn and save well enough so you can acquire those material items you feel are important. Once you've acquired these vast holdings, you attain a certain status in your community, which implies that you are successful, and thus are in a position to command the respect of others. When this state has been achieved, your inferiority complex subsides or disappears.

Those of you who haven't yet made it big will continually strive to get to the top. Many of you early in life decide that you'll be content as long as you have the comforts you need, cash saved and invested. But in your innermost thoughts and secret actions, you still try to go beyond those points to end up with your share of material wealth.

Your Negative Side

Do you miss out on good business deals because you mistrust change? Are losses attracted because you wait too long for financial transactions to jell? Do you retreat from new money-making ventures? Does your dislike for abstract or far-fetched things cause financial losses? Has steadfastness with money decisions ever been to your disadvantage? If you answered the preceding questions with a " yes", you are using the inharmonious traits you are known for, and as a result it's difficult to attract prosperity.

Do you know that stubbornness detracts from your success more than anything else? Others may call you pigheaded because there are times when you are incapable of seeing anyone else's point of view, especially if it involves something you've never heard of.

You fear losing money and the comfort and security it brings; therefore you won't take chances. Your staunch conservatism can hold a business back from growing fast. But you don't care. You'd prefer building a foundation so you can gain over a long period of time, rather than a sudden leap that may not be lasting. This same attitude is carried over if you are employed by another; thus quick promotions are not easily attained.

Your slow mind and lack of imagination can cause financial adversities. It takes you so long to absorb and comprehend a new idea that your competitors may grasp and seize the opportunities that could have been yours.

Your natural caution and prudence can degenerate into obstinacy—that's when you become a bore. Others see you as too stolid and wished you could show some sign of emotion or respond excitedly. If transactions are with a high-spirited type of person, you could lose a deal because of these personality faults.

You don't put up with any nonsense from others. Oftentimes you are too serious, driving people and business away from you. As a rule you are not easily angered. Once aroused you become furious and you explode as if a violent storm has broken loose. In an argument you will not budge. When you finally cool off you are sullen, difficult to appease, and liable to hold a grudge for a long time or to become a relentless enemy. It bothers you to lose a few bucks, but the principle of the matter takes precedence over money.

You cannot be rushed or frightened out of your slow -as-molasses pace. If someone does attempt to rush you, you will become immovable and dare anyone to approach or push you. And once you decide to move it will be at an even more tortoise-like pace than before, regardless of the dollars it may cost you or the boss.

Because you are set in your ways you don't diversify in a way that could be profitable. Ryan O'Neal wrote me that he counted too heavily on one thing when he waited two years—lost ones—for the movie *Barry Lyndon* to be released. This Taurus negative trait of his proved to be a near catastrophe for him.

You can be stingy with salaries, raises, or office supplies. If this is pushed too far, employee attrition can be high. But it's the money saved that you care about the most. Your greed can be your undoing if carried to an extreme.

Your resistance to change repels success. While other companies and colleagues are using the latest methods to operate a business, you stay far behind. You are waiting for them to fail so you can take it over. But it may be a long vigil or a wasted one.

You are rooted in monetary values to the point of becoming mentally stagnant in areas that could bring you future high earnings. Failure to read about the latest revolutions in your field, or keeping a closed mind toward them, can keep you from attaining the wealth desired.

Fear of being in debt is something you live with continually. This anxiety can lead to long hours on the job, and cheapness and difficulties in a love relationship. Because your workday never seems to end, those close to you suffer. Material gains can be such an obsession that you don't take the time to relax and enjoy life.

You go overboard on the bucks you spend on food. However, you hunt for bargains in the process. It's not the price you pay that's the problem, it's the quantity that is bought and then indulged in. No wonder you may have a weight problem!

Your hobbies for the most part are not that expensive unless you're in the upper income bracket, in which case you will still only spend what you can afford. But regardless of your earnings, you can become so fixed in the idea of owning a particular stamp, coin, painting, or antique that you will work twenty hours a day so you can acquire it. This could impair your health if done over a prolonged period. But it would be useless for anyone to try and stop you.

Money is lost through inflexibility, laziness (which many a negative Taurean possesses), deliberativeness, and bullheadedness. (Your sign is ruled by the bull.) You should learn how to avoid financial losses so you won't wind up behind the eight ball.

HOW TO HANDLE YOUR MONEY

Have you ever wondered how you can have a good time and yet have money in the bank? Wouldn't it be great if you could smile more often and light up a party instead of worrying so much about financial matters? Have you ever tried to dig deep within to see why you are so cheap? Doesn't it bother you just a little?

Don't you feel terrible that you lost out on a deal because you were too slow in making a decision? And what about your unyielding nature? Hasn't it cost you a lot in the long run? Wouldn't it be to your advantage if you could learn to be more flexible?

Wouldn't it be a welcome relief if you could trust, or be more open to, the latest "in" thing in business? And what about those expensive artistic tastes— are they carried to such an extreme that you neglect to give proper attention to your loved ones?

If you answered "yes" to the preceding questions, these are some of the areas you must work with and change. This will be an extremely difficult task because your habits are so set that to uproot them will take extraordinary effort on your part. But nothing is impossible. Don't let change cause you emotional torment; try excepting it as "growth" and you'll have a head start on the whole affair. Once initiated you won't have any difficulty continuing along the new set line. If you don't give it a try you'll miss many opportunities that could fill your pocketbook to the brim. And you're one person who doesn't want that to happen, right?

Avoid being an "old fogey;" don't judge everything new by old standards or past experiences. Keep in mind that times change and you could miss a good buy if you are a doubter. Keep an open mind. Listen to people in all fields; and mix with people in different age brackets—the young, as well as the elderly, have knowledge that may be of value. Join a club or business league. Talk over your ideas with others; follow up on an idea by pursuing, developing, refining, and adopting it to your situation. The final test is when you make it saleable.

Spend your leisure moments reading about the latest discoveries in your field. When purchasing new equipment or a computer, or hearing about it for the first time, don't dilly-dally in getting the opinions of others. A quick survey shouldn't take more than two days of your time; don't let months lapse while you make the rounds asking questions person by person. If you use your usual turtle-like methods, you'll lag behind, and it will take you that much longer to acquire the wealth desired.

Avoid being dogmatic. Realize that everyone has the right to express an opinion. Be tolerant of the other person's view and allow others a chance to make decisions once in a while. Weigh the pros and cons rather than having a fixed idea. Obstinacy doesn't pay the bills. Learn to give an inch so money isn't lost along the way.

Be prepared for others to goad you if you are languid about a decision or action. When others call you a slow-poke explain that you want to be sure that the deal will pay off for all concerned. Let them know that you must be well prepared before embarking on a project. By using these tactics it's easier for you to get their respect and understanding. Otherwise silence provokes everyone and an emotional outburst doesn't remedy the situation.

Help others and they'll help you. If someone is trying to sell you on a new concept let them know that you are the type of person who needs valid evidence of economy, money savings, design advances, and potential profit. If they can present this and similar proof that their product or idea is as good as stated, you'll be more willing to take a chance on it. Because you dislike new realms, tell yourself, "*I have* (the keyword for Taurus) to do this for my future security."

Luckily you're not the type to go head over heels in debt with a home, mortgage, or business. You are just too realistic and practical to get caught up in the blind world of overextended credit. You abhor charge accounts and, if they are used, they are quickly paid before any interest charges become due on them. Credit cards are not your folly; cash spending is preferred. The money you owe, in most circumstances, is just for regular monthly bills.

Your horror of debt has existed ever since you can remember; it's part of your Taurus nature. You do everything to prevent yourself from becoming involved in financial obligations. Your tightness with the purse strings stems from your vast concern to be free of encumbrances. Actual cash in the bank and sound investments satisfy your strong urge to be safe and secure. Thus the more dollars you save the more protected you'll feel, and the more peaceful your life will be. However, don't become so tight that you are a deadbeat. After all, your heirs will throw your money away on some of those pleasures you passed up because you were afraid you'd go broke.

Believe more in your abilities and know that you are prudent and wise. You can handle a buck better than most people. In fact, no one ever needs to give you financial advice. Because you're a master in this department, you should realize that you are wasting your time worrying about indebtedness or trying to stay clear of it. Accomplish your tasks and they'll bring you the desired monies and freedom from liabilities.

A comfortable home, and jewelry and clothes so you can dress for the occasion are important status symbols for you. Many personal sacrifices are made to obtain them. Once these and other assets have been acquired, you keep so busy working that you don't enjoy the fruits of your labor.

You can acquire a greedy streak if you don't watch out. With prices on the rise you are smart to set some funds aside; however, don't get so panic stricken that you forget how to enjoy life. Live in the present; make every moment count. Even though you like to hang on to the old and familiar, break loose from the chains that bind you and get new interests and hobbies and make new friends. Take that art course you've always wanted to.

Pay attention to your loved ones when they complain you are all work and no play. Cut down on some of your arduous tasks and indulge in sports to keep your body in good shape. Exercise is a good way to release those inner tensions that disturb you. Play golf, shuffleboard, croquet, or chess. Go fishing or rock hunting in the desert or the mountains. Take that camping trip you've been putting off. Or get your family to join you with a walk through a flower garden, park, or wood; the fresh air appeals to your senses. Go to a square dance or the country club. Listen to music. Or perhaps you'd like to attend the ballet, opera, or movies. Avoid being a stay-at-home, which leads to your getting in a rut and becoming a bore.

It doesn't cost that much to go out now and then. Art gallery openings are great for those on a low budget. Perhaps there are some department stores or exhibit centers that are giving free demonstrations and refreshments. Go to inexpensive forms of amusement like outdoor concerts. Visit the Botanical Gardens if your area has one. Perhaps you can get discount prices on theater tickets by volunteering your services or through some barter deal with the people who run various forms of entertainment. And let go of those things that upset you by working in the garden; you enjoy having your hands in the soil.

If you give more of your time, affection, and money to your loved ones, you'll be happy within when you see their eyes sparkle. Learn to laugh more and be less stiff and rigid; you'll feel years lighter. It's easy for you to stick with a budget, but don't be too stringent. Remember your family wants to have fun, even if you don't.

It's easy for you to keep track of all expenditures; they're engraved indelibly on your mind. Nothing goes unaccounted for; you must — and do — know where every cent goes. You're a great financial planner who needs to leave room for some small pleasures as well as have a big fat bankroll stashed away for those later years of your life.

A carefully considered budget can help you sort out priority spending. Consider your fixed monthly obligations before any other expenditures. Do some trimming on your food and liquor bill and give more to the entertainment and social departments.

A few raises received might help you keep up with rising costs, but you might be breaking your back to stay ahead — two jobs might be to your advantage, if the second one doesn't interfere with personal relationships. Save money, invest wisely, live a little, and you'll be prepared for your golden years.

The wealth you desire is attracted through your prudent thoughts and actions and your ability to handle finances. But don't bungle it by being too stubborn and resistant to the new. Happier days are ahead if you make a few changes. You'll discover that self-improvement is much easier if material rewards await you.

YOUR INVESTMENTS

If you want your future to be secure (and you do), set aside money now. Or, perhaps, you prefer investing in something other than a business. However, before you do, it would be to your advantage to understand your assets and shortcomings, thereby avoiding pitfalls.

Your Positive Side

A "yes" answer to any of the following questions indicates that you are expressing harmonious Taurus traits, thus enhancing your chances to gain prosperity. Are you a realist? Do you like safe and solid investments primarily? Is it against your grain to invest all the money you have? Do you shy away from unnecessary risk? With investments is everything well planned before taking action? Are you shrewd? Do you use foresight? Would you rather use your own powers of discrimination than rely on those of others? Do you make astute evaluations?

Are you aware that you're a born investor? It's vital to you that you have your money working for you. You can patiently wait for those monthly, semiannual, or annual payments to arrive in the mail. Gains over a long period of time appeal to your methodical nature. You are not a gambler. All investment plans are weighed and seriously considered without missing one detail; once they're devised, you stick to them.

You like earthy investments (you're an Earth sign) and take your time looking over land or real estate projects. In the process you keep mum about everything; you don't like to intrude upon others, nor do you want their opinion on your purchases. If someone gives you a tip, you don't act upon it right away; if it doesn't meet your conservative standards, it is discarded.

You won't allow a stock market broker to persuade you to invest in a company that doesn't appeal to you. Certainty is a must; all transactions are handled in your usual careful manner. Your powers of discrimination usually pay off. No wonder you study the prospectus so thoroughly that it's memorized!

If an art dealer mailed you a catalogue and in it you saw a figurine you wanted to own, you'd buy it at an auction if not outbid by others. You are a slow but steady bidder. Your possessiveness and innate understanding of the figurine's true value makes you more persistent than usual. However, you won't go overboard with the price unless you have the cash to pay for it.

You take great delight in hunting for gems. Your search could lead you to thrift shops or to old abandoned mine sites. Your self-reliance is shown to an advantage when you go on your own expeditions. Often times your sound judgment pays off when just browsing around.

As a disciplined investor you take a portion of your paycheck each month and put it into some form of future security. You'll go without and live a frugal existence just so you can meet your schedule. Your economizing works well for you especially when you acquire enough material goods to satisfy yourself.

Your Negative Side

A "yes" answer to the following questions indicates that you are expressing the inharmonious Taurus traits, thus lessening your chances to gain prosperity. Did you ignore a stockbroker's advice? If so, did you regret it later? When you bought stock, did you lose because you waited too long for the price to drop? When you sold stock, did you lose because you waited too long for the price to rise?

Does your resistance to change cause you losses with new investments, companies, etc.? Have you been in a no-load mutual fund that has allowed switches but because of your intransigence refused to budge when it may have been to your advantage? Have you lost money because you haven't gotten out of the bond market quick enough?

Are you aware that your being too conservative holds you back from making enormous sums of money? You live so far ahead into the future that you don't always see what's happening around you in the present time. Though you do try to keep abreast of the latest news events around the world, by the time you read, absorb, and weigh an investment possibility, the opportunity to make a killing has passed you by. And if you do get on the bandwagon at the right moment, you're afraid to lay out much dough. But you refuse to let anyone hustle or bully you into a false position or into taking action that's against your nature.

Your love for art can be costly because you are likely to donate huge sums of money to museums and individual artists. To be a patron gives you a certain sense of prestige that makes you light up. Of course, being in this position you are able to deduct the expenses from your income tax, and purchase the painting from the artist at a cheaper price than what someone else would have to pay. If the artist doesn't become as famous as you believe, your finances may suffer a little. But you figure you are still ahead of the game. And who knows, maybe you are.

You like to accumulate money, land, and properties. But you can go to an extreme, attaching yourself like a leech to a piece of sculpture, or a coin or stamp. If a fantastic price is offered, you'll turn it down. Your excuse to yourself is that it will grow in value and, later, be more valuable. You do the same with stocks and bonds. It's useless for your broker, or anyone else, to argue with you. They will get the silent treatment of a very stubborn bull. Your rigid beliefs, possessiveness, and intractable attitude can cause many losses.

But you are unshakable in adversity and able to function better than most people when under heavy pressure. You may cause considerable consternation to those who have your best interests at heart. But that doesn't faze you. When making purchases in any area you should have some liquid assets as a hedge against inflation, currency fluctuations, or economic uncertainty.

WHAT SHOULD YOU INVEST IN?

Secure ventures are a must; you need to know that your money is working in your behalf while it's out of your hands. Your best bet is to follow a long-term policy in the investment field. This type of a return appeals to your conservative nature. It's not in your makeup to take a risk.

Purchase certificates of deposit from the bank; get those which will give you the most for your money. Also plan to have some money in a regular savings account; you'll get great satisfaction in looking at those deposit mount to larger sums — it's something you can use in a tight pinch or emergency. However, you're the type who prefers to go without rather than draw out any funds.

Land for development appeals to you as well as commercial real estate. To own a skyscraper exclusively helps keep your spirits up. However, owning homes or vacant lots also gives you the solidity that is a must to you.

Treasury notes and bonds as well as U.S. savings bonds give you that safe feeling. And all other government securities, loans, and trusts are right up your alley. You know the good old U.S. isn't going to default, regardless of the economic or political situation.

Corporate bonds can be risky, but the short-term ones, which are the safest, just might be what you are looking for. They have a far lower yield than long-term corporate bonds. However, because you like to diversify, you might chance them.

All fixed-income funds (money market funds, municipal bond funds, and municipal-bond-unit investment trusts) make you feel comfortable. Ginnie Mae (Government National Mortgage Association) unit-investment trusts are based on the most conservative strategy. Sounds like you, doesn't it? In effect, they offer you a share in a pool of residential mortgages guaranteed by the government. You can't beat that, can you?

To satisfy your leanings in the direction of the artistic world, consider an art mutual fund. There are two in Europe (Knoedler-Modarco, whose stock is traded on the Geneva Exchange, and Artemis, which is traded in Amsterdam). If you're ever in the mood to take a chance on something that has a high risk and high rates of return, try getting involved with Eurodollars or foreign currency.

The collectibles make you a proud owner as well as a smart investor in terms of having liquidity as a hedge against inflation. There is risk involved; but for art you'll take your chances. In the print field you are attracted to silk-screen or serigraph prints. Tapestries, Oriental rugs, sculpture, jewelry, plates, vases, figurines, antiques, coins, and stamps — they are all your bag. The latter two are more predictable investments than fine art. Price trends are easier to track and fads are less common, though they can still mean big gains or losses. Stamps are for patient people — that's you!

Perhaps you'd like to invest in the gems your sign rules — agate and opal. Buy shares in these jewels or purchase your own mine. Other stones that are ruled by Taurus are alabaster, white coral, and white opaque. What about diamonds? Do they remind you, as they do me, of the book (also the movie and play) *Gentlemen Prefer Blondes,* written by the internationally famous Taurean author, the late Anita Loos, in which the line "Diamonds are a girl's best friend" became immortal? If they whet your appetite buy "cut investment-grade diamonds" with GIA certificates at wholesale prices. See a diamond broker for such a transaction.

In the foreign-bond market your sign is attracted to the Taurus-ruled country of Austria. If you want to invest in the foreign currency of this country, do so. But perhaps the Swiss franc would be sounder. Or bullion coins in the way of precious-metals certificates may interest you: Austrian 100 corona, Austrian ducat, or the I ducat might be what you are looking for.

To be positive that you're in a good position as prices rise, invest in a financial program designed to provide you and your loved ones with future security. The retirement age is something you think about constantly. You'd like steady monthly income for life, wouldn't you? Either one of the following two plans could be the answer to your dilemma: *Annuities* can provide regular income payments that are guaranteed by the issuing insurance company to continue for any time period selected, including your lifetime and/or that of your mate. However, if you deposit principal and defer income payments until some future date, interest is credited on a *tax-deferred* basis, thereby postponing taxes while your funds accumulate. If this is what you are searching for, ask for *deferred annuities.*

Or perhaps, the Keogh or IRA retirement plans appeal to you. If you can save a buck, you're all for it. On either of these two plans there are federal income tax savings. And you are given a guaranteed fixed income when you retire. If it's a sure thing, you'll look into it.

You may lag behind others when it comes to your daily pace, but you are abreast of the times and keep up on world affairs; this knowledge can help you to make wise investments. You may, however, want to have a broker who places your order for you, unless you go through the stock discount houses.

If you desire a broker you will definitely need one who thinks along your lines. Your best bet is another Taurus, Virgo, or Capricorn. These signs are just as practical as you; they do not like risks — only certainty and safety. Normally you don't take advice from anyone, but you will respect and listen to someone born under one of these signs.

Those brokers who encourage calculated risks and high returns on your money are Aries, Gemini, Leo, Scorpio, Sagittarius, Aquarius, and Pisces. You will run from them! Cancer and Libra on the other hand are much too indecisive for your decisive nature although they can be conservative on occasion.

Perhaps the broker you choose should belong to one of the signs just mentioned, meaning that he will enjoy taking chances and speculating, but will also follow a solid, sound, and safe investment procedure. This individual will take this stable approach, which is probably opposite his/her Sun sign traits, because he/she has Taurus, Virgo, or Capricorn as a *dominant* sign in his/her horoscope. With such a broker you'd be in fairly good hands.

When it comes to the stock market you prefer the "blue chips" and "growth stocks." Any company that is old, established, and pays good dividends through the years is your first choice when deciding what stocks you should purchase. You shun over-the-counter stocks; they are too new and thus a gamble.

Astrology can guide you in the type of bonds you should consider investing in. Be on the alert for bonds that deal with urban development, the arts, and tolls and turnpikes (tax-exempt revenue bonds which are issued by public authorities); also, firms that specialize in the building of roads. Copper, alabaster, marble, and malachite and bronze mining or refining companies are likewise attractive to you. Of the municipal bonds series, general obligation bonds are for you. You'd not only be proud contributing to your community, but they are safe, pay good yields, and are tax exempt.

Because everything in life has an astrological correspondence, each type of corporate bond, stock, or commodity has a sign/planet that rules it. Under the Taurus/Venus influence, investing in manufacturing corporations that produce hearing aids, furniture, gardening supplies and tools, musical instruments (pianos, organs, accordions, or brass), soap, purses, clothes, fibers, textiles (burlap, wool, silk, print cloth), leather, suede, artists' supplies, and aromatic products will be profitable.

Other Taurus/Venus-ruled areas that might capture your interest are companies that sell and rent furniture, brokerage firms, banks, savings and loan associations, real estate developers, gardening corporations. Or how about stock which involves seed, art, china, harmonious music, wholesale associations, trading societies, finance companies, or basic industry?

Other Taurus-ruled stocks that might intrigue you involve wine, jewelry, bronze, brass, or piped-in music firms. What about spas for vacation, beauty, weight? Or in the commodity futures, try native cow hides or cane or beet sugar.

HOW TO HANDLE YOUR INVESTMENTS

You alone must live with the investments you make, regardless of what an "expert" tells you. It's your money, so make decisions you can be comfortable with. (I doubt that you'd ever do otherwise — you are just too stable and practi-cal.) If you can't live at peace with securities, don't own them. Seek professional advice when selecting stocks, then make your own decisions based upon what your counselor tells you.

Raise your money goals as you accomplish past ones. Know where you stand financially at all times. Compare your actual income with planned outcome. Stay away from vacant land (hard for you to do) when the bank interest rates are high. If you want to build on it, the bank lending rate will probably rub you the wrong way.

Spread bank accounts over several banks in case one bank gets into finan-cial hot water. If money gets tight, or the credit cards become passé, bartering may be the "in" thing — and something you excel at! Buy goods — the long-term durables (perfect for you) — tools, raw materials, replacement parts.

The basic conservative tactic in stock investing is diversification. Owning a number of stocks reduces your risk of loss — and your profit potential — since it's unlikely they will perform in the same way. Own *different types of stock* instead of too many of the same type. This is one area you often make a mistake in.

Whether you should buy long-term, short, or intermediate bonds (five to seven years) depends on an investor's forecast of the inflation rate. If there's a sharp rise in the inflation rate you should try to stay as liquid as possible; thus ninety-day Treasury bills (keep rolling them over) are favored. Use your logic and common sense; let go of some of those long-term investments, or if you can't relinquish them due to your fixed and stubborn nature, at least invest in something that will give you a quick return on your money.

When you are investing in non-income producing assets like real estate (it's not producing spendable money unless you've leased or rented it), then you would also be wise to strive to accumulate an equal amount in cash-value life insurance, and even a pension. And with that surety, tranquillity and prosperity will be more easily attained. Of course this is the age of change; like it or not, you are a realist, so accept it and try to adapt the best you can.

Are you a winner or loser? It not only depends upon your Sun sign and how you use it, but also on the influence of Jupiter and Saturn. Jupiter attracts a gain, whereas Saturn attracts a loss. Everyone has these planets in his/her horoscope. But their influence depends upon whether their harmonious or inharmonious side is expressed at the moment a decision is made.

Under the influence of the positive side of Saturn, you are practical, conser-vative, cautious, serious, contemplative, and make a move only when you are sure the time is ripe. Long-range investments are favored. You use sound judgment, and thus can buy to advantage.

Under the influence of the negative side of Saturn you are pessimistic and cry poverty; you worry, gripe, complain, and have the blues. You are slow because you are afraid of making the wrong move, and thus can attract losses. You lack confidence and chances are if you purchase anything, it could be a real downer.

Whenever you are depressed and feel the Saturn negative traits, avoid investing in anything, because your Saturn is being stimulated in your horoscope at that moment (this could last an hour, a day, a week, a month, a year, or more). If you do invest when this inharmonious energy is being expressed, you are likely to attract a loss.

Under the influence of the positive side of Jupiter you are confident, optimistic, cheerful, easygoing, honest, understanding, happy, and generous. Speculation is favored and brings success. You use sound judgment and can sell to an advantage, take options, buy on margin, and do well all around.

Under the influence of the negative side of Jupiter you are overly confident, too optimistic, wasteful, ostentatious, extravagant, and refuse to take into account prices, expenditures, or the views of others. You are in the mood to do everything to excess. At a party you'd be on center stage making everyone laugh. If you sell an investment when you are in this frame of mind you won't get the price it's worth; your judgment will be off.

Whenever you discover you are using the negative side of Jupiter, don't take a chance with the stock market or any other form of investment. Lie low and wait until the positive side of Jupiter is being expressed, then sell. It'll be worth the wait.

In astrology *buying* is ruled by Saturn and *selling* by Jupiter. Every time you buy under a harmonious Saturn aspect your purchase will be a bargain, a good deal, or investment. Every time you sell under a harmonious Jupiter aspect your sale will be considerable gain. The moment these planets are activated in your horoscope are determined by your time, place, day, month, and year of birth. But you don't need a horoscope to know when you are in a depressed state or happy mood. By being aware of your frame of mind, you'll know how to invest wisely. The moment the negative side of Jupiter, Saturn, or Taurus is expressed, that's the time to watch out for losses; the reverse if true when their positive side is expressed.

Now that you are armed with this information you can invest wisely and be ready for whatever the world economy brings. However, you are one step further ahead than the majority of people because by using this positive energy you can improve your chances to be wealthy.

CHAPTER THREE

Gemini - Money and Investments

Those born from May 21 through June 20 have the Sun in the sign Gemini. Every sign of the zodiac corresponds to a particular type of prosperity; it's what you do and how you use it that determines whether you'll be successful or not.

Do you want to wind up in a mess because of your chaotic spending habits? You probably would. Instead, wouldn't it be better if you could banish financial upheavals, nervousness, and uncertainties? By knowing your faults and how to correct them you can enjoy life more, save money, and, be in tip-top shape. And that's well worth the effort, isn't it?

YOUR MONEY

Your sign is represented by the Twins; thus there are two of you: One Twin is practical and the other scatters money to the winds as fast as he/she can get his/her hands (Gemini-ruled zone) on it. This duality can cause quite a conflict with yourself. You never know which one of you is going to emerge. However, most of the time it is the impractical Twin that dominates your life.

It doesn't take you long to go shopping; you dart in and out of a store in a jiffy. You glance at everything as you hurry by. When your eye catches something of interest, you stop, touch it, and immediately make up your mind whether you should buy it or not. Later you wonder how your bucks could have disappeared so fast.

Your generosity is shown by your lavish spending on your friends and loved ones. Half of the time you forget what you bought them, or may not remember spending a cent on them. A pal may wear a gift you gave him/her, but you may not recognize it. That's because you bought it so quickly.

The price you pay for something is not important to you; if you have the cash you won't quibble over whether you can or cannot afford it. Books, education, and travel are your weak points. The knowledge you gain from them is worth every penny they cost. They are your first loves; everything else is secondary.

Your expenditures are numerous: clothes, hats, gloves, shoes, sports, movies, restaurants — you name it. Because you get bored easily, you need a large wardrobe. You like an outfit for every occasion and may change three times a day. Your closet is so jammed full that you have to tug to get something out. But that doesn't stop you from spending more.

The one Twin wants to hang on to every garment for security; the other Twin is known to give a sweater or coat to a buddy on the spur of the moment. And so it goes, back and forth; your duality befuddles you occasionally. You are not stupid. You have a brain and know how to use it. In fact, you're really an intellectual.

Because you have above average intelligence (very likely a high IQ and maybe even a member of Mensa) and use your mind to the fullest, you manage to earn a good income. You know the value of your skills and usually earn what you're worth; however, you're not money hungry.

You are self-sufficient and don't want to have to answer to anyone. Although you freely spend, you can also save a few dollars. You look out for number one first, and a flock of others if you've got it to spare. However, you've got to handle your own money. You can't stand anyone to place limitations or restrictions on your finances, or on anything else in life for that matter.

Your dough is spent, without hesitation, on those brainstorm ideas you get in the middle of the night. Not only are they costly, but they give you insomnia, especially when they cause losses. But it doesn't take you long to forget about them, because suddenly you're off on another kick.

One Twin can keep your head above water and do well with finances, whereas the other one blows his/her earnings carelessly. There's a positive and negative side of Gemini, and if the positive side is expressed you have a better chance of becoming financially secure.

Your Positive Side

Are your income and expenditures subject to constructive thought and action? Does your mind express itself readily with money? If so, have gains resulted? Are you quick-witted with financial deals? Is it an enjoyable challenge to solve money problems by applying reason and knowledge? Are you interested in stashing away a few bucks for a rainy day? If you answered the preceding questions with a "yes," you are using the harmonious traits you are known for, and as a result, prosperity can be more easily attracted.

Do you know that you have invaluable ideas? Profits can be made when you push them through. However, you may not know which notion to initiate first. It seems that the wheels of your mind are constantly chugging away and every few minutes new ideas are springing up.

You are stimulated by taking chances in the money market. It goes against your Gemini nature to put all of your eggs in one basket. In fact, diversification must have been invented by you.

Your versatility shows up when you make a bundle through several jobs you hold simultaneously; a tennis tournament, a song you wrote, an essay contest, the lottery, a band you played in, and your investments. It seems you hit the jackpot every time you have a bright idea to leap into something new. And you are never content with sitting still because you bore much too easily; therefore you're always ready for a new adventure.

And what about that money you made so easily? Does it disappear on a good time or on your loved ones? You spread it around: a little fun and a little in the bank. The dividends earned from stock are reinvested in the same stock. This is the practical Twin using common sense and looking ahead to the future.

If you have a financial problem it doesn't take you long to solve it. Your mind jumps so fast from one stored piece of knowledge to another that in seconds of time you've got the answer. And all of your decisions are made just as quickly. No wonder people need and like you around.

You are abreast of the times; the new "in" equipment, machinery, techniques, and telephone system must be tried. If you want it, you'll get it and spare no expense. And, most likely, you'll be able to take mechanical or electronic equipment apart, if it should break down, and put it back together again. You are extremely skillful with your hands as well as knowledgeable with your brain.

Going to school and taking short courses on a variety of subjects is something you feel is worth every nickel spent. It's not unusual to find you taking some class or another during most of your lifetime. It seems there's always something more to learn. Money spent in this direction is not wasted, in your opinion, because somehow you always make use of the information gained. And while studying, you get a lift that sends you soaring. You are more actuated by mental expression than material gains because to you the mind, and its intellectual expression, is a material reward, especially when it pays off in dollars and cents at the bank.

An idea for a new ad campaign may pop into your mind. So you get the ball rolling and get everybody interested in it only to later change everything around. Your sign is known as "The Thinker." Once you've given it some thought you realize that the improved way is better.

You are a real joiner and probably belong to almost every club in your area: tennis, golf, bowling, business leagues, health, yoga, gourmet, literary, and the country club. It's all because you enjoy the company of others as well as being interested in every phase of life. The price of membership and the cost each time you attend isn't of much concern to you. It's the group get-togethers, conversation, and the enlightenment gained that make it all seem worthwhile. The more people you meet, the happier you are — money is no object. And besides, you tell yourself, maybe you will make some good business contacts that could further your career.

One of your greatest pleasures is to travel. Also, you can earn money through this diversion. Income may be through the airlines, an agency, or as part of your job. You may decide to spend a few bucks on a trip and while you're there you make the rounds of a few antique stores and gift shops. While there you chit-chat about what they may need. So while you enjoy yourself on a vacation you also purchase what the shopkeeper wanted. By doing this you deduct the trip from your income taxes.

You guys/gals can economize while dating. Because you like variety there's an endless array of places you frequent; some are free (like outdoor concerts) and others may cost a little. You are not one to impress your date with where you go; it's what is there to see that dominates.

Your Negative Side

Have you lost money through vacillation? Do you have insomnia after you've been on a big spending spree? Are you constantly making errors handling finances? Do you have an inner turmoil related to monetary concerns constantly gnawing at you? Are you wasting your greenbacks on your ideas? For the most part, are money matters unsettled? When you lose a few bucks, do you react with irritability, uncertainty, or confusion? Do you save a little, but spend most of your funds haphazardly on some impulse? If you answered the preceding questions with a "yes" you are using the inharmonious traits you are known for, and as a result, it's difficult to attract prosperity.

Is your point of view in financial areas frequently changed? One day you want to make a million bucks on a notion that just flashed into your mind. Then the next day you don't care about its net worth, it's the idea put into reality that becomes your chief concern. Your friends and associates throw up their hands in despair when you go through one of these capricious moods.

And then there are those occasions when you conceive something without thinking of it from a money-making angle. You fail to see the business side because you are too mentally tuned in to the creative side. And when you are made aware of its cost, you suddenly switch the other way and dump the whole project.

When a new computer or office equipment is demonstrated, you buy it only to get rid of it the next month when a different model is shown by a salesman from another company. You are a pushover when people appeal to your intellectuality; the details and practical side are overlooked until someone points them out to you. This habit can be expensive and keep you in debt over a long period of time.

Too much talk, worry, or anxiety over money can cause you nervous exhaustion, especially after you've been unwise in a financial deal. You are a bright person, but most of the time your mind is so busy jumping from one subject to another that you don't always stop long enough to think anything through. And when you do, you're horrified that you didn't catch your mistake earlier. But do you think that will slow you down and stop all of those foolish expenditures? No, because you turn right around and do them again.

And then those moments of indecision arise: Should you, or should you not, spend the money to buy a new car? Back and forth you go as you ask your friends. One pal may say to go ahead and purchase it, whereas another tells you not to, that your old automobile is still in good shape. This only confuses you all the worse. How does it all end? Usually by parting with your dough when you suddenly decide it's a good deal, whether it really is or not.

You guys can spend a lot of your dough on dating. Because you tire easily, you have many girls on the string. If there's one gal only in your life, and she's full of surprises, you may stay away from the others. But, regardless of how many women you take out, it's going to cost you an arm and a leg because you like to go to all forms of entertainment and amusing places.

You Gemini gals go overboard on the money you spend on clothes and makeup. You tell yourselves it's so you will look your best when you're out on a fling. Actually, it's the love of variety that makes you buy all those different colors of lipstick and eye shadow. But you figure it's worth it because it will benefit your love life. But tell me, do you have to own every new shadow that comes out?

Your ability to make a buck from a great variety of interests amazes your pals. A winning streak at the racetrack puts you on top, so you turn around and splurge your earnings on your buddies. And what about that tennis tournament you entered? It paid off, too. And wasn't everyone happy for you when you won a cross-word puzzle contest? And then the sweepstakes followed; it seems you've got all of the right answers — with your intellect it stands to reason.

And, of course, each time you make a bundle, there goes another party thrown for your friends. Unless you decide to take them all on a chartered bus to a football game. Or perhaps you'll settle for a picnic.

Your expenditures are bigger than your income. Look at a perfect example: the late Judy Garland, a Gemini, who received tons of publicity for being in debt and having to skip out of back doors of hotels because she couldn't pay her bill. Your sign should learn how to control your impulses and budget yourself so future money difficulties won't occur.

HOW TO HANDLE YOUR MONEY

Wouldn't you like to avoid those panic-stricken moments when you realize you've run out of funds and don't know what you're going to do until the next paycheck arrives? Have you ever thought that those circumstances can be avoided? Is your money going out on a multitude of unimportant things that you never use again or at all?

Is transportation high because you spend on the fastest means available, or because you like to disappear in your car to the beach or the mountains, or to a nearby city? If so, is this a regular pastime? Are you paying rent beyond what you can really afford? Is your food bill enormous because you seldom eat at home?

If you answered "yes" to the preceding questions these are some of the areas you've got to work with and change. It's not impossible to break a bad habit, but it's difficult for you because you are so variable and have difficulty concentrating on one topic. Moreover you forget those past mistakes; your mind is on the present and the future. But because you are bright, why not try to remember by tying a string around your finger for a bad habit you are trying to break? But only one string and one habit at a time; otherwise you may become too scattered and confused and nothing will work.

Your signing up for lessons and then dropping out can be costly when you don't get a refund. If this was an every-now-and-then occurrence it wouldn't hurt your pocketbook as much as it does when it happens several times a year. Next time you enroll in a class analyze your true reason for taking it: Is it going to bring you future security? Is it a passing fancy? Or is it just to satisfy your curiosity? Could you be putting that money to better use with an investment fund or war bond, thus giving you solidity later on? If you try short courses you may find them easier to stick with.

Because you are born under the sign of the Twins, you like to have two of everything. Can't you settle for one and save your nickels and dimes for a rainy day? And keep in mind, you only have *one* pair of lips, so try to curb your compulsive spending on every new lipstick that comes out on the market. By having a few basic colors you still will have your lipstick colors match those outfits you change several times a day.

When you gals go shopping try to buy skirts and blouses that can be mixed and matched; and you guys try to purchase pants and shirts that can be interchanged colorwise. By using common sense you can save money and still have the variety you crave. Realize that clothes may look good and sell you in business, but your greatest asset is your witty personality.

To keep you busy and to save a buck, why not sew your own wardrobe? Buy a wine-making kit and make your own; that'll help you save a few pennies. And make your own furniture from scratch, or buy it unpainted and stain or paint it. Not only will it be something new for you to do, but it's being practical.

Buy a do-it-yourself book and see what fun you can have — get your pals or loved ones to join you — I'm sure this type of action will satisfy that inquisitive nature of yours. But just think of the dollars you can save, and when enough accumulate you can invest them in something solid. Or if you must spend your cash, buy something that can increase in value: tapestries, Oriental rugs, gold coins, paintings, or antiques.

You bit off more than you can chew and have to learn to live within your means. It's very difficult for you to trim down those expenses. But if you don't you'll never be financially solvent. Try some comparison shopping. Think of it as a game and that you want to see what store will be the winner with the cheapest price.

See what stores have the best value for your money. Look for bargains; the flea market is a gathering place for your sign — not because of the prices or unusual buys, but because you can engage in conversations with strangers and enlarge the circle of your friends. So frequent them, and you'll enjoy yourself and probably come away with something you've wanted for ages.

And if you want to cut down on some big spending go Dutch treat with your buddies rather than footing the bill yourself. Small amounts add up over a period of time and turn into large sums. It's really not obvious until you do add them up; try it, you'll be in for a shock.

Next time you want to move to a new place, think about how costly it will be. After all, you probably just moved a few months ago and now because you're restless you are ready for a change to another abode or locale. Don't sign papers for the first place you see. First look around and imagine living in it. Then walk around the neighborhood and see if you like it and if the people are friendly — that's a must with you.

To become financially solvent and have a few bucks saved for your future is important. To do this you should first cut up all of your credit cards and throw them out. Second, you should adopt a budget — a lenient one, otherwise you won't give it a whirl. It will take some talking to yourself to economize, but you can do it if you really want to.

List your earnings (job, inherited investments, etc.) and how much it will take for you to live on (rent, gas, electric, telephone, food, medical, dental, and transportation to and from a job, including insurance on a car, but not the car payments). The areas you can now list and cut down on in order to save money and/or to invest wisely are: clothing, membership dues, entertainment, eating out, recreation, and the gifts bought for people throughout the year.

Make an itemized list of all the money you owe your various creditors. Pay them off as quickly as you can to save interest charges. Rather than missing a payment to someone, send something; it shows good faith. If you have difficulty in meeting any debts, contact the lender; perhaps they can be deferred until you're able to get caught up.

If your rent is more than you can afford, perhaps a less expensive apartment would suffice. You are creative and can decorate a place nicely. However, don't splurge on fixing it up. Try to find hobbies that will satisfy your desire for change and relieve your boredom. For fun, disco-dance, ride a bike or a horse, or go hang-gliding. If you want something cheaper to do, jump rope or play handball, volleyball, horseshoes, or, because you're agile, try doing some gymnastics. Attend neighborhood theaters, concerts, movies; but don't go every night to one or the other of them unless it's free.

Try on a regular basis to save a certain amount of your paycheck each week. Don't skip putting money aside or it'll be difficult to get back on schedule. Plan for the future rather than living for the moment. Stick with the plans and you'll be in control of the future.

Allot a portion of your paycheck for fun and the rest for the usual living expenses and debts; put the remainder (seven percent of your earnings) in a sound investment program. Don't be too strict with yourself. Make allowances now and then for your see-saw spending whims. You can goof every now and then, but don't fall off. Allow for some socializing and don't spend more money than you make.

Work another job to help pay off some of those loans. If you get a brainstorm of an idea, seek financial help before leaping in. Always know where you stand. Review your goals periodically; don't make changes without first weighing the pros and cons. Don't consider your budget as a barrier to your happiness, but as a saving grace for your future due to the rising costs that could arise.

YOUR INVESTMENTS

You can benefit by setting aside money now so your future will be secure. Or perhaps you prefer investing in something other than a business. However, before you go leaping into any undertaking, it would be to your advantage to understand your assets and shortcomings, thereby avoiding pitfalls.

Your Positive Side

A "yes" answer to any of the following questions indicates that you are expressing harmonious Gemini traits, thus enhancing your chances to gain prosperity: Do you profit from the stock market through analyzing the "how" and "why" of everything before investing? Is it necessary for you to be well informed about an investment? Do you derive pleasure from studying each company's prospectus? Are you intuitive with the stock market? If so, has it paid off? Do you scrutinize your finances before investing? Do you think and act fast when speculating? If so, has it been to your advantage?

Are you aware that you're a born speculator? You like to experiment and usually wind up ahead. All stock market records are kept straight so you can go to them, size them up, and make sudden moves. You are able to adapt quickly and to changing stock-market conditions. No wonder you come out a winner. And the knowledge you possess is put to use with your wise financial maneuvers.

Your dual personality comes in handy with bonds and money market funds. You switch back and forth from long term to short, depending upon the current interest and inflation rate as well as which Twin decides to emerge: the one who wants quick gains or the one who wants long-term ones.

You're the type who buys real estate, improves the place, and sells it a year later for a nice fat profit. And you are into everything from shopping centers to motels to private homes. And you don't mind taking a risk on REIT's (a fund, organized as partnerships, that invests in pools of income-producing property) over-the-counter on the stock exchange; you favor office buildings. Perhaps you'll be as rich as Geminian Bob Hope, who is alleged to be one of the wealthiest movie stars in Hollywood due to his sound and extensive investments in real estate.

Or will you gain enormous sums of money by wheeling and dealing in commodity futures? It takes nerve (and you've got it) to speculate in this area by buying on margin. These futures contracts on certain U.S. government securities are purchased as a speculation on future changes in interest rates. You use logic and intuition and hit it with a lucky streak when the interest rate, by the date your contract stipulates, goes in the direction you said it would.

Your desire to travel is partially satisfied when you buy stamps for investment purposes. While putting them in the books you mentally escape to the country of origin. Not only do they satisfy your desire for variety, but they are valuable and you can sell or trade them for profit at any time desired. Your love of knowledge is gratified, as well as your desire to attain security, when you purchase rare books. This hobby for investment purposes keeps you busy running to auctions.

Your Negative Side

A "yes" answer to the following questions indicates that you are expressing inharmonious Gemini traits, thus lessening your chances to gain prosperity: Did your so-called intuition ever backfire in relation to an investment? Does investing in stock or speculating in commodity futures or options make you so nervous and tense that you wind up with insomnia?

Do you have expensive losses because you can't concentrate properly on stock market records, reports, or statistics to make the right moves? Does indecision cause a loss when investing in real estate, stocks, commodity futures, or options? Do you lose money constantly because of an untimely switching of your interests from mutual funds to bonds?

Have you made many quick decisions with investments you've later regretted? Part of the problem stems from your association with people who try your patience to the point where you just leap in blindly, taking your chances come what may. Later, listening to the stock market reports, you realize that you made a mistake. So what do you do about it? The next day you sell it at a loss and buy some stock in a company that really hits a low point in a few days. And, without thinking it might go back up again, you sell it and continue in the vicious circle of being in and out of the market almost on a daily basis. It might not be good for your pocketbook, but it satisfies your craving for change and variety.

Ideas to make a fast buck run pell-mell through your mind. You get a little high when you think of those millions you're going to reap. Your dual nature has you flip-flopping among stocks, bonds, real estate, gold, silver, art, rare books, and stamps, and anything else you get wind of. There's never an end to what you will try. The gambler in you wants to pick a winner; however, you usually wind up the loser.

If a pal tells you to bet on a particular horse, you will. Likewise, if you are listening to someone talk about how much he made on trucker's stock, as soon as you can get to a phone you call your broker and buy shares in it. And what's more, you fail to make inquiries about it first.

Your sullen moods come right after you've had a heavy loss. But within an hour you bounce back with the desire to give it another shot. And you wonder why you are always on the losing side, regardless what it is you touch.

When it comes to options — it's difficult for you to resist the temptation to get involved with abnormally high premiums for calls on volatile, speculative stock. Let's say you are convinced that a specific communications stock selling at fifty dollars is going to rise in a price by a specific date. So you buy a call option at fifty on one hundred shares of stock. And you pay a premium of six hundred dollars for your option. When it is time for your option to expire, the stock has fallen and is selling at thirty dollars; therefore, you guessed wrong and lose your six-hundred-dollar premium. The daily excitement of wondering what its final destination will be has you like a yo-yo. But you enjoy every nerve-jangling moment of it, even when you lose.

You consider all investments a game, one that can be won. It's the mental challenge that spurs you into taking risks. Your need for constant excitement adds to it; the results are of little consequence to you. You'd be better off by putting your money into safe areas so you'll be in good shape in the future.

WHAT SHOULD YOU INVEST IN?

Calculated risks are preferred; however, it would be wise not to take too many chances. Short-term investments which can net you a good return for your money would be more advantageous. If you diversify, which I'll wager you will, you can have better protection for your dollars and at the same time enjoy being involved in more than one area.

Actually, everything interests you; however, the greater the risk, the greater the thrill. Commercial paper could really interest you because it may mature in thirty or ninety days. This promissory note floated by a major corporation which wants to raise money is not guaranteed. You could lose everything from it if the company doesn't have the money to pay its debt; but then again, you could make quite a bundle in a hurry if it did meet its obligation.

Telephone (ruled by Gemini/Mercury) utility company bonds may interest you; it pays to invest in something you use and your sign is known for yakking constantly on the phone. The U.S. (also ruled by your sign) dollar in the currency-investment field may be something you'd like to invest in; but watch the futures market. It's too hazardous for you, although the excitement of it is exactly what you want. But that's not the way to be financially secure.

Traveler's checks in foreign currencies appeal to you because they satisfy your urge to go to faraway places. By owning them you might get a yen (not to be confused with the Japanese one) to take a trip to another nation. Because you need diversification so you don't get bored, be sure you don't go whole hog by purchasing traveler's checks in every country's currency. Of course, they are one of the most profitable hedges against the dollar if it declines in value.

In the collectibles there's enough to keep you busy running in circles (you delight in doing that) for a long time. Collect autographs of celebrities; rather than buying them from a store that specializes in autographs, go and meet the people in person. Your great gift of gab will come in handy. Later you can sell these to dealers or collectors.

Buy finely bound and inscribed first editions of books as well as rare ones if you can afford them. Start a stamp collection by getting free stamps from everyone you know. If someone works in an office that gets a lot of foreign mail, ask that individual to save you the stamps.

Contemporary prints made from woodcuts, lithography, engraving, or etching processes may interest you. Graphic posters could be your particular favorite. Buy a print that not only pleases you, but has material value as well. If you can't or don't have the money to buy originals, why not form a partnership with a friend? The small investor with limited funds may find prints a more satisfying market than oils. If you buy what you like, be prepared to make mistakes; but even then you may be ahead of the game. By the way, according to the experts, well-chosen prints can be expected to appreciate by thirty percent a year!

Comic books are a big "in" thing; perhaps you saved some when you were a kid or perhaps you've collected them through your parents or other channels. Hang on to them and sell them later, if you wish. They can be traded through magazine ads or other markets.

Perhaps you'd like to invest in the gems your sign rules — beryl, golden beryl, cat's-eye chrysoberyl, alexandrite, aquamarine? Buy shares in them, purchase your own mine, or go into them as a business or as a collectible for a hedge against inflation.

In the foreign-bond market, your sign is attracted to the Gemini-ruled countries of Denmark, Norway, Sweden and the city of London, England.

To safeguard your future against inflation and currency fluctuations, considering your gambling nature, you need to invest in a financial program designed to provide future security. A tax-exempt bond fund, if you qualify financially, can bring you income from relatively long-term tax-exempt investments without your losing the ability to withdraw any part of your money if the need arises (and with you, it will). This is good for someone as busy as you are because you don't have to supervise it yourself, and you receive a monthly income check exempt from federal income taxes!

You keep up with world affairs; therefore, your ideas to make money can be based upon current trends. However, because one never knows which Twin will emerge (the one that attracts financial gains or the one that attracts financial disasters), it's to your advantage to seek the advice of an expert.

A broker who thinks along the same lines as you may be desirable. Therefore deal with another Gemini, Aries, Leo, Scorpio, Sagittarius, Aquarius, or Pisces. These signs will encourage calculated risks because they, like you, are nervy, quick, and take chances. From a strictly financial standpoint, however, they may not be the best signs for you to listen to or be involved with.

You really need a broker who is analytical, practical, and able to provide the balance you so sorely need. Therefore, consider Capricorn, Taurus, and Virgo as your best bet. They are slow thinking and acting because they want to be sure of all transactions. However, accept daily differences of opinion with them and expect to be annoyed by their deliberation.

Cancer and Libra are indecisive and changeable just like you. Libra weighs the pros and cons and wants to balance everything in its proper perspective. Cancer may do something on a whim, if he/she gets too bored thinking about what to do or what not to do. Therefore, these signs as a broker could either be beneficial financially or cause losses, depending upon which way they swing.

Perhaps the broker you select is born under the sign of Aries, Gemini, Cancer, Leo, Libra, Scorpio, Sagittarius, Aquarius, or Pisces, and he/she chiefly follows solid, safe, and sound investment procedures. This individual takes this approach, which is opposite his/her Sun sign traits, probably because he/she has Taurus, Virgo, or Capricorn as a *dominant* sign in his/her horoscope. If this occurs, you're in fairly good hands.

Astrology can guide you in the type of bonds your sign should consider investing in. Be on the alert for bonds that deal with education and mass-transit systems, tax-exempt revenue bonds which are issued by public authorities and involve bridges, ferry systems, railroads, and city transportation, and firms that specialize in communication, distribution, and transportation, or are involved with the metallic element Mercury (also known as quicksilver).

Because everything in life has an astrological correspondence each type of corporate bond, stock, or commodity has a sign/planet that rules it. Under the Gemini/Mercury influence you should invest in manufacturing corporations that produce information-handling devices, respiratory equipment, air filters, wind instruments, windmills, bicycles, copying and duplicating machines, pencil sharpeners, communications equipment, air freight, educational articles, and tissue paper or other allied paper products.

Other Gemini/Mercury-ruled areas that might capture your interest are companies which are involved with the making of type and all forms of printing or periodicals, newspapers, magazines, books, telephone, telegraph, railway, railroads, transportation, truckers, travel, rapid transit system, and instruction (teaching).

Still other Gemini/Mercury-ruled areas are the literary field, correspondence schools, mail-order houses, catalogues, and distributors for consumers and of automobile replacement parts.

HOW TO HANDLE YOUR INVESTMENTS

Diversity is the answer for you. It makes you happy to dabble in variety because you feel secure in the fact that if one fails, you've got the others. Keep in mind that if you have non-income producing assets like real estate (if it's not producing spendable money) then accumulate liquid assets. This liquidity can be in cash or savings accounts, foreign currency, traveler's checks, bonds, stocks, gold, cash-value life insurance, or even a pension.

The short-term bonds you favor are generally considered the safest but lowest yielding, so invest in them to get the quick returns which you like. As for stocks, if you can't live at peace with your nerves, don't own them. You alone must live with the investments you make; therefore, make decisions that you can be fairly tranquil with (although that's a difficult state for you to reach regardless of the situation you find yourself in).

Your desire for experimentation should be curbed. Check out all the new companies and projects before shelling out your dough on them. Get the opinion of more than one expert before taking action. Weigh the pros and cons in relation to how you may profit or lose. Put on your Gemini thinking cap and you'll probably do the right thing.

Stay clear of margin accounts. Don't burden yourself with excessive debts. Watch out for consumer hustles and rip-offs such as London options and mail-order diamonds.

If you don't know anything about prints you could invite disaster by buying one that is a reproduction rather than genuine. Read books or attend art classes before making firm decisions in this area. The print should be signed by the artist and should not say "in the stone." Have a dealer guarantee the authenticity of his prints in writing.

Are you a winner or loser? It not only depends upon your Sun sign and how you use it, but also on the influence of Jupiter and Saturn. Jupiter attracts a gain, whereas Saturn attracts a loss. Everyone has these planets in his/her horoscope, but their influence depends upon whether their harmonious or inharmonious side is expressed at the moment a decision is made.

Under the influence of the positive side of Saturn, you are practical, conservative, cautious, serious, contemplative, and make a move only when you are sure the time is ripe. Long-range investments are favored. You use sound judgment, and thus can buy to advantage.

Under the influence of the negative side of Saturn you are pessimistic and cry poverty; you worry, gripe, complain, and have the blues. You are slow because you are afraid of making the wrong move, and thus can attract losses. You lack confidence and chances are if you purchase anything, it could be a real downer.

Whenever you are depressed and feel the Saturn negative traits, avoid investing in anything, because your Saturn is being stimulated in your horoscope at that moment (this could last an hour, a day, a week, a month, a year, or more). If you do invest when this inharmonious energy is being expressed, you are likely to attract a loss.

Under the influence of the positive side of Jupiter you are confident, optimistic, cheerful, easygoing, honest, understanding, happy, and generous. Speculation is favored and brings success. You use sound judgment and can sell to an advantage, take options, buy on margin, and do well all around.

Under the influence of the negative side of Jupiter you are overly confident, too optimistic, wasteful, ostentatious, extravagant, and refuse to take into account prices, expenditures, or the views of others. You are in the mood to do everything to excess. At a party you'd be on center stage making everyone laugh. If you sell an investment when you are in this frame of mind you won't get the price it's worth; your judgment will be off.

Whenever you discover you are using the negative side of Jupiter, don't take a chance with the stock market or any other form of investment. Lie low and wait until the positive side of Jupiter is being expressed, then sell. It'll be worth the wait.

In astrology *buying* is ruled by Saturn and *selling* by Jupiter. Every time you buy under a harmonious Saturn aspect your purchase will be a bargain, a good deal, or investment. Every time you sell under a harmonious Jupiter aspect your sale will be considerable gain. The moment these planets are activated in your horoscope are determined by your time, place, day, month, and year of birth. But you don't need a horoscope to know when you are in a depressed state or happy mood. By being aware of your frame of mind, you'll know how to invest wisely. The moment the negative side of Jupiter, Saturn, or Gemini is expressed, that's the time to watch out for losses; the reverse is true when their positive side is expressed.

Now that you are armed with this information you can invest wisely and be ready for whatever the world economy brings. However, you are one step further ahead than the majority of people because by using this positive energy you can improve your chances to be wealthy.

CHAPTER FOUR

Cancer - Money and Investments

Those born from June 21 through July 22 have the Sun in the sign Cancer. Every sign of the zodiac corresponds to a particular type of prosperity; it's what you do and how you use it that determines whether you'll be successful or not.

Do you know that your emotionalism, which leads to foolish spending, would make this a difficult objective to achieve? Instead, wouldn't it be better if you could prevent losses, shortages, and banish negative thoughts from your mind? By knowing your faults and how to correct them you can enjoy life more, save money, and, be in tip-top shape. And that's well worth the effort, isn't it?

YOUR MONEY

Money clings to you like sand does when your hands are wet. However, you are a bundle of contradictions and inconsistencies. You believe that "variety is the spice of life;" as a result your dough may go fast. But then you turn right around and become tighter than most misers.

You have to be in the mood to go shopping; otherwise you'll put it off until another day. The Cancer "crawl" is used when moving about; you don't go sideways like a crab (the animal representative of your sign), but you do manage to go almost as slowly.

In the store you can drive your pals crazy because one moment you want to buy a specific item and the next you decide against it. By the time you arrive home you may not have purchased anything because the frugal part of you won over the whimsical part who wanted to go on a spree.

As a rule you will do comparison shopping before spending a cent. If you feel sorry for someone you are likely to buy a gift for him/her. Your desire to be needed can overpower your conservativeness. You have a strong maternal instinct, which, when given in to, can make you loosen the purse strings. Your loved ones will never be in want with you around.

Most of your money is spent on food and things for the home: accessories, furnishings, plants, cooking utensils, dishes. These are the areas you weaken in the most. Although you like clothes of all types (to give you the diversity you like) this is not an area that's going to make you part that quickly with those hard-earned pennies you've managed to put away.

You tend to eat at home more often than you eat out. Your own good food, in unlimited quantity, is preferred. To cook for and feed others is one of your greatest delights. Your friends can drop by any time if they are hungry and you'll go out of your way to fix them a good meal. The expense is no object, although the price you usually pay for groceries is not exorbitant.

It's imperative to you that money be stashed away for the future either in the bank or in the form of investments. In fact, a fair portion of your earnings will always be hidden away, perhaps in the cookie jar or somewhere else in the kitchen, a room ruled by your sign. You like wealth and are not content until you've acquired it. Security is important; without it you'd go to pieces. You will work hard for the money it brings. However, first you must be content in your environment and enjoy the labor you perform. Any financial success you have is usually due to your own perseverance and industrious nature.

You gals can be dependent upon a man who has material assets. However, you may want to supervise the expenditures and make sure there's something left for that rainy day. You know the value of money, although when emotionally frustrated you may spend it foolishly. However, there's a positive and negative side of Cancer, and if the positive side is expressed you have a better chance to be on the winner's side.

Your Positive Side

Do you persistently stick with your financial objectives? Is it easy for you to save money? Do you hold out tenaciously on business deals until you get the monies desired? Are you shrewd in financial transactions? Do risks frighten you? Is the need to conserve money stronger than the desire to spend it? If you answered the preceding questions with a "yes," you are using the harmonious traits you are known for, and as a result, prosperity can be more easily attracted.

Have women been influential in your making a living? Your mother, friend, counselor, or wife encourages you to be successful. Or perhaps your money comes in through a business that caters to the female sex.

Money is gained through your careful and prudent actions. You are not about to leap blindly into a deal. You must absorb all ideas given to you and after digesting them you are able to divert them to your own use. This process of assimilation is the only way you can deal with anything.

Your slowness at making decisions may upset others, but it hasn't hurt your bank account. You must carry out your own ideas in the way you see feasible for yourself. The dog-eat-dog world of competition turns you off. Your lack of aggression is made up for when you succeed through tenacity.

It's the old and familiar that you have sure footing on. Your sign is known for having "gut feelings" over most things. Many times a financial gain comes through following such a hunch. However, all new products as a rule are tested for performance and durability before measures are taken to release them.

Your ability to mentally grasp the likes and dislikes of the public, and to understand their tastes and views, earns you a lot of bucks where it counts. If you are in retail (a Cancer-ruled area) you can really clean up because you sell only that which you know the populace will buy.

Your bank account grows when you rent garden space to others so they can grow their own vegetables in the city. So not only is the vacant lot on your property put to good use, but you've given others a means to put food (your favorite word) on their table.

And to make an extra buck you just might decide to raise African violets in your basement or grow plants and sell them for profit to your neighbors, banks, libraries, office buildings, restaurants, and the like. You have a green thumb and care for your plants just as you would for children.

Money is earned through a variety of sources. If you had to make it all from one area you'd get a little bored. You know your own mind, although it may not seem so. Once you've really made a decision you stick to it. However, you are occasionally changeable but generally only in personal, not in financial, matters.

You worry over those greenbacks even when you're quite well off. If you're in a business where your income fluctuates because of supply and demand, your insecurity is considerably higher than it would be if you had steady earnings.

Office equipment is handled as carefully as your wallet; it's even polished! You do what you can to keep up with the times, but you don't go out of your way to do so. You'd rather keep computers or machinery and have them repaired or overhauled from time to time than to be investing your dough continually in the latest models.

The possible dangers in the business world make you worry. Just the *thought* of taking a risk on some new venture exhausts you completely. Difficult chores are seldom approached head on; instead they are worked on calmly and with circumspection. You accomplish more than others do, working in this quiet way. It's music to your ears when the cash comes flowing in.

You can make a buck through being dramatic and being before the public in some way or dealing with them privately in business. Creativity is accomplished with great depth of feeling. The emotion that goes into it pays off at the box office.

Domestic and family matters exercise an influence on money. To provide your loved ones with the comforts of life you think of additional ways to earn income, like making colorful pillows for sofa and floor use or heirloom quilts. Wise investments are part of your plan. Or you may take on a sideline to make a few extra dollars, like selling hermit crabs as pets. Because you are extremely conscious of your ancestry and enjoy delving into the past, you may find genealogy fascinating. Your friends who want theirs researched could pay you handsomely. So you take them up on it without boasting what exactly you are going to do or why. You just go ahead in your usual calm and gingerly manner.

Your Negative Side

Are you an emotional spender? Do losses occur through inconsistency on your part when it comes time to make a decision? Have losses occurred as a result of too much diversification? Is it difficult for you to regulate expenditures?

Does your restlessness cost you money? Do women cost you lots of dough either because you listen to their advice or spend money on them? Do your finances fluctuate too rapidly for you? Does it frustrate you that your income is irregular? If you answered these preceding questions with a "yes", you are using the inharmonious traits you are known for, and as a result, it's difficult to attract prosperity.

Are you changeable where money matters are concerned? One moment you want to make your fortune and will deny yourself everything but food. Later you don't believe you'll ever hit it big so, "Why go without?" you say. This swinging back and forth drives your loved ones up the wall. When the urge to be here today and gone tomorrow strikes, your pocketbook becomes quite empty. You don't care. But the next day when you wake up, you are horrified at how much you spent the day before. And you just don't know what gets into you at times. On these occasions you go overboard with the money you spend on food and living quarters. The cupboards and freezer are stacked with enough food to last months, which gives you a feeling of security. And more pots and pans are purchased: one for fondue, the other for crepes — then there are the dishes for the escargot.

You delight in gossiping with others about their money. You are curious about how they make and spend their dollars. By hearing them talk you may get a few ideas as to what you should or should not do. Because you are an impressionable person, you learn by the mistakes and profits of others. You tune in as if it is happening to you — and with your active imagination you can make yourself believe it is!

When it comes to your own finances you dislike telling others about the condition you are in. You are extremely sensitive in this department. And if money doesn't come in the way you like, you get yourself all worked up into a tizzy. And then the crying jag starts. True to your Water sign nature, the tears that flow are enough to fill a few buckets.

If you're not making money, your mental state doesn't improve. In fact, it deteriorates. Betty Hutton, a Cancerian, was a big movie star who did very well until acting roles stopped coming in and her finances dwindled down to nothing. She left Hollywood and many years ago received publicity to the effect that she had been broke and was now working happily in a church doing housework (ruled by the sign Cancer). These changes of fortune are a complete drainage of energy for anyone born under your sign.

If you're not earning a living through work or investments, you become so restless that others have difficulty keeping up with the emotional scenes you put yourself through. Money affects your mental attitude more than it does that of other signs. You have a flair for melodrama which is seen when you pour your heart out to your loved ones telling them about your financial straits.

There are times when you just can't cope with your problems and you turn to liquor to lighten your load. If you don't go the booze route, then you alternate between the weepy mood and the compulsive eating kick. You beg your friends and loved ones to be understanding and sympathetic to your cause. But you manage to stay in that scene for only a short time. It isn't long before you come out of the crablike shell you've been hiding in and smile at the world as if nothing ever happened.

All projects are entered through your feelings rather than reason. Often a loss occurs through your following a hunch. Or you may lose out on an enormous deal because you took too long to decide whether you should get involved. It's in your nature to mistrust anything that sounds too good.

Your money, like everything else with you, depends upon your moods. If you're morbid, you avoid others and indulge in bouts of self-pity and depression. Once you emerge from that role you enter the spotlight for the attention you secretly crave, but are too shy to admit you want. This new part you're playing costs you a few bucks, which are shelled out hesitantly.

Debts are frowned upon and are seldom incurred. It's important for you to be financially solvent; otherwise, insecure feelings dominate, resulting in negativity. A certain sum is set aside and, regardless of the circumstances, not touched. If it is used, it's only because you're desperate. Your emotions are your downfall. When you get upset it affects your job and your wallet where it hurts most. That's when you're most apt to go off the deep end with a spending spree. To have a large bank account, learn how to handle your feelings and money.

HOW TO HANDLE YOUR MONEY

Wouldn't you like to avoid those mental flip-flops you go through in relation to finances? Doesn't it bother you that you lost a pile of dough because you were too slow in acting upon a business deal? Have you ever wondered how to get the most out of your money and thus avoid those worrisome nights?

Is your food bill high because you overeat? Do you spend your money on some fanciful whim of the moment? Did you lose to a competitor because your old-fashioned computer or machinery couldn't produce the workload required and his/her modern computer or equipment could?

If you answered "yes" to the preceding questions, these are some of the areas you've got to work with and change. It's not impossible to break bad habits. You can channel them through constructive outlets, though it will take a lot of effort on your part — at *all* times, not just when the mood strikes.

A lot of money could be saved if you cut down on what is spent on home furnishings, on garden supplies or tools, and on kitchen remodeling. Next time you get the urge to buy something, think about where you will put it. If the entire room has to be changed around so this new object can fit in, that means you really don't need it, especially if it is for show rather than use.

Instead of taking forever to deliberate on a business transaction, discuss the subject with others; perhaps this method of operation could help you in your conclusions that much faster. Think to yourself, "I know I can be slow, so rather than losing out entirely, I'd better get the opinions of others and weigh everyone's advice. Then perhaps I won't lose the deal like I did the last time."

Keep up on the latest computers and equipment and, if possible, try to figure out if it would be wise for you to get rid of outdated computers or machinery. Think, "If I do purchase this could I cut down on employees and save on the payroll? If I buy this will I be able to do more work quickly and thus attract more clients and in the long run make more money?" Discuss the idea with an accountant and see if it's advisable.

One of your main problems is that if you are an employer, you don't like to let people go. Your employees are like your family and you want to protect them. Because of this trait, many times you will not buy new computers or equipment that could replace workers. That's something that can hold you back from being extremely wealthy, but another part of you would rather not make that kind of money if you had to let an employee go. So it's ultimately your decision and something you have to live with.

Your desire to help anyone who is in need can become an expensive hobby. It's easy for people to get your sympathy, although you appear aloof and unapproachable. But once you've heard a sob story, and feel sorry for the person, there go your dollars. You have to be careful that others don't take advantage of this wonderful trait you possess. It could cost you a lot more than you'd like and may not be repaid. However, if you've been stung in the past, you may not come to someone's financial rescue that fast the next time around. You learn from your mistakes. So the next time you are ready to go on one of those emotional spending escapades, think about the past (which is very real to you), and that could easily stop you from getting carried away.

Instead of weeping over your upsets, do something physical: Clean the house, go scuba diving, water skiing, shoot the rapids, compete in water sports, or go snowshoeing if possible. Because you are a Water sign, water is your natural habitat; it soothes your emotions. So rather than going on a money-spending binge, be around water, even if it's just to look at it. A soak in a hot tub may suffice.

Or if you're an artist paint water scenes on canvas to get those frustrations out. Or sew. Do some needlepoint, knit, or crochet — all favorite activities of your sign. Sell or give them away. You'll be proud of your accomplishment and the new owner may feel blessed. And that in return will make you glow. This is a good new habit to build to replace your emotional tizzies.

When you get in one of those restless moods, keep an eye on your pocketbook; otherwise it may wind up empty. Spend only what you can afford. To break up monotony and perhaps save a few quarters, play bridge or backgammon (without playing for too high stakes).

Or get your pals or loved ones to go to a country or old-fashioned dance. After you've kicked up your heels a little you will have forgotten what caused your crying jag in the first place. Or just listen to peppy music. Stay away from torch songs. And instead of cooking up a storm or nibbling (you're a snacker) go for a long walk where food isn't handy. But don't take any to eat along the way. Think about what excessive food expenditures do to your pocketbook — a pound saved is a pound earned!

Avoid betting on *every* horse at the racetrack just because you want to win. You may want to follow your hunches, though, because you are psychic. However, very few people have been a hundred percent correct with ESP all of the time.

If your earnings are irregular, take on another job (part time) and the fluctuations you've experienced will be lessened. Or put your money in investments that could bring you extra income, then when there's a delay in getting money from your regular profession it won't send you into a panic-stricken mood.

Set up a goal for money and give yourself a deadline to meet it. Compare your actual income with planned income. But what you really need is a budget that allows you a little spare money for those melodramatic scenes you go through. You wouldn't feel comfortable if you couldn't splurge every now and then — just don't make it too costly. With good budgeting procedures you can have more money to buy those things you want when that urge strikes.

Credit card buying is not your cup of tea, though you like to have a charge card handy in case you get your feelings hurt and can compensate by spending money. But think of what you can save on interest if you pay cash for everything. It's best to get all loans paid off as quickly as possible and save on those interest charges.

Your food bill is what you really need to revise, although that is extremely difficult for you to do. To make it a little easier, don't lump your eating-out money with that which is set aside for groceries. The dollars you spend for restaurants should be part of your entertainment funds. However, you really must do something about buying food just because you want it handy for your hunger pangs. Your diet and pocketbook are not helped when you buy too many perishables because this forces you into eating them quickly. Learn to curb your expenditures in this direction, and not only will you save a buck, but you may lose some weight.

You may wonder how much you should allow out of your paycheck for every item: food and money owed on loans should be twenty percent each; medical and dental five percent; clothing and entertainment should be ten percent; rent, gas, lights, telephone should as a total unit be twenty-five percent; transportation (car payments are not included, but insurance is) should be ten percent; the money you save or invest should be seven percent; the miscellaneous items you can't recall spending on should be three percent.

These percentages are, however, viewed as traditional guidelines. Due to your circumstances they may vary. Perhaps you are living with a roommate or spouse and share the rent, or are living at home with your parents, and so on. Whatever your budget consists of, there must be room to goof off with or you will not stick with it at all. Although your sign is tenacious, you do get bored easily and can quit the best of projects in midstream. So make it like a game that has to be played all the way to the end before the winner is known. And you'll be proud of yourself when you've come out ahead.

YOUR INVESTMENTS

You can benefit by setting aside money now so your future will be secure. Or perhaps you prefer investing in something other than a business. However, before you get involved in any undertaking, it would be to your advantage to understand your assets and shortcomings, thereby avoiding pitfalls.

Your Positive Side

A "yes" answer to any of the following questions indicates that you are expressing harmonious Cancer traits, thus enhancing your chances to gain prosperity: Do you buy and sell stock in volume and profit by it? Are you successful when you play your hunches with investments? Do you prefer conservative investments over speculative? Is it a must with you to diversify? Do commodities, most of the time, go the direction you want? Do your shares in stock fluctuate in your favor? Are you easily influenced by others? If so, has it paid off?

Do you invest according to the mood you're in? There are many changes where speculative ventures are concerned: Your apprehension fights against your curiosity until one wins out. The stronger of the two is your whimsical mood that becomes a reality when you invest. It's to your advantage to follow those inner feelings when they give you the "go" signal.

You are full of contradictions, constantly swinging back and forth between long- and short-term investments. The cautious and practical side of your nature wants a sure thing, whereas another part of you wants excitement in taking a chance.

Your favorite speculative sport is a dangerous one: futures commodities. Perhaps it's the food that appeals to you in the commodity market, or maybe the constant fluctuation that breaks up boredom and monotony? You enjoy watching the market every few moments, anxiously waiting to see if the price will drop or rise. It's the constant up-and-down motion that really turns you on. And when you're lucky, you may make a killing of six thousand dollars in one day just because you followed a hunch and guessed right!

Over-the-counter stocks and new issues of corporations going public for the first time and of smaller companies seeking equity financing are hazardous. They are fabulous profit-making opportunities which are difficult for you to turn down. However, you find them particularly appealing because they are new, and you are sympathetic toward helping the underdog get ahead.

Real estate is a natural for your sign because it deals with home-sweet-home; a typical Cancerian scene is a living room with the dog lying on the floor and a woman sitting by the fireplace knitting and a man reading the newspaper. Thoughts of this domestic bliss make you desirous of owning your own abode. When you have a roof over your head that you own you feel safe, secure, and comfy. And your judgment is excellent when it comes to buying. Once a house is bought you like to hang on to it, unless you're in the real estate game of buying and selling in short periods of time.

You're a real collector, whether it be of china plates drawn and signed by the artist, old phonograph records, or antiques. You are sentimental and become attached to the collectibles; however, they are also valuable and could bring a good price if you ever had the heart to part with them. Meanwhile, they are your security.

Your Negative Side

A "yes" answer to the following questions indicates that your are expressing the inharmonious Cancer traits, thus lessening your chances to gain prosperity: Are you indecisive about investments? If you speculate and the stock fluctuates, do you become an emotional mess? Do you lose when you play your hunches with investments? Are you inconsistent with investing and do you attract losses as a result?

Do you panic easily when the stock market takes a plunge? Have you been wiped out from speculating with commodity futures? Would you emotionally cling to an investment even if it meant a loss? Do you buy and sell stock over a short period of time (days, weeks) rather than holding on for the advisable six-month capital gain period?

Are you aware that boredom can get you into hot water with investments? When you are in that restless mood and pace the floor with nothing else to do, you are likely to get involved in risky ventures. To pep up your day you may decide to take a fling with options.

The six-month option period is preferred because you tire easily of one stock. The short sale is your favorite: This is stock you borrow from your broker and sell, then later buy the stock to replace what you borrowed. Your belief is that a profit can be obtained if the stock *declines in price* between the sale and the covering purchase. Of course, when you're running an unlucky streak the stock *increases in price* during your option period and there goes all of your money; this can literally wipe out not only your savings but your personal chattel. Your love of the home and land keeps you from putting that up for security with the broker; however, you will sell your antiques to cover yourself. Once you've lost with options, or any margin-account commodity, you'll never forget it and will not try again.

After an enormous loss you really go into your shell and pout. Your home life and everyday affairs become dissatisfying. You wonder where you erred and how that stock could have gone up instead of down in price. If you stop and think, you'll realize that you were indecisive before deciding to sell short. And because time was running out, you had to move fast, which is against your nature, and that forced you to rely upon a hunch that didn't pay off.

Of course, the tears fall for days when you realize the gravity of what you did — all because you wanted to put some spice into your life. But what about the time you purchased stock and were informed by the broker that you should sell because the company could go bankrupt? What did you do? You couldn't bring yourself to sell because you had faith that the corporation would be back on its feet again and your investment would be intact. It's difficult for you to let go of something you are emotionally tied to and that stock was with a company that manufactured your favorite food. You put the Cancer stomach before the Cancer money, which is not odd for anyone born under your sign to do. However, it isn't the way to be ahead of the game.

WHAT SHOULD YOU INVEST IN?

Due to your changeable nature you should follow a short-term as well as a long-term policy. That way, you'll see your money working for you constantly. Then those quick profits you anticipate bring you joy and the ones not expected are pleasant surprises when the dividend checks arrive in the mail.

Your desire for variety has to be satisfied by diversification. Number one on your priority list is purchasing a home. Once that has been taken care of, other areas are entered. Fast-food franchises appeal to your tummy and pocketbook. Six-month certificates of deposit bought from the bank make you feel secure.

Get involved with government funds, which are short term, safe, and pay well. These are bills and notes issued by different agencies of the government and you can buy or trade them. Other short-term investments that could keep you contented as a mother hen with her chicks are "families" of funds. Different investment groups have made it increasingly easy to move from one of their funds to another, just by a phone call, at little or no cost. These "switching privileges" appeal to your sign because it is possible to split your money among different types of investments and change the balance with changing conditions. It must have been dreamed up by a Cancerian because its method of operation is typical of your sign.

Another short-term investment that could keep you happy is commercial paper, which, if the corporation pays back its debt, could give you a nice return on your money after a thirty-day period. The most risky areas are commodity futures and stock options. This is nothing more than pure gambling. In the commodity futures market, your sign rules silver, food (Maine potatoes, eggs, dressed poultry), beverages (orange juice), chicken feed, the Canadian dollar, cocoa beans, Treasury bills and bonds; therefore these areas may interest you the most. If in the past you've come out ahead with commodity futures and stock options, continue along these lines.

As money becomes worth less and less, more and more people in all countries are turning to tangible commodities such as precious metals. These have maintained their positions through wars, depression, and runaway inflation. Silver is used in a wide variety of electronics applications — from electronic calculators to transistor radios — and in the manufacture of film. Stock in silver mines or corporations which deal with silver might be hazardous than the commodity futures market. Or to compensate, perhaps you'd like to buy silver flatware, serving trays and dishes, etc. You are silver happy and may believe these silver items will grow in value. Besides, they are practical (you tell yourself) because you can use them when you entertain. Once you've become the proud owner of silverware you will not relinquish it. Because you are extremely family conscious it will be left as an heirloom.

Perhaps you'd like to invest in the gems your sign rules — emerald, pearl, moonstone, and opal - or the soft and white stones, selenite and chalk. Buy shares, purchase a mine, or go into them as a business.

Because land and property mean so much to you, purchase real estate mutual funds or buy shares in property syndicates such as REIT's. Also, conventional mortgage pass-through certificates attract you, although they lack liquidity, are costly (usually a twenty-five thousand dollar minimum), and are not guaranteed by the government. With them the originator of the mortgage passes through to you monthly payments of principal and interest as well as any prepayments that are received on the mortgages in the pool.

To get the most out of your money continue to save it, but invest in some worthwhile areas. A family trust for your children can save you tax dollars. The important retirement age is on your mind; therefore you want to provide for your own and your loved ones' futures. A refund annuity may appeal to you because you receive a steady monthly income for life. Or for tax savings, what about deferred annuities?

Astrology can guide you in the type of bonds your sign should invest in. Because you are patriotic, buy what your nation sells: in the United States of America the Series E bonds or Treasury bonds are for you. Regardless of where you were born, be on the alert for bonds that deal with Cancer-ruled areas: land development, housing projects, dams, waterworks, rivers especially, with tax-exempt revenue bonds in the municipal field. One example is the water and power company of the city you live in; you might want to buy the bonds of Cancer-ruled New York. If you want a "quickie" return for your money go for trans bonds, which are tax-exempt municipals with a three-, six-, or nine-month, or one-year duration.

In the foreign bond market, your sign is attracted to the Cancer-ruled countries of Argentina, Canada, and Italy. Invest in the Canadian dollar if the foreign-currency department appeals to you. Perhaps you'd be lucky trading commodities, stock, silver, or art in any of these countries.

Before you become involved in any type of investment, it's imperative that you should be abreast of current world affairs; otherwise, wrong moves may be made. Because you are so changeable and indecisive it would be to your advantage to seek the advice of an expert.

A broker who thinks along the same lines as you may be desirable. Therefore deal with Aries, Gemini, Leo, Scorpio, Sagittarius, Aquarius, and Pisces. These signs will encourage calculated risks (not necessarily a wise idea) because they, like you, take chances. However, Pisces may not move fast enough for you. And from a strictly financial standpoint, these signs may not be the best for you to listen to or be involved with.

You really need a broker who is conservative and stable, and uses logic; he can provide the balance you so sorely need. Therefore consider Capricorn, Taurus, and Virgo your best bets. You will respect their slowness because you understand that they want to be sure of all decisions.

Another Cancerian or a Libran would be too moody and whimsical for your pocketbook. They weigh the pros and cons, but continually alter their opinions. If they swing the right way they may be beneficial, but if they don't you're out a few bucks.

Perhaps the broker you select was born under the sign of Aries, Gemini, Cancer, Leo, Libra, Scorpio, Sagittarius, Aquarius, or Pisces and he/she chiefly follows solid, safe, and sound investment procedures. This individual takes this approach, which is opposite his/her Sun sign traits, probably because he/she has Taurus, Virgo, or Capricorn as a *dominant* sign in his horoscope. If this occurs, you'll have the best of two worlds: a broker who speculates but uses prudence.

Because everything in life has an astrological correspondence, each type of corporate bond or stock has a sign/planet that rules it. Therefore, under the Cancer/ Moon influence, invest in silver, aluminum, music (recorded, rhythmic, country, western), silverware, silver plate, land, property, real estate, motels, hotels, mobile homes, prefabricated homes, miniconglomerates, home furnishings, retail stores, and discount department store chains.

If these areas don't capture your interest, try barge fleets, bottle water (spring, distilled, mineral, soda, sparkling, carbonated), swimming pools, water boards, fishing, liquids, beverages, soft drinks (including diet ones), or the milk and dairy industry, including yogurt.

Other Cancer-ruled areas are articles for women and family, or products for the home. And of course there's your favorite subject — food: the grocery industry, supermarkets and food chains, and bread-baking companies. Or how about canned, packaged, or frozen foods? Dehydrated foods, of which there are a wide variety (nearly one hundred), have nutritional value and can be used in the home or for wilderness camping, institutions, or survival programs. Chickens are also ruled by your sign. Perhaps you'd rather raise, sell, and package them?

Because you enjoy being surrounded by plants and flowers, buy stock which deals with garden supplies and tools. If you wish, try the vending-machine industry, because there are enough kinds to satisfy any Cancerian.

HOW TO HANDLE YOUR INVESTMENTS

It would be wise to seek safe and sure areas rather than the risky ventures which excite you because they bring constant change. You can still make that big killing, and in the process neither your health nor your bank account will suffer.

It's good to diversify, but if you spread small amounts around in *everything,* you will not gain as much as you would if you had *larger* sums tied up in *fewer areas.* You are afraid that one may fail; thus you are insuring a return on something. You should stop worrying that some are going to fail. Your active imagination works overtime and if you are negative, "you attract what you think."

If you get involved in REIT's, stay clear of any "C & D" trust which makes short-term construction and development loans. Runaway inflation or a recession hurts them, and in the past their trusts were in a horrendous bind; it the bank hadn't saved them, they would have collapsed. REIT shares are liquid, and many are listed on the stock exchange, whereas if you are an investor in a partnership fund you may have difficulty selling out. Ask a lawyer, accountant, or broker to give you all the pros and cons so you won't get stuck in the wrong type of deal.

Before investing in real estate, shop around for the lowest interest rates. If big-apartment ownership is desired, it can be risky if rent controls are imposed. A duplex close to home can be managed and owned by one person and will bring income. Vacant land can be risky because of the problems with building: high labor prices and interest on the loans. To own your own residence outright is a hedge against future currency fluctuations or changes in a country's monetary system which could lead to a recession.

If you buy silver, take delivery and have it stored. Avoid silver future commodities because of the volatility and lack of liquidity. Keep your money in several different banks in case one major one has a disaster. Generally your sign is psychic; however, if your ESP hasn't paid off in the past, don't take a chance that it will in the future.

Try to stay clear of margin accounts. Don't buy something unless you can afford to lose it. Invest in some blue chips on the stock exchange and satisfy your gambling instincts with a few wild shots. You alone must live with the investments you make, regardless of what an "expert" tells you. It's your money, so make decisions you can live with peacefully and thereby avoid an ulcerous condition.

Are you a winner or loser? It not only depends upon your Sun sign and how you use it, but also on the influence of Jupiter and Saturn. Jupiter attracts a gain, whereas Saturn attracts a loss. Everyone has these planets in his/her horoscope, but their influence depends upon whether their harmonious or inharmonious side is expressed at the moment a decision is made.

Under the influence of the positive side of Saturn, you are practical, conservative, cautious, serious, contemplative, and make a move only when you are sure the time is ripe. Long-range investments are favored. You use sound judgment, and thus can buy to advantage.

Under the influence of the negative side of Saturn you are pessimistic and cry poverty; you worry, gripe, complain, and have the blues. You are slow because you are afraid of making the wrong move, and thus can attract losses. You lack confidence and chances are if you purchase anything, it could be a real downer.

Whenever you are depressed and feel the Saturn negative traits, avoid investing in anything, because your Saturn is being stimulated in your horoscope at that moment (this could last an hour, a day, a week, a month, a year, or more). If you do invest when this inharmonious energy is being expressed, you are likely to attract a loss.

Under the influence of the positive side of Jupiter you are confident, optimistic, cheerful, easygoing, honest, understanding, happy, and generous. Speculation is favored and brings success. You use sound judgment and can sell to an advantage, take options, buy on margin, and do well all around.

Under the influence of the negative side of Jupiter you are overly confident, too optimistic, wasteful, ostentatious, extravagant, and refuse to take into account prices, expenditures, or the views of others. You are in the mood to do everything to excess. At a party you'd be on center stage making everyone laugh. If you sell an investment when you are in this frame of mind you won't get the price it's worth; your judgment will be off.

Whenever you discover you are using the negative side of Jupiter, don't take a chance with the stock market or any other form of investment. Lie low and wait until the positive side of Jupiter is being expressed, then sell. It'll be worth the wait.

In astrology *buying* is ruled by Saturn and *selling* by Jupiter. Every time you buy under a harmonious Saturn aspect your purchase will be a bargain, a good deal, or investment. Every time you sell under a harmonious Jupiter aspect your sale will be considerable gain. The moment these planets are activated in your horoscope are determined by your time, place, day, month, and year of birth. But you don't need a horoscope to know when you are in a depressed state or happy mood. By being aware of your frame of mind, you'll know how to invest wisely. The moment the negative side of Jupiter, Saturn, or Cancer is expressed, that's the time to watch out for losses; the reverse if true when their positive side is expressed.

Now that you are armed with this information you can invest wisely and be ready for whatever the world economy brings. However, you are one step further ahead than the majority of people because by using this positive energy you can improve your chances to be wealthy.

CHAPTER FIVE

Leo - Money and Investments

Those born from July 23 through August 22 have the Sun in the sign Leo. Every sign of the zodiac corresponds to a particular type of prosperity; it's what you do and how you use it that determines whether you'll be successful or not.

Do you want to wind up behind the eight ball because of your showy spending habits? Instead, wouldn't it be better if you could prevent losses and financial difficulties, and avoid disasters in general? By knowing your faults and how to correct them you can enjoy life more, save money, and, be in tip-top shape. And that's the position you'd like to be in, isn't it?

YOUR MONEY

Not only are you known as the king of the zodiac but also as "the last of the big-time spenders." You are a high roller from the word go. Your friends may call you a giant among men, because your philanthropic deeds are so magnanimous that you shine like the star that you are.

When you go shopping it's first class all the way. Expensive gifts are bought for your friends and loved ones. You give — and give — and give until there's nothing left to give. The price you pay is dear. You live in the lap of luxury whether you can afford it or not. Because you're a princely sign you must have the best that money can buy. The late Jacqueline Kennedy Onassis, a Leo, was fortunate enough to experience this without suffering financial disaster.

You have a high standard of living and believe that you must outdo the Jones'. Money is a status symbol and ego trip to you. It means that you have power and can associate with the élite on an equal basis.

Your clothes are chosen carefully. They are sumptuous and when donned give the respect and authority you so hungrily crave. Your expensive tastes and gourmet life-style show that there's a burning fire (you're a Fire sign) raging within you to live it up to the very hilt. And you do, regardless of the exorbitance.

You take on unnecessary burdens, especially when a buddy is in need. If you don't have the cash, you'll borrow it from a loan institution just to help out a pal. Your pride is such that you could never let him/her know you didn't have the dough in your bank account. Your generosity is unlimited and others envy your loyalty.

Your friends are entertained in a royal manner. If you're in a high-income bracket the table is set with the finest china, crystal, and silverware. If you're in a low-income bracket everything will look as elegant as is possible within your means. You dine out a lot and go to topnotch restaurants. If you're not well heeled you will save your money until you can go to a well-known eating establishment. You'd rather not go at all if you can't be seen in the swank places. You think everyone judges character through the wealth a person has.

You are a real money-maker with such expertise you make most signs sit back and take notice. The female lion (representative of your sign) rules the roost and may be an entrepreneur just like her male counterpart. The late Lucille Ball, a Leo, amassed a fortune, not only from her acting performances, but from the studio she owned, headed, and rented to other television companies.

Just the thought of having, or spending, a few bucks increases your vitality and puts you in command of all situations. That's when you are at your very best. There's a positive and negative side of Leo, and if the positive side is expressed you'll wind up in tip-top shape financially.

Your Positive Side

Does having money make you gain and retain self-esteem? Are your interests centered on finances? Is it important that you reach the pinnacle of material success? Do you pursue ambitious goals for the dough it will bring? Are lavish parties given for business purposes? Is accomplishment a necessity? If you answered the preceding questions with a "yes," you are using the harmonious traits you are known for, and as a result, prosperity can be more easily attracted.

Do you have large and majestic ideas? You will take a chance and profit by your ideas because you are industrious and know influential people who can aid you in their realization. It doesn't take you long to reach desired goals.

The love of the grandeur is intense and acts as a spur to ambition. You appreciate and must have all the good things life has to offer. In the process your unquenchable thirst for personal glory is not denied. And along with it are the riches that belong to you — but you've earned them through your determination to rise to the highest point without allowing any obstacle to interfere with your plans. Your competitors drop by the wayside because they don't have your guts or willpower.

Before and after reaching the zenith of your career, you spend an enormous sum of money on your appearance. You're a sharp dresser and like to flash expensive jewelry. It's as if you are putting on a show to attract wealthy people. And you are. Your belief that the outward impression of affluence will draw people to you does just that. You associate with those who are somebody. And, of course, that makes you feel extremely important.

It's the faith you have in your own abilities that pays off at the bank. Thoughts of failure are never entertained. There is no limit put on what you can achieve. Those dollars are gained through those social activities where you mix business with pleasure.

You are charming, warm, and popular, but manage to keep your distance. However, considerable monetary gains are made through your always being out front where you can easily be seen. You are so sure of yourself that others can't help feeling confident about your talents. They will enter into profitable financial transactions with you. If they don't have the necessary funds to invest, they'll introduce you to the right people.

Your desire for recognition makes it appear that you are power driven — and you are. In your opinion, if one has material assets, one can buy center stage. Therefore, you go out of your way to satisfy your ambitions. And all the time as you climb upward you concentrate on the limelight that is soon going to be yours.

You are daring and take risks. Along the way financial reverses may occur, but they are ignored. It won't be long until your strength and strong recuperative powers put you right back in the chips.

Quality is preferred over quantity. If you own a business you purchase the most expensive office equipment, computer, and machinery that your money can buy. Your office is plush, a real showplace where you entertain your clients with your own private bar. The debt incurred doesn't disturb you in the least; in fact, it's forgotten until the accountant reminds you of it. However, you are a person who pays your bills on time. Your pride wouldn't let you do differently.

Lots of dough is spent on creative projects. It's the applause that is more important to you than the income earned. However, you will make a staunch attempt to amass large sums from any enterprise undertaken. Most of the time you take the bull by the horns and come up as the winner. You are the type who could turn a money-losing coin-operated laundry into a success by adding a snack and liquor bar and a few go-go dancers.

You are a true gambler in every sense of the word, forever optimistic that you are one person who can reach the pot of gold (ruled by your sign) at the end of the rainbow. An exhilarating thrill is felt when you wonder whether your horse will come through with flying colors, or on the dice roll you'll make your point, or you'll hit 21 with blackjack. Because you enjoy sports, you are the perennial bettor who takes a shot at baseball, football, and basketball or any other game that whets your interest. And when you've won a wad of cash, it's time to throw a victory party for all your friends.

You can gain money through entering tournaments that have a good purse prize. Also, financial rewards are earned through show business, politics, or your work as administrator, executive, official, director, leader, or owner of a business.

Your Negative Side

Can people flatter you to the extent you'll spend money on them, or a project of theirs? If so, does this result in a loss? When you have plenty of cash burning in your pocket, do you throw your weight around and lord it over others? Do you brag about the way you make or spend a buck? If you answered the preceding questions with a "yes," you are using the inharmonious traits you are known for, and as a result, it's difficult to attract prosperity.

Have you experienced losses through listening to others about money ventures? Are you kindhearted with your dough — to a fault? Do you tip big just to make others kowtow to you? Do you believe in putting on a big front to attract money? If so, did it put you behind the eight ball?

Will you demand a raise even if it isn't merited? If you don't get it, or it's a small one, you feel that your superiors didn't think much of your work. This action could lead to such an ego deflation that you may quit and look for another job.

Most of your actions spring from pride, especially when your vanity has been wounded. To compensate you become an egotistical spender who has to be a big shot whether you can afford it or not. Your family may be shocked at the debts incurred and the money that is tossed in the air as if it meant nothing more to you than scratch paper. But you boast and tell your loved ones not to fear because you're going to be in the pink in no time.

It won't be long until you try your luck with a project that is purely speculative. The gambler in you will defend it by saying that if one doesn't take a chance in life, nothing will ever be gained. You believe that whatever you set your mind to getting can be obtained.

When you wish to impress someone you are likely to exaggerate the profits that can be gained. You expect others to go along with your grandiose ideas. If they don't, you become a demanding and incensed lion who refuses to admit he's/she's wrong. The person who crosses you is dropped and you tell yourself that he's/she's inferior to you and would have been a detriment. Immediately you accept party invitations to meet new people who have money and prestige, and who will flatter you when they accept your propositions.

Enterprises are initiated with you in full command. You resent anyone telling you what to do. Everything must be run your way; if others find fault with your methods your temper flares. You feel that no one is in a position to criticize or lead you.

Often you overshoot your mark and go too far, too soon, with the outlay of expenditures piling up quite high. Lack of experience, impulsiveness, and a hypersensitive ego could bring on financial problems to the extent that a business is bankrupted.

You assume an air of self-importance and blame everyone except yourself for your monetary predicament. But you will go out and take a temporary job so you can get back on your feet. While working your mind is geared toward success. In your spare moments you make inquiries into anything you hear about that has a possibility of bringing in a quick buck.

Once enough money is in your pocket you feel powerful and authoritative; it's time to try again. Only this time you plan to choose your associates a little better. Or perhaps you'll go it alone because that is preferable to partners. You feel quite capable of handling your own affairs. It's only when you don't have the capital needed that you team up with someone.

You expect your employees to toe the mark and obey your every order. Often you take the credit for something you didn't do. But, because others realize that you're a braggart and not about to let anyone steal the spotlight from you, they let it stand. This could cost you a pretty penny if several of them walk off the job at the same time.

Your pocketbook gets emptied quickly when you buy all those lavish presents for others. It's not only the desire to please someone, but you want that individual to think well of you. A show of wealth makes you strut like a peacock and feel important. But this can be a steep price to pay on a daily basis. It is one of the causes of financial adversity that can strike if you're not more careful.

You don't like your good-hearted nature taken advantage of by anyone. If someone is in serious financial trouble you will come to his aid even though it may put you in a bind. This could become a problem. Often you lend the money because you need a favor, want to be in a superior position, or your vanity is fed by the person complimenting your greatness as he/she asks for the loan.

It's extremely difficult for you to control your extravagant monetary habits and build up a sizable bank account. You always have an excuse to spend a buck: the bills, clothing, food, gifts, entertainment, and to reinvest it in projects that can bring you enormous sums of money. It seems like there's never an end in sight. If you don't curb or quit some of your ostentatious spending, inflation is going to hit you where it hurts the most — your pocketbook.

HOW TO HANDLE YOUR MONEY

Wouldn't it be good for your ego if you really did have all the money you try to impress others as having? Do you realize that by going on a budget and saving a few bucks, you could be in the position you dream about? Are you tired of silently worrying about how the bills are going to be paid?

Did you lose out on a lucrative business deal because you were so in debt you couldn't raise enough funds for it? Wouldn't you like to be prepared so the next time an opportunity arises you can grasp it?

If you answered "yes" to the preceding questions these are some of the areas you've got to work with and change. Because you are a fixed sign, it's going to be rough for you to do. But you've got that tremendous willpower that you're known for working on your behalf. And once you've found the road to take, which doesn't interfere with your pride or let anyone know what you are up to, you'll be ready to make the trip to the bank.

It's important for you to have your place in the sun. But at the same time it would be wise to have some money stashed away in a bank or investments. Your love of display is looked upon as a showy egotism rather than that of true wealth. Your desire for status can be achieved when you accomplish a worthwhile merit. True success is not always the outward appearance but what your net worth totals. If you're in hock up to your ears and continue to throw cash around freely, it'll be difficult for you ever to get out of the red. You must learn to see that your extravagance doesn't become unreasonable and put you in the hole.

Your inner reason for flaunting your dollars is to impress yourself and show others that you've arrived. It gives you a wonderful feeling of power to let people know you're in a top-income bracket: So you buy a large wardrobe, pick up the dinner tab for a large group, and purchase expensive presents for friends and loved ones. Realize that you are trying to buy others with your money to cover your own inferiority feelings. When it's gone (and it won't be long at the rate you go), so are the people. Forego a little bit of ego-playing and you won't have such a dent in your wallet.

A classy car, beautiful jewelry, a luxury home, and clothes are more important to you than a sizable bank account or a few bucks wisely invested. You want money for *now*, not for some future year that you may not live long enough to reach. At least that's what you tell yourself. But deep down you do want to be secure.

You can still put on the dog and appear as if you are loaded without actually getting in debt. Shop around and buy an outfit that is in the medium price range or is discounted rather than one that is a designer label at full price. You carry yourself with such class that no one will know the difference.

Avoid making goals so high that you can't keep them. The fast buck made on a whim usually turns out a nightmare, especially if you jump in impulsively. Over-enthusiasm for something that your associates frown about only makes you more daring. Check it out with an accountant and lawyer to see if it's affordable and practical. Don't get angry when others oppose you. Listen to their reasoning and advice. Guard against being so stubborn that you wind up with an empty wallet.

Give credit to others when deserved; try not to steal it for yourself. Your employees will admire and respect you, especially if you compliment them. They'll work harder and bring you the profits desired. That's better than having them walk off the job, isn't it?

Your superior and haughty mannerisms attack the other person's ego, thereby encouraging resentment because you've tried to make him feel inferior. This action can chase people away and you could lose money in the process.

Flattery is your downfall and you foster it by selecting associates and friends who feed your ego. Don't give in to their wishes, especially if they first compliment you and follow with a request for a loan. Think things through, otherwise you may be the victim of your own vanity. And then where would your bank account vanish to?

Plan your future now before you take any other kind of action. You don't have to be a slave to money when you're on a budget. Fun and pleasure can be indulged in. You need something in reserve for the later years of your life. Your pride is such that you wouldn't want your relatives, or anyone else, to have to support you. Because you don't like anyone telling you what to do, tell yourself, "I *will* (the keyword for Leo) save for me."

It's necessary for you to make a budget. The idea turns you off; the details of it even more so. If you have an accountant, or someone you feel comfortable with, let him take care of it for you. But you should keep receipts and records of the money spent. Turn them over to whoever is going to keep your books for you. Don't neglect any small amounts; it bugs you to count pennies, but every cent adds up. You'd be surprised if you totaled these little sums at the end of the year.

If you decide to figure your own budget, write down how much you earn and what is needed for living expenses (housing, gas, lights, telephone), food, medical, dental, and transportation to and from the job, (don't include car loan payments, but do include car insurance).

Take into account how much you spend on clothing, entertainment, recreation, dining out, and gifts purchased throughout the year. These are the areas you can cut down on in order to save money and/or invest wisely. Put aside at least seven percent of your earnings, or more, for a trust fund for your future years.

List the dollars you pay out in loans, charge accounts, or credit cards. Cut the cards up and throw them out. Pay off all debts as quickly as possible. This avoids the interest trap that puts you into such hot water — add up how much interest is paid in a year and you'll be amazed at what you could have bought with it.

Because you are a very proud person, you don't want to tell anyone about your budget. If you're married, swallow your pride and tell your spouse the truth. You can still enjoy living and having a good time. Buy the jewelry, car, clothes desired, but don't go overboard. You don't need such a large wardrobe that you can't wear everything in a year's time. Cut down on luxuries and not only will you be ahead financially, but you'll enjoy them more. Also curb some of your daily expenses.

Set aside some money for gambling if that's your interest. Never bet more than you might spend on some other form of recreation. Don't think about how much you'd like to win; instead keep in mind what you can afford to lose at the races, crap tables, roulette wheel, Lottery, etc. If you've reached the limit allowed on your budget, stop. Don't continue to play or you'll start a bad habit and will find it difficult to be in command of the situation. And because you must be in control of everything, be in the driver's seat with your budget.

If you can swing it, buy a home rather than rent one. Keep entertainment expenses down to a minimum — this is what you have to watch the most. Your tendency to live high off the hog has to be changed or you'll wind up without a cent.

Go to as many free places as you can: outdoor concerts and so on. See museums and local theater plays or musicals. Get outdoors and become involved in the sports you enjoy: horseback riding, tennis, squash, racquetball, baseball, handball. Or, if you want to exercise to keep that proud Leo figure trim, try aerobics, gymnastics, jump rope, or take ballet lessons — they aren't that costly.

If you find that you are spending more than you should or need to cut down, don't take away money that should be set aside to provide for your future security. This fund is never to be touched; cut corners in other departments. Make a compromise in some way if you want something but can't afford it. Guard against blowing your budget and savings on something you see and desire. Be your usual firm self and a recession can't hurt you that much.

YOUR INVESTMENTS

You can benefit by setting aside money now so your future will be secure. Or perhaps you prefer investing in something other than a business. However, before you go leaping into any undertaking, it would be to your advantage to understand your assets and shortcomings, thereby avoiding pitfalls.

Your Positive Side

A "yes" answer to any of the following questions indicates that your are expressing harmonious Leo traits, thus enhancing your chances to gain prosperity: Are influential people helpful to you in relation to speculating or investing? Do you want to control the stock you own by being chairman of the board or the largest shareholder? Are you impulsive when buying or selling stock? If so, has it paid off? When you purchase stock, do you prefer buying many shares in one company rather than diversifying?

Is gold one of your pet investment areas? Are you a conscientious investor? Do you take pride in the way you handle your investments? Your broker and associates respect your judgment and admire your courage to take risks that later prove to your advantage. Their compliments give you such a mental high that you go out of your way to do even better.

Speculation is your sport; it's a game of pleasure for you. A fast buck is desired, therefore short-term maturation is preferred. You want to see activity with investments; if any are moving too slow, you get right out. New ones are attacked with zest and vigor similar to the lion when on the hunt.

You are a typical options trader who is known to be a natural-born risk-taker. Your strategies are researched by others (you can't be bothered with details), regardless of the time and money involved. Reports are read and studied for the overall picture. It's important for you to know your subject thoroughly so you can display your knowledge when discussing it with experts *and* also so your pocket-book will be filled after you've jumped in whole hog.

At an auction if there's any ostentatious furniture, e.g., from the Louis XIV period, you get so enthusiastically carried away with bidding that you're not aware of the escalation price. Furthermore, if it's something you want, you don't care how much it costs. Luckily it is usually something that years later proves to increase in value. But it's also used as a conversation piece to impress your visiting guests.

Gold — gold — gold; you are gold happy. No wonder it's ruled by your sign! It's a weakness that's difficult for you to resist. Your home or office may be furnished or trimmed in gold — accessories, drapes, sculpture, etc. Your loved ones and friends know how obsessed you are with owning gold jewelry — that's one gift they know you'll be pleased with. You are gung ho on valuable gold coins and can't seem to surround yourself with enough of them. And, of course, you've got gold bullion stashed away in a Swiss bank and hold a certificate on it.

You move with the times and keep abreast of new developments, therefore know what to go after to achieve your investment goals. Your optimism makes you a winner all the way.

Your Negative Side

A "yes" answer to the following questions indicates that you are expressing the inharmonious Leo traits, thus lessening your chances to gain prosperity. Do you lose through speculating because you fail to listen to the advice of others, or to take the time to check the details? Will you buy enormous shares in a particular stock only because you want to boast that you're the largest shareholder or chairman of the board?

Do you spend a fortune on entertaining others in grand style just so your wealthy guests can give you some tips? If so, did the amusement cost you more than you gained? Are you an impulsive buyer? If so, do you lose money as a result? Do you sell stock at the wrong time because you are too impatient to wait for it to escalate?

Are you impractical with most investments? Your ideas are probably shot down by a financial counselor or your accountant. But you are so willful and rigidly self-possessed that they can't talk you out of going into something that you'll lose your shirt on. You think in big terms and must have the most expensive stock, property, painting, etc. — all to arouse envy and feed your ego. You don't count the cost of it or the loss it brings you.

Your boldness is seen in the way you speculate: in and out of deals faster than most people can blink an eyelid. It's difficult for you to accept failure; in fact, you don't even consider it a possibility. You could be another Bernard Baruch, a Leo, who had a seat on the stock exchange and made millions but went broke several times. You never give up and keep hoping that a killing will be made quickly.

However, it's not solely for a huge profit that you play the market. All investments are made because of the recognition they bring. When you go to a party you are on center stage while bragging about all the money you have tied up in various ventures. It makes you feel superior that you own more stock, bonds, gold, and real estate than your associates. Your conceit can cost you a fortune, especially if you hit an unlucky streak.

You find commodity futures as exciting as watching the horse you bet on come around the bend. Will you gain or lose with gold futures? It all depends upon which way you speculate that the price of gold will go: up or down. If it does the opposite of what you want, during the time specified on your gold futures contract, and the margin account is called, you are hanging on a limb. You've lost everything you pledged as security and now you may want to fall off and break your neck. But because you're a strong Leo you rise above it with your head high; after you've recovered, you'll be back for more. Of course, you might get a bright idea that it's better to buy gold bullion outright. That will be fine, except you can't stand it being stored in a bank vault when it can be in your private safe at home. That way, every day you can look at it shining brightly. It will light up your face, and the burglars', if word gets around that you hold it in your possession. And being the boaster you are, it would be known far and wide. And you'd be up a creek, but not a gold one! Purchase gold as an investment, but, please, can't you let it be stored in a safe place?

WHAT SHOULD YOU INVEST IN?

You enjoy plunging in to scoop the market. It's not the safest policy to follow, but you derive such pleasure with taking chances that to be happy, and yet be reasonably secure, stay with short-term investments such as thirty-, sixty-, or ninety-day bonds or Treasury bills.

Because you are a fixed sign you have your pet objects you like to hang on to: large oil paintings and statues, antiques that are ostentatious with lots of gold leaf or inlay. These can be valuable as collectibles and used as a hedge against inflation.

Satisfy your love of sports by becoming part owner of a nationally famous football team or whatever athletic event turns you on. Then watch your gambling streak come to the fore when you bet on it to win. It's more exhilarating when you have big stakes in a game from more than one angle. Or purchase bonds or stocks in a city-owned stadium or arena, such as Madison Square Garden in New York City; make inquiries for your local area.

Investment notes (also called thrift certificates) pay high interest but you may have to sacrifice some safety — they are not insured and vary in risk. As for commodity futures and options — if you've been successful with them in the past, it could happen again. But the moment they start to turn sour, get out as soon as you possibly can. The up-and-down emotional turmoil you go through with them makes your pulse beat fast and could cause some heartaches (Leo rules the heart) — but you'll love every exciting moment!

A thirty-day commercial paper note floated by a large corporation may appeal to you; it can be risky if the company doesn't do so well. In the mutual fund department, your sign likes the common-stock mutual funds, although for regular stock purchases you swing from preferred to new issues and over-the-counter. The preferred gives you a fixed and usually generous amount of income from their dividends. The new issues and over-the-counter stocks are extremely risky, but you are attracted to the high and quick profit that can be made from them.

Bonds are a great favorite for you Leos. There are those corporate ones that have good liquidity even though they are speculative. And the high yield bonds, which are a class of mutual funds; they are also risky but have diversification and can prove financially rewarding. And then there are trans bonds, which are short-term (three-, six-, and nine-month) municipals. And utility company bonds, which are not tax exempt. (The *power* company is ruled by your sign.) And then there are the safe government bonds which would be good for you to think twice about.

Your sign rules the sun, so you'll find stocks in the Sun Banks of Florida intriguing. Gold stocks would interest you, but due to political uncertainties in the countries of origin, such as South Africa, they can be risky. Or buy a gold-bullion precious-metals certificate with domestic or international storage — you don't take possession so there's no assay hassle. Or if that's too expensive for your pocketbook, try gold coins (the most popular are the Krugerrand, Mexican fifty peso, Austrian hundred corona, Canadian maple leaf, or Austrian ducat).

Perhaps you'd like to invest in the gem your sign rules — the ruby? Buy shares in this jewel, purchase your own mine, or go into rubies as a business. Or perhaps the other Leo-ruled stones would appeal to you: chrysolite, hyacinth, and soft yellow minerals.

In the foreign-bond market your sign is attracted to the Leo-ruled country of Peru. Speculate on dollar fluctuations by purchasing foreign currency.

Invest in some safe financial programs which are designed to provide future security for those years you want to avoid having your Leo pride hurt. No-load (no sales charge) tax-deferred annuities might be a good one. Or try the fixed-income funds which are trusts based on the most conservative strategy (something you don't always like but need). The government puts its backing behind certificates sold to you.

Because you keep up with world events, you are one step ahead when it comes to investing wisely. However, it never hurts to consult with an expert for advice, although your sign generally doesn't like to ask for it.

A broker who thinks along the same lines as you may be desirable. Therefore deal with another Leo (if your egos can take it), Aries, Gemini, Sagittarius, or Pisces. They are as gutsy and fast-moving as you are. They will encourage risks, so from a strictly financial standpoint they may not be the best sign for you to listen to or be involved with.

You really need a broker who is practical and uses a conservative approach; however, this is the opposite of what is desired. This individual could annoy you with his/her slow and analytical methods. Therefore, if you decide you'll "chance it," your best bet is Capricorn and Virgo.

You might find Cancer and Libra's indecisiveness appealing — at least they weigh the pros and cons and let you see both sides of everything. These signs could be beneficial for you and they certainly know how to admire and handle you to your liking.

Taurus runs from anything speculative, whereas Aquarius and Scorpio run toward it. However, these signs are fixed (stubborn, rigid) like you so there would be too many clashes of opinion with stalemate results.

Perhaps the broker you select is born under the sign of Aries, Gemini, Cancer, Leo, Libra, Sagittarius, Aquarius, or Pisces and he/she chiefly follows solid, safe, and sound investment procedures. He/She takes this approach, which is opposite of his/her Sun sign traits, probably because he/she has Taurus, Virgo, or Capricorn as a *dominant* sign in his/her horoscope. If this occurs you'll have a risk taker combined with a conservative strategist.

Astrology can guide you in the type of bonds your sign should invest in. Therefore, be on the alert for bonds that deal with playgrounds, public schools, power plants, and solar energy.

Because everything in life has an astrological correspondence, each type of corporate bond or stock has a sign/planet that rules it. Therefore, under the Leo/Sun influence, invest in toys, games, hobbies, schools, sports arenas, or circus companies.

Or perhaps you are a movie-theater fan and so would like the motion picture industry; or do you prefer to be a Broadway angel? Also in the glamour field are interior decorating companies, catalogue showrooms, and all places of amusement.

If these areas don't capture your interest, why not try firms researching in solar energy or companies that manufacture solar products (watches, calculators, swimming pool heaters, cigarette lighters, water and home heating systems)? Or other Leo/Sun-ruled areas: bathing suits, sunglasses, sunburn ointments — all perfect for a day at the beach. You should invest in something you use yourself. And nothing makes a Leo recuperate faster than a day in the sun.

Also, as a Leo, you'd enjoy stock in the gourmet food industry, vacation hotels, motels, spas — the classier the place, the better. And gambling casinos in resort areas are tailored just for you. It is a known fact that gambling is one business where the recession seems to have little negative effect on earnings. The records of casino operators indicate that the amount of money each individual bets goes up with a recession. Thus the expert stock market counselors have said that during dull economic periods, earnings of gambling stocks tend to outperform those of other industries. However, these gaming stocks are usually volatile and are not for the weak at heart. If that's a problem, a stock that might be useful is a company that manufactures cardiac pace-makers, also ruled by your sign.

HOW TO HANDLE YOUR INVESTMENTS

Write down your investment goals. Guard against making them so unrealistic that they are difficult to attain. Instead of trying to show off to others, impress yourself with the solid and steady money you derive from following wise investment procedures.

You can still make that big bundle by setting aside a certain sum of money that is called your gambling fund. Go have a fling and indulge in all those risky ventures you hungrily crave. The hottest games in town are commodities futures and options. they are for the guy/gal who is nervy and can adapt to rapid price fluctuations without having a heart attack in the process. The money gained from them is spectacular — right up your alley. And the losses are just as spectacular, especially if you lose your home in the process.

As for your precious gold, Europeans have a high respect for it and so has all mankind — even killing for it, so keep it stored in a bank. Short-term bonds are generally considered the safest but lowest yielding. They attract you mainly because of the time limit; however, long-term bonds appeal to you because they are the riskiest and highest yielding. But the experts say that whether to buy long-term or short-term bonds depends on the inflation rate. If it is not too high, buy long-term bonds; if it is high, buy short-term bonds.

In times of a sharp rise in the inflation rate, it's best to stay as liquid as possible. Buy ninety-day Treasury bills and keep rolling them over. Buy corporate bonds, which are traded on the New York or American Stock Exchange. Smaller issues trade less frequently and are hard to sell unless you knock the price down to little or no profit to yourself.

Don't burden yourself with excessive debts when, with inflation, other costs are likely to go up. You may have difficulty coping with the payments — and that would bother your pride. Instead of splurging when you receive a dividend check, reinvest it in more stock.

When purchasing rubies, find a reputable expert such as a retail jeweler who will act as investment advisor for a small fee. Get the "fluorescence test" to determine the value of your ruby.

If you want a long-term objective like real estate, take the interest earned from bonds, stocks, savings, or your gambling profits and invest in a house you can live in or rent out.

Are you a winner or loser? It not only depends upon your Sun sign and how you use it, but also on the influence of Jupiter and Saturn. Jupiter attracts a gain, whereas Saturn attracts a loss. Everyone has these planets in his/her horoscope. But their influence depends upon whether their harmonious or inharmonious side is expressed at the moment a decision is made.

Under the influence of the positive side of Saturn, you are practical, conservative, cautious, serious, contemplative, and make a move only when you are sure the time is ripe. Long-range investments are favored. You use sound judgment, and thus can buy to advantage.

Under the influence of the negative side of Saturn you are pessimistic and cry poverty; you worry, gripe, complain, and have the blues. You are slow because you are afraid of making the wrong move, and thus can attract losses. You lack confidence and chances are if you purchase anything, it could be a real downer.

Whenever you are depressed and feel the Saturn negative traits, avoid investing in anything, because your Saturn is being stimulated in your horoscope at that moment (this could last an hour, a day, a week, a month, a year, or more). If you do invest when this inharmonious energy is being expressed, you are likely to attract a loss.

Under the influence of the positive side of Jupiter you are confident, optimistic, cheerful, easygoing, honest, understanding, happy, and generous. Speculation is favored and brings success. You use sound judgment and can sell to an advantage, take options, buy on margin, and do well all around.

Under the influence of the negative side of Jupiter you are overly confident, too optimistic, wasteful, ostentatious, extravagant, and refuse to take into account prices, expenditures, or the views of others. You are in the mood to do everything to excess. At a party you'd be on center stage making everyone laugh. If you sell an investment when you are in this frame of mind you won't get the price it's worth; your judgment will be off.

Whenever you discover you are using the negative side of Jupiter, don't take a chance with the stock market or any other form of investment. Lie low and wait until the positive side of Jupiter is being expressed, then sell. It'll be worth the wait.

In astrology *buying* is ruled by Saturn and *selling* by Jupiter. Every time you buy under a harmonious Saturn aspect your purchase will be a bargain, a good deal, or investment. Every time you sell under a harmonious Jupiter aspect your sale can be a considerable gain. The moment these planets are activated in your horoscope are determined by your time, place, day, month, and year of birth. But you don't need a horoscope to know when you are in a depressed state or happy mood. By being aware of your frame of mind, you'll know how to invest wisely. The moment the negative side of Jupiter, Saturn, or Leo is expressed, that's the time to watch out for losses; the reverse is true when their positive side is expressed.

Now that you are armed with this information you can invest wisely and be ready for whatever the world economy brings. However, you are one step further ahead than the majority of people because by using this positive energy you can improve your chances to be wealthy.

CHAPTER SIX

Virgo - Money and Investments

Those born from August 23 through September 22 have the Sun in the sign Virgo. Every sign of the zodiac corresponds to a particular type of prosperity; it's what you do and how you use it that determines whether you'll be successful or not.

You'd like to wind up ahead of the game, wouldn't you? However, getting bogged down by detail and missing the overall picture could attract financial difficulties. Instead, wouldn't it be better if you could prevent losses and hardships and banish worry? By knowing your faults and how to correct them you can enjoy life more, save money, and, stay in tip-top shape. And that's worth changing your bad habits for, isn't it?

YOUR MONEY

You are known as the "Harvester of the Zodiac" because you gather knowledge, assimilate and utilize it, and reap the profits. Money is gathered and stored in a safe place rather than freely spent. Perhaps another Virgo originated the idea of burying cash in the ground, an act which is typical of the Earth sign you were born under.

Consumer goods are bought only when necessary. Discount coupons are saved and used. You know that the department stores have special sales in January and other months, so you patiently wait for these bargain days. When you do go to the store everything is scrutinized to the nth degree. You want the best value for your money. Every dime spent can be accounted for.

Seldom do you give a present unless it's someone's birthday or a holiday or special occasion. The gifts purchased must be useful. All spending you do for yourself, or others, is planned carefully. You are a wise shopper.

All the clothes and shoes in your closet are used until they almost fall apart — shoes are repaired and clothes mended. You are *not* one who has to be "in" with the latest style. Your wardrobe consists of conservative garments that always look good and are never really considered outdated. No wonder your pocketbook never suffers!

You live simply and frugally. Most of the time you cook your own meals. Food is not wasted; casserole dishes are made from the leftovers. If you eat out you shy away from the fancy restaurants, but the dining establishment you go to has to be clean and serve a well-balanced and tasty meal.

Money is not spent on living it up and having a ball. The library is visited frequently because you enjoy reading. If a book you want can't be found there, you may buy it in a store. Your other big splurge areas (as you may call them) are lectures, museums, and classes. In other words, acquiring knowledge is your specialty.

Your love of studying is put to practical use, either in your job or daily living. You are prepared for whatever may crop up. It pays off in times of emergencies when you come to the rescue of others. Because you are quiet like a mouse, everyone is amazed that you know so much. When you help others through being well versed with information, this reaffirms your belief that the few bucks you spent were well worth the price paid.

Your strong need to be financially secure makes you feel driven to save for unforeseen expenses. The future is planned down to the very last detail. With your unpretentious life and level-headed management, you are able to amass enough to live comfortably on for the rest of your life, which is something the late Greta Garbo, a Virgo, was able to do.

All mistakes are viewed as bitter experiences that will never be repeated. There is a positive and negative side of Virgo, and if the positive side is expressed you can wind up with the material assets desired.

Your Positive Side

Do you stretch your salary and still have sufficient dough to save? Are you always looking for new ways to increase your savings? Do your practical ideas bring you a few extra bucks? Are you cautious with financial deals? Do you keep a wary eye on expenditures? Are you conscious of the value of money? If you answered the preceding questions with a "yes," you are using the harmonious traits you are known for, and as a result, prosperity can be more easily attracted.

Do you limit your spending because you want to? You make your own rules when it comes to dollars and cents — and you have plenty of sense. Clear-cut objective thinking is practiced continually. After reading the statistics and analyzing everything on hand, you are able to come up with the best ways to earn a living and handle your assets.

Money is gained through hard labor, which you thrive upon, and by performing a service in which your mental abilities are put to use. Your resourcefulness pays off at the bank time and again because you can get right down to the meat of the matter.

You will never risk security and go out on a limb, especially if someone tells you about a way to make an overnight fortune. Seldom are you attracted to, or carried away by, fantasy. You believe in keeping your feet solidly planted on the ground — and that's where they always are. However, you do scout about for a means to better your pocketbook. But whatever is undertaken is going to be a sure thing and only after it has been seriously and contemplatively approached. Thus your method to gain a few bucks requires a lot of time before a decision is made. But you are not about to do it any other way.

As a rule you shun anything that is new or too impractical. You prefer making money through old and reliable methods. Your critical and discriminating outlook governs all of your actions. Before you are convinced of anything you must see, know, and understand the project to a "T."

When anyone tries to approach you to buy the latest equipment or machinery, he will have a difficult time convincing you that it's to your advantage to purchase it. The "how" and "why" of everything is questioned by you so thoroughly that the salesperson had better know his subject backward and forward.

Data is gathered, evaluations are made, and conclusions are drawn after everything has been dissected. When the time is ripe, estimates are given and agreed upon. Your sound judgment pays off handsomely when the profits of the transaction have been completed. Your sign is one that certainly reaps what you sow.

The material blessings of life are desired but not easily acquired. Seldom do you truly earn the money deserved for the labor expended. You are able to analyze what the public wants and then can give it to them with a service unequaled by most people.

You get ideas to make money through reading books, magazines, and periodicals. A neighborhood is surveyed carefully before you open a business. You begin on a small scale and hold the purse strings tight all the way to the bank.

A few extra bucks could be made through your love of animals. You might find raising rabbits in your spare time a profitable hobby, especially since they don't make noise, require little space, and eat lightly. Or with owning a breeding pair of llamas, the dollars gained from the sale of their wool might be music to your ears.

You do not enter any partnership until you've grilled the person to your liking. He has to be as conservative as you. If he's the bossy type it doesn't faze you because you enjoy taking orders from others. Your adaptability with everyone helps you keep the cash flowing in.

As a rule you are so good with handling a buck that you don't have any serious financial problems. If any do arise, you get an extra job and work day, night, and weekends to get straightened out. But you probably do that anyway, so it's doubtful you will ever run into many monetary upsets.

It's the love of actual work, and having the fruits of your labor pay off with a sizable bank account, that make you want to succeed. You are inclined to make dough using brains rather than brawn. And when those greenbacks come rolling in, peace of mind is achieved.

Your inquisitiveness takes you down many paths. But you won't be led astray. Your objective is always kept in mind. In fact, you will put aside other things, if necessary, in order to attain a goal.

Your Negative Side

Do you worry about finances? Have you ever lost money from a "sure thing"? Are you overly concerned about security? Have you lost opportunities to make a buck because you were too cautious to invest? Did you ever lose dough because of overemphasis on logic and/or reason? If you answered the preceding questions with a "yes," you are using the inharmonious traits you are known for, and as a result, it's difficult to attract prosperity.

Are you distrustful of the money-making ideas of others? If so, have you lost out because of it? Is it difficult for you to get ahead because you are afraid to take chances? Has your tight rein on finances made you lose the very person for whom you desired solvency? Do you have such a deep-rooted fear of debt that you sit on your money?

Have you noticed that you get so involved with the details of a business deal that by the time you get around to telling the person you'll accept, it is too late? Your being over-careful of what you say and do about money is going to make it difficult for you to acquire the material possessions desired. You struggle so hard to make ends meet and then when you have a chance to get out of this rut, you blow it on over-fastidiousness with those who are trying to help you.

You are one of the most industrious signs of the zodiac; however, you are not ego-driven enough to have your eye on a higher position. This, combined with your shyness and introversion, is one of the chief reasons why you don't earn a larger income than you do.

You lose money through being too critical. When you use one of your worst traits, which is being a nit-picker, you rub others the wrong way. Your lack of tact and diplomacy, when you attack others verbally, can cost you your job or, if you're self-employed, enormous sums of money in business.

Some of your financial difficulties are attracted as a result of your getting too bogged down by detail and not looking at the overall picture. You do everything the hard way. Old and outdated equipment is used because you want to pinch pennies and also because you enjoy working with the familiar rather than having to slow down production by learning how to use something new. But in the long run you turn down work because you're not able to keep the same fast pace your competitors can with their computers or other modern equipment. So there goes that big money you'd like to get your hands on!

Your hard-earned bucks go out quickly on your greatest weakness: factual books and instruction courses. You are the perennial student who studies one subject after another. It takes you a long time to assimilate what you learn; thus the knowledge gained isn't applied immediately. (It could take you twenty years to make use of it.) When a job opening arises in the area you've got a diploma in, you may turn down the offer of a better position and salary because you don't think you're ready for it. And then, later, you wonder why you don't have the cash flow your associates enjoy.

Did you know that there are more bachelors and old maids under your sign than any other? Did you ever wonder why? How can anyone know you exist if you stay home and read a book (Agatha Christie was a Virgo recluse who stayed home and wrote books), or take on extra work so you can get ahead financially? Your excuse for not going out and socializing is that it costs money. So fun and pleasure are forsaken and a possible lifetime companion is denied. And you don't change once a sizable bank account exists. Your preoccupation with security can make you wind up a lonely old person.

Those of you who do marry, before you get into the stay-at-home rut, expect others to be the same necessity-minded spender you are. If they aren't, your criticism of how they spend their nickels and dimes could cause rifts that later lead to divorce. Moderation is a virtue, but being a downright tightwad is not — and that is something you are guilty of.

There's nothing wrong with being materialistic. To just exist and miss out on all the joys that life has to offer can make you a dull person and can later affect your health.

You're a picky eater and go for simple and bland food. Others in your household have to put up with your cost-saving meals. You are great with the meat-stretchers (if you haven't become a vegetarian) and can eat the same diet daily. But you are too cheap to spend a few pennies on something that's off limits to you — a dessert. So your family goes without any treats. But you are always explaining to them that it's for their own good because they won't get fat or have cavities that need filling. Thus you can save a buck on sweets as well as the dentist's bill!

Happiness comes not only from having security, but in living a full life which requires some spending. You can learn how to handle your money so you'll have a sizable bank account and, simultaneously, enjoy yourself.

HOW TO HANDLE YOUR MONEY

Are you ready to have a good time and yet have money saved for that rainy day? Wouldn't you like to go to a party and meet new and interesting people instead of staying home and worrying about finances? Wouldn't you like to see a loved one's eyes light up when you give a gift that is a little impractical?

Doesn't it disturb you that you are not in a bigger income bracket? Would you like to do something about it? Has your desire for perfection made you lose a few bucks? Wouldn't you like to avoid financial losses in the future?

If you answered "yes" to the preceding questions these are the areas you've got to work with and change. It's not easy to break a habit, or to alter some of your personality traits, but they can be channeled into constructive outlets. And if you think of the profits you'll reap, and the fun you'll derive from it, you'll find it that much easier to do.

Learn to discuss your money-making ideas with your associates. Realize that they can dissect information also. And remember, "two heads are better than one." If you don't talk it over immediately with someone, and you wait for months to pick it apart, a competitor can beat you to the draw. And you do want to make a few bucks, don't you? Also be alert for stiff competition which could make your company lose profits simply because you refuse to modernize your operation. Stop and think about how much time could be saved (you're an efficiency expert) because your business would be more productive and increase its financial flow if everything were streamlined.

Guard against becoming so over-involved with detail that the perspective is distorted or lost and the overall picture is left hanging somewhere over the horizon and out of sight. If you continue along these lines, your project will disappear as the sun does when it sinks below the horizon. However, unlike the sun, it may not rise the next day; so you could be out some dough if this occurs.

Your sound judgment and quiet manner attract the attention of your boss. But if you want a pay raise, as well as a promotion, add another dimension to your personality. Instead of being so reticent and hoarding your knowledge, speak up and share it. Sometimes when you add a little showiness to your intelligence, it fattens your wallet.

Be cheerful: A serious countenance repels whereas a happy one is an attractive influence. Project a warmer appearance. Not only is this good for climbing the corporate ladder, but if you're in a public-service business your client relationship will improve and you'll watch those greenbacks come flying in your direction.

If you don't become a little "livelier" and you are in an occupation where you deal with the general populace or clients, you are likely to stay in the same position with a few salary increases for the rest of your life. If that is your "bag," then the alternative would be to scrimp and save every penny (which you do anyway) and when you've got enough, invest it in a financial program where your dollars are working for you, earning more than a bank would pay in a regular savings account. Then your later years could be lived in some sort of peace and prosperity.

You expect people to be perfect and when they aren't you go bananas. When you seek out the weaknesses in people, or in projects, use your critical eye to look for the good points as well as the flaws. Give compliments on anything you like instead of keeping them to yourself. Use tact lest you undermine a person and lose a client, job, or money in the process. Realize that no one, including yourself, is perfect — "It is human to err."

When you become concerned about security it makes it so much more difficult to attract. It's imperative for everyone to set aside something for those retirement years. (You love to work so much you may never give it up.) But if you continue to worry, it'll be difficult for you to make headway in the areas that can bring you the increased sums desired.

You are your happiest when sticking to a budget. If you haven't got one yet (which is rare for a Virgo) now is the time to start. Thus when you're older or retired, you'll be sitting pretty. You are so careful with the way you handle finances that it'll be a breeze for you to stick with a monetary plan. Nothing is shelled out without your first having thought about it. You are aware of where every cent goes at all times. In fact you are a planner from the word "go."

With your analytical ability you're too smart to fall into the interest trap by using credit cards, opening charge accounts, or taking out a loan, unless it's for property or something that's essential. And then you try to pay it off so quickly that you sacrifice fun and games, which puts you right back into your old rut again.

The traditional rules of your budget should follow this broad guideline:

Living expenses (rent, telephone, gas, electric) 25%
Food (eaten in as well as out) 20%
Repayments of loans, charge accounts 20%
Transportation (car insurance, not payments) 10%
Savings 7%
Clothing 5%
Dental and Medical 5%
Life and Health Insurance (if job doesn't cover it) 4%
Recreation 3%
Miscellaneous 1%

The preceding figures should be more or less switched around according to your needs, family, and life-style. Perhaps you live in a big city and don't need a car so you can save on loan payments. Or do you live rent free with a relative or share the rent with a pal?

The *miscellaneous* is for the little "extras" which might crop up in the way of gifts throughout the year. The *savings* represents money that you invest in or put in the bank to earn interest. You are one person who doesn't have to be told never to touch this account except in dire emergencies. You could loosen those purse-strings just a little and see more of your family and life in general. But while you're sitting on some of that dough, purchase goods that will cost more later on when inflation has risen to a higher point.

You can go places and do things *and* still have a buck stashed away for a rainy day. Plan your fun as you would a savings program. Because you're accustomed to (and delight in) a work schedule, why don't you also have one for those pleasurable pastimes that you are going to indulge in? You'll find it that much easier to swing into a new life-style.

Get rid of some of those strict rules for your household members. Spend a few dollars on treats, like buying a cake, or bake it yourself. Don't expect others to live up to your standards or follow in your footsteps. Rent a cabin in the woods to hibernate and enjoy nature. Or add a library room to your house, if you own it and have the space to do so. Then you can have more room to store all those books you buy.

Spend some money for those tailored clothes you enjoy. Take a sightseeing trip to see historical houses, spots, or museums. Or better yet, join a historical society and maybe you'll get a cut rate on a group chartered journey. Join literary clubs and go to meetings and social functions; just think of all the knowledge you'll gather there!

Go to a health farm if you're a vegetarian. Or do something that's inexpensive: Attend cooking, or health food exhibits, go to street, city, or state fairs. For recreation try your hand at croquet, shuffleboard, golf, or chess. Take a walk in the park or forest. Climb a mountain — you don't have to go very far up. Read books on rocks and hunt for them in the desert. Or collect herbs in the countryside with a group of herbalists.

Attend dances; you might find the social contact enlightening. Do you realize that you can have fun and discuss intellectual subjects at the same time? Just think, you may learn something new and it won't cost you that much dough.

Now that you are enjoying life, and have money saved in the bank, a recession won't creep up on you so quickly because you're prepared for it.

YOUR INVESTMENTS

You can benefit by setting aside money now so your future will be secure. Or perhaps you prefer investing in something other than a business. However, before you go leaping into any undertaking, it would be to your advantage to understand your assets and shortcomings, thereby avoiding pitfalls.

Your Positive Side

A "yes" answer to any of the following questions indicates that you are expressing harmonious Virgo traits, thus enhancing your chances to gain prosperity: Do all investments have to be a "sure thing"? Do gambling and taking a risk go against your grain? Do you have a systematized formula for investing? Is foresight used before investing? Are you a practical investor? Do you only invest after a thorough intellectual examination? Are you able to adapt and move quickly when stocks fluctuate in price? If so, have you gained as a result?

Because of your logical approach, have you always done well with your investments? It's probable that a lot of time is spent reading and studying the stock market encyclopedia or the Internet and anything else you can get your hands on. A corporation's prospectus is analyzed and thought about for a long time before any dough is spent on stock or options. You're not in a hurry to put your money on anything unless you think it'll pay off. Because you are patient, you don't mind waiting for long-term maturation on your bonds. However, if the inflation rate shoots way up, some of your long-term investments are sold and short-term ones are bought. You feel safe by leaving some where they are because you believe that the inflation rate may go down and as a result your bonds will be worth more.

If a pal gives you a tip to buy some over-the-counter stock, you refuse to purchase it right then and there. You must get all the facts on the company and evaluate its worth through a complete study of whether that corporation's type of business is a necessity in the world of commerce and everyday living. Usually your sound judgment proves to be right.

Probably you started your stamp collection as a child. What began as an enjoyable hobby became, because of the knowledge gained from it, a profitable one. It shouldn't take you long to decide about becoming a member of a stamp club. To attend shows and sales is a delightful pastime. You can't wait to get there so you can pick the dealers' and auctioneers' brains before and after public business transactions. Later, at home, you can sift through the information gained and weed out the unessentials. You can follow up by wisely purchasing the stamps you know that can be valuable as a hedge against inflation.

Margin accounts and taking risks are shunned like the plague. However, you are known to speculate on something you believe is going to be a winner. Seldom are you fooled by superficialities. You are going to break everything down to such minute detail that nothing is going to escape your critical eye. Once you are sure that you're on the right track you leap in. This method of operation generally reaps outstanding profits for you.

Your Negative Side

A "yes" answer to the following questions indicates that you are expressing the inharmonious Virgo traits, thus lessening your chances to gain prosperity: Has fear of taking a risk held you back from investments that later brought gains to your acquaintances? Do you worry about stocks and bonds? Have you ever been wrong in your analytical observations concerning an investment?

Do you find options mentally stimulating, but too nerve-wracking? Are you too picky about what you should invest in? If so, did this cause a loss? Because you must be sure of an investment, do you wait too long to take action? Have you attracted losses because you were so bogged down by detail that you couldn't see the overall picture?

Do you have so many notebooks full of stock information that by the time you've thoroughly studied them, all of their prices have drastically changed? Of course, when this occurs confusion reigns and you have to start all over again from scratch with other corporations that you had ignored previously. All this work you do is so time consuming that you miss out time and again. But one thing is sure — you know everything about a company's operations and statistics. This knowledge alone makes you happy; so you do not consider it a waste of time.

Your lessons are learned bitterly; once you've had a loss you never repeat that form of investment again. As an example, "puts" in the option market appeal to you because you are a cautious investor who believes that the stock market is going to decline as a whole. Therefore "puts" are considered to be your hedge. When stocks go down this insurance method pays off. But it can make you a nervous wreck during the six months and ten days your option period is in effect. If the stock goes up, instead of down, your "puts" are worthless and you've lost your initial investment. This is one time your negativity and over-conservative strategies can cost you a lot of your hard-earned dollars.

When you go to the races you are so busily engaged studying the handicap sheets and horses' histories that by the time you get to the betting window the race has started and it's too late to place a bet. After a while this disgusts you to the point of deciding that you'll bet two dollars on every horse in a race, and just maybe one will be the long shot coming in to pay you a nice bundle of cash.

You are so skeptical of money-making propositions that you lose out on them because you don't take advantage of a good thing when you hear about it. And in the process you are so busy picking everything apart and destroying the ideas given by others that your criticism costs you not only the profits you could have gained, but the friendship of a pal or broker. But that doesn't faze you. However, this type of action does not put you ahead if you're looking for a hedge against a recession.

What Should You Invest In?

Safe ventures are preferred, even though you may not make the "killing" you could if you speculated. You are evenly balanced as to liking short-, medium-, and long-term investments. Your best bet is to follow the method you think best for that particular moment. In other words if the inflation rate is up, short-term bonds are favored; otherwise, long-term ones are chosen. Or because you're a middle-of-the-road type of person, select medium-term maturation periods.

Your love of books makes them ideal to collect, especially finely bound and inscribed first editions as well as rare books. Luckily you're knowledgeable enough to purchase those books which are genuine and valuable. You are one individual no one is going to gyp!

Because you're an Earth sign you are more interested in undeveloped land than structures. However, real estate as income property gives you a solid feeling of security. So, as Virgo Greta Garbo did, you could purchase it. Or perhaps like another Virgoan, Lauren Bacall, you may want to buy your own co-op apartment in a very old and historic building.

You may not want to risk putting your hard-earned money in the stock market. Perhaps you'd be interested in purchasing as many long-term durables, tools, raw materials, replacement parts, etc., as you can lay your hands on, regardless of whether they are bought at retail or wholesale prices. Then you'd be ready if bartering became the "in" thing.

If you decide the stock market's for you, you're the type who will read every book, newspaper, magazine, and scan the Internet, so you're informed about world conditions and can buy stock accordingly. You'll do anything to improve your portfolio. Perhaps you'll go to the extreme of my friend the late Billy Rose, a Virgo billionaire, who had a ticker tape in his New York City townhouse. He told me that he analyzed stock, then jumped in and never lost one cent along the way. Of course, his having been the secretary at one time to financier Bernard Baruch gained him knowledge that he utilized, Virgo style, later.

Or perhaps, like Billy Rose, you are turned on by art and sculpture. In his home he had masterpieces worth millions, which, before his death, he donated to Israel for his memorial gardens. If you aren't in an income bracket to afford expensive objects d'art, with your keen eye for detail you can spot a good buy in an area that does fit your pocketbook.

In the options market you may be interested in becoming a straddle player (a combination of a put and call option at the same striking price is the price which is fixed in the option contract at which the option may be exercised). By purchasing a "put" and "call" on the same stock, you can make money whether the stock goes up or down. Of course, its high cost may be a disadvantage because two options cost more than one; therefore the stock must move further for you to win. But just think about how much more peaceful your life will be because you know you're going to make a buck one way or the other!

If in the past you've gained through speculation, then continue along these lines; however, if the reverse holds true, stay away from it because you are expressing the Virgo traits on their negative side and are likely to get a repeat performance. Abide by this rule with any area that is known to be risky.

In the collectibles, contemporary prints made by the lithograph process appeal to your sign. Many of these original graphics have increased in value by thirty percent in a ten-year period. And of course there's philately for those who enjoy putting stamps in books knowing that they are going to escalate in price as the years go by. Or maybe you are turned on by collecting "First Day of Issue" stamps on postcards. They not only are attractive, but can be valuable at a later date. Or perhaps you like to collect priceless historical documents?

Perhaps you'd like to invest in the gem your sign rules — jasper? Buy shares in this jewel, purchase your own mine, or go into jaspers as a business. Or do the same with the stone that rules you sign — flint — which may pay off if sold to the manufacturers who use it in their products.

You feel safe with the guaranteed fixed-income funds and U.S. savings and Treasury bonds. With your analytical mind you may think that convertible bonds are a smart buy in a confusing market. Because they pay fixed interest instead of variable dividends, yields are more predictable than those on stocks — and that is something which appeals to your practical side.

To look out for your later years, you need to take advantage of all you can. The deferred Swiss franc (ruled by your sign) annuity may solve your problems. Or perhaps you're eligible for the Keogh or IRA retirement plans. Just think of the money you can save on your federal income taxes by having one of them. Or of course any deferred annuity might do just as well, if not better.

In the foreign bond market your sign is attracted to the Virgo-ruled country of Switzerland. Or perhaps the Swiss franc, ruled by Virgo, appeals to your sign for investment purposes.

You are one person who definitely knows what's going on in the world; therefore you are one step ahead when it comes to investing wisely. You may want to place your order with a broker instead of going through a stock discount house.

A broker who thinks along the same lines as you may be desirable. Therefore, deal with another Virgo, Taurus, Scorpio, or Capricorn. These signs, like you, want safety and surety; however, watch Scorpio — this person takes chances! However, Scorpio may *also* have Taurus, Virgo, or Capricorn as a *dominant* sign in his/her horoscope. If this occurs, you'll have the best of two worlds: one who is inclined to speculate but uses sound judgment.

The signs that will encourage those calculated risks are Aries, Gemini, Leo, Scorpio (on occasion), Sagittarius, Aquarius, and Pisces. So from a financial standpoint, they may not be the best sign for you to listen to or be involved with. And knowing you, you won't pay attention to them, so it may be wasted effort even talking to them.

Cancer and Libra may cause you too much confusion with their indecisiveness. However, they do weigh everything, not quite as thoroughly as you do, and may not be a bad influence. At least you can give them a chance and make your own decisions — which you'll do anyway.

Astrology can guide you in the type of bonds your sign should consider investing in. In the municipal bond area, the tax-exempt revenue bonds which deal with parking areas and municipal garages are Virgo/Mercury ruled and may appeal to you.

Because everything in life has an astrological correspondence, each type of corporate bond, stock, or commodity has a sign/planet that rules it. Therefore, under the Virgo/Mercury influence invest in manufacturing corporations that make dining room furniture, home bars, refrigerators, food freezers, non-perfumed soaps, cleaning materials (mops, brooms, solvents, etc.), vacuum cleaners, food counters, and supplies for the food industry.

If these areas don't capture your interest, why not try companies that make office equipment and machines (rubber stamps, pencil sharpeners, filing cabinets, briefcases, typewriters, calculators, information-handling machines and devices, and the following machines: adding, data processing, word processor, duplicating, mimeograph, printing). Or you could purchase stock in stationery manufactures or stores.

Other Virgo-ruled areas are stocks in paper companies like tissue paper, etc., or map companies or manufacturers of office supplies. For those of you who are health conscious (and most of you are) try health resorts (fat farms), spas, fitness resorts, weight-control centers, health food or colonic irrigation machine manufacturers, or magazines that deal with diet, health, and weight. Or what about owning stock in a cereal company?

And for you animal lovers there are animal food, toys, accessories, and clothes. In the commodities futures try grains and feeds. Or how about linseed, meal, sorghum, or flaxseed? — all are ruled by your sign.

HOW TO HANDLE YOUR INVESTMENTS

You'll never have to worry about the wool being pulled over your eyes. Your highly selective nature keeps everything pretty well intact. What you don't know about, you'll investigate and dissect. So it's unlikely that you'll ever get stung. However, you are susceptible to losses as mentioned previously in this chapter.

Continue you safe and sure road. It's the one you are familiar with; detours aren't as lucky for you. Keep in mind that when you invest in non-income producing assets like real estate (it's not producing spendable money), then you should also strive to accumulate an equal amount in liquid assets. This liquidity can be cash, bonds, stocks, cash-value life insurance, or even a pension.

Perhaps you'll invest most of your money in blue chips and put aside a small amount for those near-risky areas. You are attracted to the basic conservative tactic in stock investing which is diversification. By owning a number of stocks you reduce your risk of loss — and your profit potential too — because it's unlikely that they will all perform in the same way.

If you want to get involved in real diversification, own stock not only in different industries but also of different types. As a conservative investor you have to be careful of making the mistake of owning too many stocks of the same type.

A good way of obtaining a portfolio which is conservative and diversified is to buy shares in a mutual fund that has performed best over the past several years. Make sure the mutual fund is one that is an income or income-and-growth fund.

If you are retired or nearing the retirement age, you are going to be interested in preserving capital and obtaining a good income, which is the strategy employed by the conservative investor. Regardless of your age, your sign tends to follow these lines. However, if you have a desire to take a risk now and then, aim at capital growth.

If you are in the moderate (and many of you Virgoans are in the middle between conservative and risk taking) category you are concerned with safety and income, but also want growth and as an in-between type you have to be willing to take moderate risks to achieve it. So, with your usual way of going over everything with a fine-toothed comb, you shouldn't really have any problems. In fact, the experts could consult you and learn a few new facts.

Are you a winner or loser? It not only depends upon your Sun sign and how you use it, but also on the influence of Jupiter and Saturn. Jupiter attracts a gain, whereas Saturn attracts a loss. Everyone has these planets in his/her horoscope. But their influence depends upon whether their harmonious or inharmonious side is expressed at the moment a decision is made.

Under the influence of the positive side of Saturn, you are practical, conservative, cautious, serious, contemplative, and make a move only when you are sure the time is ripe. Long-range investments are favored. You use sound judgment, and thus can buy to advantage.

Under the influence of the negative side of Saturn you are pessimistic and cry poverty; you worry, gripe, complain, and have the blues. You are slow because you are afraid of making the wrong move, and thus can attract losses. You lack confidence and chances are if you purchase anything, it could be a real downer.

Whenever you are depressed and feel the Saturn negative traits, avoid investing in anything, because your Saturn is being stimulated in your horoscope at that moment (this could last an hour, a day, a week, a month, a year, or more). If you do invest when this inharmonious energy is being expressed, you are likely to attract a loss.

Under the influence of the positive side of Jupiter you are confident, optimistic, cheerful, easygoing, honest, understanding, happy, and generous. Speculation is favored and brings success. You use sound judgment and can sell to an advantage, take options, buy on margin, and do well all around.

Under the influence of the negative side of Jupiter you are overly confident, too optimistic, wasteful, ostentatious, extravagant, and refuse to take into account prices, expenditures, or the views of others. You are in the mood to do everything to excess. At a party you'd be on center stage making everyone laugh. If you sell an investment when you are in this frame of mind you won't get the price it's worth; your judgment will be off.

Whenever you discover you are using the negative side of Jupiter, don't take a chance with the stock market or any other form of investment. Lie low and wait until the positive side of Jupiter is being expressed, then sell. It'll be worth the wait.

In astrology *buying* is ruled by Saturn and *selling* by Jupiter. Every time you buy under a harmonious Saturn aspect your purchase will be a bargain, a good deal, or investment. Every time you sell under a harmonious Jupiter aspect your sale will be a considerable gain. The moment these planets are activated in your horoscope are determined by your time, place, day, month, and year of birth. But you don't need a horoscope to know when you are in a depressed state or happy mood. By being aware of your frame of mind, you'll know how to invest wisely. The moment the negative side of Jupiter, Saturn, or Virgo is expressed, that's the time to watch out for losses; the reverse if true when their positive side is expressed.

Now that you are armed with this information you can invest wisely and be ready for whatever the world economy brings. However, you are one step further ahead than the majority of people because by using this positive energy you can improve your chances to be wealthy.

CHAPTER SEVEN

Libra - Money and Investments

Those born from September 23 through October 22 have the Sun in the sign Libra. Every sign of the zodiac corresponds to a particular type of prosperity; it's what you do and how you use it that determines whether you'll be successful or not.

Because of your luxurious living habits would you want to wind up in a mess? Instead, wouldn't it be better if you could prevent losses, shortages and hardships? By knowing your faults and how to correct them you can enjoy life more, save money, and, be in tip-top shape. You'd like that, wouldn't you?

YOUR MONEY

Just like the Scales, which represent your sign, you are known as the "Balance Seeker of the Zodiac." You are always trying to equalize the debits and credits of your life. But unfortunately in trying to seek equality you become unbalanced. When you feel on top of the world, you dip into your pocket and spend extravagantly. Then, suddenly, you reach into your pocket and it's empty — you are broke. And with that, you sink to the very bottom.

Once you've regained your equilibrium you are at peace with the world. However, the moderation discovered doesn't last for long. All you have to do is glance at that sizable checking account and you're off and gracefully running again. You may tell yourself that you are just going to window-shop. But that is where you make your first mistake; your second is in the store when you purchase not only what is outside on display, but anything pretty you happen to pass along the way.

Beauty and luxuries are the rulers of your life; you are their helpless slave. They keep you in financial bondage — you try to break free, but can't escape. They are your weakness and, regardless of what they cost, you pay the price every time. You will do almost anything to possess and own them. The road they lead you down appears to have no ending.

One expensive garment is preferred over several inexpensive ones. What you can't pay for in cash, you charge and quickly forget about. When the bills arrive in the mail, they aren't always paid on time. And that doesn't concern you in the least.

Your world is that of the jet set. If you're not with the élite in reality, your daydreams temporarily satisfy that longing. But meanwhile your pocketbook suffers along the way because you buy what you want whether you can afford it or not.

Money is your ticket to a good life. You dislike ugliness and discord; therefore, you pay heavily for that luxury car, home, jewelry, and all the finery that dough can buy. You must surround yourself with beauty — it gives you the harmony you hunger for. In fact, you can't exist without it.

Your loved ones and friends are treated royally. The gifts you give have a high price tag, but the compliments received are well worth the extravagant sums paid. The rounds of parties you attend are endless. You are known as a social butterfly. Party invitations are accepted because you have difficulty in saying no. And when you make your appearance you are elegantly attired. You may not have a dime on you, but your furs and diamonds are all the security you need.

Wealth can be drawn through your pleasing personality, beauty, artistic talents, or ability to counsel others. Money is desired so it can be spent on pleasure and an easy life. There's a positive and negative side of Libra, and if the positive side is expressed perhaps the scales will tip to the middle and offset financial disasters and bring lasting material assets.

Your Positive Side

Has honesty paid off with money dealings? Is it easy for you to balance your checkbook? Do you go out of your way to attain status and a sizable bank account? Is a lot of money spent on entertaining? If so, does it reward you later with a financial increase? Do other people help you materially? If you answered the preceding questions with a "yes," you are using the harmonious traits you are known for, and as a result, prosperity can be more easily attracted.

Are you aware of the real reason you spend so much dough on all those expensive clothes? It's because you know that, besides your talents, it's your charm, looks, and good manners that are your greatest assets; and, if you play them up to the hilt with a wardrobe that dazzles, you've got it made in life. And you do!

You can hobnob with the most aristocratic part of society and feel right at home. Your innate ability to handle yourself politely and properly on all occasions is something you were born with. You didn't have to read the late Libra Emily Post's book on etiquette. But, because you excel in the social graces, the money comes rolling in.

You are one of the luckiest signs of the zodiac because those greenbacks seem to fly in your direction without too much effort on your part. Not only do you decorate an office with your delightful personality, but you are talented and can work at a hectic pace.

Often money is gained through others who seek your advice. You are a good troubleshooter and are know to be fair and just. You see both sides of the coin and thus can be invaluable in certain business transactions.

When an opportunity arises to make a buck, you do not jump in immediately. Friends and associates are asked about what they would do if they were in your position. Once you've heard everyone's opinion, you weigh all the pros and cons and then, finally, make your decision. Usually you select the right road; the one that's paved with riches.

Those dollars may be gained through selling a product with such finesse that the buyer doesn't even realize he's made a purchase. That light sales pitch and the friendliness that goes with it are difficult to resist.

Your desire to socialize takes you into many homes and places of entertainment. Not only do you enjoy the company of others and their conversations, but your bank account gets fattened in the process. Perhaps you sell cosmetics, paintings, or jewelry, or are in your own business. Regardless of what career you are into, it's your winsome smile and soft voice that makes people want to cater to you.

Your beauty may bring you lots of money as a model. Or perhaps you make a lot of cash through demonstrating beauty products or operating a self-improvement salon. Whatever you do, it's done in good taste. People who can pay your high prices are attracted.

Dollars may be gained through the ideas you possess. You know how to make use of them. The right people are met, or contacted — usually through a party or the countless friends you have. Partnerships may be started, or perhaps you sell your brainchild outright. Either way, you've got a good deal all the way to the bank.

You're the type who may pioneer in the literary field. Maybe you're another Truman Capote or Arthur Miller; both were born under the sign Libra. Your creative talent can bring in lots of royalty checks.

You are accustomed to your financial affairs going up and down continually. It could make you negative for a short while. When these low moods are felt, you become reclusive. But, because you have a changeable nature, it doesn't take you too long to swing back into a cheerful frame of mind. And that's the time you seek companionship and, once again, the dollars start to flow in. But they'll go right out again. And so it goes with you.

Time-saving machinery is desired in your business to increase production, and because you don't have a lot of energy to spare. You do not buy computers or equipment from the first salesperson who comes bouncing through the door. Prices from every manufacturer are compared carefully by you and your associates. Only after many meetings and discussions will you purchase a new computer or office machine. When you make your final move it's because you are sure that your company will profit by it.

You may spend a few bucks on education, but only with the thought of the remuneration it will bring; otherwise you're not one to give up your social pleasures for any schooling, unless it's something to do with the arts. However, the monetary gain anticipated usually measures up to your expectations — and then some.

Your Negative Side

Do fun and pleasure come before financial common sense? Do you try to buy friends? Have you lost out on money because of laziness? Do your unrestrained emotions cause you to go on spending sprees? Is it difficult for you to save a buck because you continually change your profession?

Do unwise social relations result in foolish expenditures? Does money go out on that which pleases you rather than that which is of necessity? Is your attitude toward bankruptcy nonchalant? Is ugliness in all forms so despised that you'll pay any price to avoid seeing it? Are you a spendthrift?

If you answered the preceding questions with a "yes," you are using the inharmonious traits you are known for, and as a result, it's difficult to attract prosperity.

Have you noticed that you are easily influenced by others on financial deals? It's difficult for you to say no to a potential money-making proposition. You want so desperately to be liked that it costs you an arm and a leg in the process. But if it's only money that is lost, you don't care. It's the friendship that means the most to you.

Love of ease is your main reason for wanting money. And as soon as those dollars come in they go right out again. You live it up just as the late Libra F. Scott Fitzgerald did. He spent a fortune on his social life, making the rounds by wining, dining, traveling with the smart set, and blowing every cent he had on overdoing his zest for living. Does it all sound familiar?

Peace and harmony are so important in your working environment that you have been known to quit a good paying job for a lesser one, only because the new place grants you the serenity desired. This can be a steep price to pay if it's kept up on a continual basis.

Many of you Librans are extremely mercenary and will yield to the unscrupulous ideas of others to make a buck dishonestly. Those of you who fall into this trap are the wayward ones who lie around doing nothing. And when the money comes in through this destructive channel, it disappears just as fast. So eventually some of you wise up; those of you who don't become the victims of your own greed.

Flattery can be your downfall. If praises start pouring in, you are so attentively engaged in listening to those sweet words that you aren't aware you're being conned into investing in a scheme to make a quick buck. When you realize it, it's too late — the person and your dough have vanished! This pattern is repeated time and again. You tell yourself that it'll never happen again — but, oh, those compliments are so irresistible, aren't they?

Some people may say you're vain, but you aren't. You despise ugliness and worship beauty. Therefore you spend large sums of money on cosmetic surgery, hair treatments, facials, massages, spas and anything else that pampers your body and countenance. In fact, you'd spend your last penny on this rather than for food. You know that when you look great you can get a date and be taken to dinner.

Your sign is in love with love. Emotional disturbances in this department unbalance you completely. The only way you can compensate for being hurt is to buy yourself something pretty. So off you go to an expensive store where you have an account. Not only do you charge purchases up to your limit, but every cent you have in your wallet is spent.

Whenever possible you entice a coworker to take over some of your job responsibilities while you sit back and watch everyone work. The praises you bestow on them, as well as your delectable smile, make them eager to please you. If you arrive late for work your associates cover up for you with some excuse or another. When the boss catches you off guard you get fired and your pocketbook takes a real beating.

Both sides of an issue are weighed with all business transactions. When a time limit for a decision is set, you are thrown for a loop. Either you lose out on the deal entirely because you are indecisive, or you rush in and regret it when it doesn't pay off as anticipated.

Your expenses exceed your gains. If you don't learn how to change your spending habits and handle your money better, financial binds will continue. And with a recession you would be caught in a mess.

HOW TO HANDLE YOUR MONEY

Wouldn't you like to find that balance you so avidly seek? Don't you think it would be great if you could buy some of those luxuries desired and yet still have money in the bank? Are your personal expenses so high that you can never seem to get ahead?

Do you have so many clothes that you are late to work because you can't decide what to wear? Are you in debt because you have a housekeeper's salary to pay? Is it because you don't want to get your hands dirty or are too lazy to do any cleaning? Do you buy a particular car solely because it's expensive?

If you answered "yes" on the preceding questions these are some of the areas you've got to work with and change. You are always interested in improving yourself, so here's your chance. However, when you weary of something you swing the opposite direction — so this is one pitfall you will have to learn to avoid if you are going to stay out of financial slumps.

You have to learn not to spend more than you make. Tear up all charge cards so you won't be tempted to make purchases when you go off the deep end. When your love life gets topsy-turvy, instead of getting yourself in a hole financially, be creative.

If you are an artist, draw, paint, or sculpt. If you're not adept along these lines take a class related to them or learn to make ceramics, pottery, or jewelry. The profits made from these hobbies could give you that extra income you need for those beautiful clothes you like to wear. And just think about all those wonderful compliments you will get on your creative talents. And whatever upset came about with a sweetheart has a better chance of disappearing when you've diverted destructive emotional energy into constructive emotional energy. So you wind up with a few bucks, compliments, and will be proud of your achievements.

To get out of debt and to supplement your income go into a side business of selling in your leisure time. Because you are so into fashion, why not sell gorgeous clothes by giving parties in your home? Throw in a few fragrances and your friends may buy them also. Or try selling furs, cosmetics and jewelry in the privacy of your living quarters. You can even buy them for yourself at the wholesale price you pay; then you can have your heart's delight at a big savings. Because you enjoy sending greeting cards, sell them in your spare moments. All of these Libra-ruled areas should keep you happy, especially when the dollars come rolling in from them.

Or start a mini-gift shop from your abode; buy the presents you give others at a discount price. Keep in mind that when you give something to another, it's the thought behind it that really counts, not the price paid: So curb those enormous expenditures on your loved ones and associates and get it at a cut-rate figure.

When you see an ad for an outfit that you think you'd like, ask yourself if you really need it. In other words, "Can you get by with what you already own?" Nine times out of ten you'll answer "yes." Try doing some comparison shopping; you'll be so indecisive that maybe — just maybe — you won't wind up with anything. That's one way to curb you from spending your dough!

Your three biggest expenditures are with clothes, home, and entertainment. You tend to overdo them all. If you are renting, try not to live in the most expensive apartment building. Save your dollars by either owning your own home, co-op, or condominium, or renting a place that is within your means. But before you buy a place, think about the money going out in mortgage payments. Can you afford it? Will it force you to cut down on your wardrobe or partying? If it won't, go ahead. But if it does, you'll be in bad shape because you'll want to have your cake and eat it, too — and that means going head over heels into such debt that you may never be able to balance those scales. And that would be real havoc, wouldn't it?

Now, to counteract any future ruin in the financial department of your life, you need to start by making a budget. Once you see your debits and credits listed in black and red, the reality of it all will become quite clear. And that makes it easier for you to follow.

Write down every penny you spend on the so-called nonessentials: candy bar, cab fare, new gloves you don't need, etc. Keep a daily record of all expenditures and you will be amazed at where your money goes so quickly. These are some of the miscellaneous areas of a budget that you can try to cut down on.

On a separate piece of paper jot down how much you earn, how much is needed for the basic living expenses (rent, utilities, telephone), food, medical, dental, and transportation to and from the job (include car insurance, but not car loan payments). Figure out how much is spent on clothing, eating out, entertainment, recreation, and gifts bought throughout the year — these are the areas that you can also cut down on in order to save money and/or invest it wisely. When you are figuring your budget you should set aside seven percent of your earnings, or more, in savings or investments.

Now what about those dollars you pay out in loans, credit cards, or charge accounts? Write them down and save interest by paying them off as fast as possible. That interest adds up and can buy you a new hat. Try to pay all your creditors each month rather than taking turns each month with different ones. If you need help with balancing your budget consult your telephone book for the number of the local consumer credit counseling service. As a rule they don't charge for their services; perhaps they can help you get new, lower monthly payments on your outstanding debts.

In red ink outline all of your desires to save money. Look at this sheet of paper every day. When you start to spend, first look at your budget and see if you can afford to. Take your lunch to work; to keep your spirits high, eat out once in a while with your pals and coworkers.

Curb your entertainment expense; don't go to every new play, movie, or concert that comes to town. Go dancing (ballroom is your favorite) or take ballet lessons to keep your figure trim. Play racquetball, tennis, or squash. Or float on a raft or in a swimming pool. Go ice skating and show off your gracefulness; the flattery received will make you glow. And for those quiet moments to balance your body, mind, and soul — get into yoga.

Are your car payments high? Do you have a Jaguar or some other foreign sports car? Does it cost a fortune? If you can get by with a cheaper automobile, try to cut expenses in this department. If you just have to drive around in a luxury car, then you must sacrifice in another area of your budget: Eat out less, or don't buy so many furs. Isn't one mink coat enough?

Instead of buying carpeting which won't last forever, purchase that Oriental rug you fell in love with. It will last beyond your lifetime if cared for properly and will increase in value. If you ever wanted to sell it because you got tired of it, you'll make a nice profit.

Is your salary so large that you can afford to have a daily housekeeper? If it's not, why not have her come once a week? Or better yet, hire a teenager who wants to make a few extra bucks after school lets out.

Instead of splurging all your dough on those facials at the beauty salon, buy the masques at the drug or health-food store and give them to yourself. If those massages are costing you an arm and leg, exercise at home. Instead of going to an expensive beauty parlor every week, try the beauty schools where it costs less. Who knows, you may get a more talented hairdresser there than you do in your fancy place.

Start a financial plan that will still let you enjoy yourself now and when you are older or retired you'll have something to fall back on. Stick with your budget — watch that swinging back and forth. It'll be difficult for you to be financially solvent unless you learn how to tighten your purse strings and control your desires. It's advisable you start now in case a recession occurs.

YOUR INVESTMENTS

You can benefit by setting aside money now so your future will be secure. Or perhaps you prefer investing in something other than a business. However, before you go leaping into any undertaking, it would be to your advantage to understand your assets and shortcomings, thereby avoiding pitfalls.

Your Positive Side

A "yes" answer to any of the following questions indicates that you are expressing harmonious Libra traits, thus enhancing your chances to gain prosperity: Before investing, is everything seriously considered from every angle? Are liquid investments preferable? Is money gained by slowness of decision and action? Do the tips you get from your friends pay off? Is cash spent on art objects? If so, have your investments been profitable? Do you like to balance your portfolio with an equal amount of currency tied up in stocks and bonds? Is diversification your "bag"? Do you listen to the advice of your investment counselor? Has it proven advantageous?

Are you aware that you are a conservative speculator? The risks are exciting, but so are those sure gains. As with everything else you do in life, you go from one extreme to another. But before you spend one penny, you weigh the pros and cons. The past and present record of a stock is read and studied. Your fiends and broker are questioned relentlessly. When you are ready to make a move, it's done fast.

Because you like to be fair and give all types of investments a chance to work well in your behalf, you are likely to be equally interested in short-, medium-, and long-term maturation periods. You figure that you are covered in case of any sudden financial disaster and yet you have low, medium, and high yields as a return on your money. Also, this makes it easier for you because you avoid indecisiveness.

You may attend expensive auctions just for the sheer excitement of being around people who are well off. But the moment you see those beautiful antiques and paintings, you find yourself right in the middle of things bidding. However, before you get too carried away, you regain your equilibrium and stop just in the nick of time. There are some days that you come away with a lucky buy and others you go home empty handed because you were in a cautious mood.

If a buddy tries to talk you into taking a chance to make a big killing in the options or commodity futures market, your pleasant smiles says "yes" but your mind says "no." At least you are aware that you have difficulty making decisions. You know that if you had to decide whether a particular stock is going to go up or down in price within a specified time period, you'd feel as if you were dangling from a swinging chandelier and couldn't get off.

Your fondness for the social scene can be quite profitable, especially when people talk about how they make money. You are curious and enjoy listening to all the different avenues others are involved in. Perhaps you'll learn something you can use someday yourself. But in the meanwhile you take it all in mentally and then go through your usual weighing process. And there's been many a time that the knowledge gained at these gatherings has paid off handsomely later.

Your Negative Side

A "yes" answer to the following questions indicates that you are expressing the inharmonious Libra traits, thus lessening your chances to gain prosperity: Are you so desirous of pleasing others that you'll invest in whatever they tell you just so you don't lose their friendship? Is it difficult for you to make up your mind about whether you should or should not invest in a particular stock? Because you feel hurried, do you jump in and take a substantial loss?

Do you spend lavishly on something that fails to bring immediate returns? And then do you start all over again on something new? Do you wait too long to bid on a piece of property? As a result, do you generally lose out?

Are you aware that you repeat past errors? It's because you live for one day at a time — today. The past is over and forgotten and the future — tomorrow is another day. This attitude could make you wind up losing more than just that pretty shirt of yours.

It's difficult for you to choose the type of stock you should invest in. All the different corporations' prospectuses are gone over time and again. One company may have certain features you like, and another may not. Finally you end up purchasing stock in a cosmetics firm because makeup beautifies — your love of beauty even extends into investment areas. However, do you recall those countless losses from other cosmetic firms that fell by the wayside?

If you get a hot tip at a party that a new issue on the stock exchange is going to go big in two months and that you should buy it now and sell it in seven weeks because you'll make an enormous profit, you are likely to chance it. Five weeks later when the corporation goes bankrupt, you can't understand where your mind was when you invested in all those shares. But individually they were so cheap you didn't realize their overall cost, nor that the business was not organized very well.

And what about the time you saw an exquisite Oriental ivory figurine in an auction catalogue, borrowed a wad of money from the bank, attended the auction, bid on it (and a few other items), and happily went home with your purchase? A year passes, you change your decor, take the Oriental figurine back to the auction house to be put on the market. Instead of making a profit, you take a substantial loss — half of what you paid for it. Why? Because a law protecting animals whose tusks supply the ivory restricts sales and made your statuette go down in value. That's when you realize that you should have been more informed before buying it because that law had been in effect at the time it was purchased by you.

As a hedge against recession, you may decide to be practical and buy silver bullion because it's cheaper than gold. Both appeal to your esthetic senses because they are shiny and pretty. But silver is the riskier of the two because it is so volatile. Losses occur when it hits bottom. That's one time when you would have been better off indulging your expensive tastes!

WHAT SHOULD YOU INVEST IN?

A balanced portfolio is necessary: short-term, medium-, and long-term maturation dates plus diversification which minimizes risks. For excitement you need to speculate; for safety you require some solid conservative investments. This method of operation satisfies your desire to have everything equal.

The thirty-, sixty-, and ninety-day bonds, government funds, treasury bills and notes, commercial paper, and certificates of deposit appeal to you because you can see instant returns on your money. Intermediate bonds that mature in five to seven years are in the medium range and pay more than short-term bonds. And those that yield the most are the long-term bonds which mature in around twenty years. If a recession occurs it would be in your best interest to be in the short-term bond market.

Your sign rules art, so this is an investment area that gratifies your love of the esthetic. Art as a collectible is being used by many as a hedge against inflation.

The lithograph, silk-screen, and serigraph processes are favored when purchasing contemporary prints. Posters and prints that show loving couples, picturesque scenery, and the dance put you in a romantic mood.

In the fine-art field you like the oils to be in the pastel shades — form, harmony, and the right blend of colors are important to you. You have a keen eye and deep appreciation of the artistic and to invest in it is your greatest delight.

An art mutual fund such as Knoedler-Modarco (stock traded on Geneva Exchange) and Artemis (stock traded in Amsterdam) could certainly give you that lift when those blue moods strike. Eurodollars, if you can afford the, would interest you.

Perhaps you'd like to invest in the gem your sign rules — the diamond? Or what about the stones ruled by Libra — white marble, white quartz, white spar, alabaster, or malachite? Or there are the metals your sign rules — copper, bronze, and brass? Buy shares in diamonds and/or the stones and metals mentioned; or purchase your own mine or go into these areas as a business.

It's interesting that my dear friend Mickey Rooney, a Libra, chose to use bronze when he got involved in producing his Leg-ics in limited editions as a collectible. Leg-ics is a new word that was coined by Mickey to replace the word medallion; these Leg-ics are legends of the motion picture industry. So collect them if this appeals to you.

Perhaps you'd enjoy collecting marble or bronze busts or statues. Or become a patron of the arts and help support some struggling and talented artist, or the ballet or opera house in your local area. Just think how much more enjoyable everything is when you have a part in it.

"Jingle, jingle, jingle;" those light, ringing, twinkling sounds are like music to your ears when you collect coins and run your fingers through them or wear them as medallions or on a charm bracelet. Rare coin collecting is a more predictable investment than either fine or junk art. The market is wider, price trends are easier to track; though they can still mean big gains or losses for speculators. You may want a diversified basic portfolio.

If in the past you've gained through speculation, then continue along these lines; however, if the reverse holds true, stay away from this because you are expressing the Libra traits on their negative side and are likely to get a repeat performance. Abide by this rule, especially with anything that is known to be risky.

In the foreign bond market you may be attracted to the countries of France, Germany, or China (ruled by Libra). Or if you want to invest in foreign currency, try China's (Libra-ruled, too) dollar. Or perhaps stock on the foreign exchange, which has companies listed for these same countries, would appeal to you.

It's important that you offset your chances of being in a poor position if a recession occurs. Due to your conservative-speculative nature, you should invest in a financial program designed to provide future security. Annuities may be just what you are looking for, or perhaps deferred annuities are preferred because you want the opportunity to realize attractive appreciation potential without the burden of immediate taxation.

The socializing you do can keep you abreast of the trends and what's going on around the world; therefore, this is an aid when it comes to investing wisely. You may wish to seek the advice of an expert because, like the pendulum, you swing back and forth trying to decide what you should put your money into for the best results.

A broker who thinks along the same lines a you may be desirable. Therefore, deal with another Libra, Gemini, Cancer, Scorpio, or Aquarius. These signs tend to be both risk takers and conservative. Cancer gets as indecisive as you; Scorpio calculates ahead, then jumps in; Aquarius is erratic and, like Gemini, you never know if this person's in a speculative or conservative mood. It may be better to have a broker who is practical and able to provide the balance you so desperately seek and need. Therefore, consider Capricorn, Taurus, and Virgo. They are the best suited for safe and sound investments. They are slow to action, but then so are you — at times.

If you're interested in a broker who encourages calculated risks and making "big bundles," try an Aries or a Leo, Sagittarius, or Pisces. Beware of the wild chances they take, though. From a financial standpoint they may not be the best signs for you to listen to or be involved with.

If you are lucky you might find a broker who is an Aries or a Libra, Gemini, Cancer, Leo, Scorpio, Sagittarius, Aquarius, or Pisces Sun sign and this individual *may also have* Capricorn, Taurus, or Virgo as a *dominant* sign in his/her horoscope. If this occurs, you'll have the best of two worlds: one inclined to speculate but who uses sound judgment.

Astrology can guide you in the type of bonds your sign should consider investing in. Therefore, be on the alert for the Libra/Venus-ruled municipal bonds that deal with public projects or parking areas. The municipal tax-exempt revenue bonds that deal with your sign are playgrounds and municipal garages.

Because everything in life has an astrological correspondence each type of corporate bond, stock, or commodity has a sign/planet that rules it. Therefore, under the Libra/Venus influence invest in manufacturing corporations that produce or use in their products copper, bronze, brass, malachite, white quartz, white marble, white spar, amber, diamonds, fine china, porcelain, or crystal stemware.

If these areas don't capture your interest try companies that produce artists' supplies, stringed musical instruments, brass instruments, harmonious or piped-in music, fine wines, perfume, toilet articles, aromatic products, cosmetics, beauty products, perfumed soap, spas for beautification or leisure, and vacation hotels or motels.

Also, as a Libra you'd be intrigued with stock or bonds in firms that manufacture weighing scales (sound familiar?), measuring devices (tape measures and scales), jewelry, lingerie firms, textiles, suede and leather goods, furs, wigs, hairpieces, vases, figurines (ivory, porcelain, china, marble, etc.), mattresses, furniture, gourmet delicacies, and luxury items.

Because you love clothing and finery, why not try stock or bonds in the fashion industry, or decorating companies on the exchange? Or because you're an

Air sign, try investing in stock or bond corporations which manufacture air filters or air-conditioners. Because you're sweet and your sign rules candy and sugar, why not try that with bonds or on the stock exchange? Or if you've got the nerve (and sometimes you do) try sugar (cane, beet) in the commodity futures market. Other Libra/Venus-ruled "futures" are flour, potatoes, corn (including corn gluten feed), hominy feed, cottonseed meal, cotton, fibers, textiles, and flour.

HOW TO HANDLE YOUR INVESTMENTS

Safe and sure areas are sought as well as risky ventures. When that new get-rich-in-a-hurry investment opportunity comes sailing along, be leery of it. Your weak moment will come when you think about all those beautiful clothes and luxuries you can buy when your ship comes sailing in. But stop and think: Perhaps it may bypass your port and dock somewhere else or get sunk along the way!

Do your usual weighing of the pros and cons before investing. Never leap into anything just because you want a new car, mink coat or a yacht. Inquire around and get the opinion of people you feel confident with, such as an investment counselor.

Ask an accountant to guide you as to how much you can afford to lose. Some blue-chip stocks or bonds might be well worth considering as an investment. You may want to put aside a small amount to gamble with so you can make a fast buck and take off on a Mediterranean cruise.

If you're into diamonds, be on guard against falling for in-house certificates, high-pressure sales, unusually low prices — the so-called "bargains" — and your adoration of the gem itself. Get a certificate from an independent gem lab, such as Gemological Institute of America, European Gem Lab, or United States Gemological Services. Don't buy mail-order diamonds!

Because you like to diversify, perhaps you'd like to invest your money according to how the experts think a typical investor should do it: twenty-five percent of your savings in a savings account; fifty percent in bonds — municipal bonds, especially if you're in a high tax bracket, or a bond fund; thirteen percent in the stock market; twelve percent for a gambling fund — so you can take chances and make enough loot so you can afford to indulge in fun and games.

The only problem with a savings account is that when an urge to go on a spree strikes, you are likely to withdraw every cent and splurge it all on pampering yourself. Don't burden yourself with excessive debts when other costs are likely to go up. If you do, your fight against inflation may turn out to be your defeat.

You alone must live with the investments you make, regardless of what anyone tells you. It's your money, so make those balanced decisions that ensure your comfort. If you can't live at peace with securities, don't own them.

Are you a winner or loser? It not only depends upon your Sun sign and how you use it, but also on the influence of Jupiter and Saturn. Jupiter attracts a gain, whereas Saturn attracts a loss. Everyone has these planets in his/her horoscope. But their influence depends upon whether their harmonious or inharmonious side is expressed at the moment a decision is made.

Under the influence of the positive side of Saturn, you are practical, conservative, cautious, serious, contemplative, and make a move only when you are sure the time is ripe. Long-range investments are favored. You use sound judgment, and thus can buy to advantage.

Under the influence of the negative side of Saturn you are pessimistic and cry poverty; you worry, gripe, complain, and have the blues. You are slow because you are afraid of making the wrong move, and thus can attract losses. You lack confidence and chances are if you purchase anything, it could be a real downer.

Whenever you are depressed and feel the Saturn negative traits, avoid investing in anything, because your Saturn is being stimulated in your horoscope at that moment (this could last an hour, a day, a week, a month, a year, or more). If you do invest when this inharmonious energy is being expressed, you are likely to attract a loss.

Under the influence of the positive side of Jupiter you are confident, optimistic, cheerful, easygoing, honest, understanding, happy, and generous. Speculation is favored and brings success. You use sound judgment and can sell to an advantage, take options, buy on margin, and do well all around.

Under the influence of the negative side of Jupiter you are overly confident, too optimistic, wasteful, ostentatious, extravagant, and refuse to take into account prices, expenditures, or the views of others. You are in the mood to do everything to excess. At a party you'd be on center stage making everyone laugh. If you sell an investment when you are in this frame of mind you won't get the price it's worth; your judgment will be off.

Whenever you discover you are using the negative side of Jupiter, don't take a chance with the stock market or any other form of investment. Lie low and wait until the positive side of Jupiter is being expressed, then sell. It'll be worth the wait.

In astrology *buying* is ruled by Saturn and *selling* by Jupiter. Every time you buy under a harmonious Saturn aspect your purchase will be a bargain, a good deal, or investment. Every time you sell under a harmonious Jupiter aspect your sale will be a considerable gain. The moment these planets are activated in your horoscope are determined by your time, place, day, month, and year of birth. But you don't need a horoscope to know when you are in a depressed state or happy mood. By being aware of your frame of mind, you'll know how to invest wisely. The moment the negative side of Jupiter, Saturn, or Libra is expressed, that's the time to watch out for losses; the reverse is true when their positive side is expressed.

Now that you are armed with this information you can invest wisely and be ready for whatever the world economy brings. However, you are one step further ahead than the majority of people because by using this positive energy you can improve your chances to be wealthy.

CHAPTER EIGHT

Scorpio — Money and Investments

Those born from October 23 through November 21 have the Sun in the sign Scorpio. Every sign of the zodiac corresponds to a particular type of prosperity; it's what you do and how you use it that determines whether you'll be successful or not.

Do you want to wind up behind the eight ball because of your compulsive spending habits? Instead, wouldn't it be better if you could prevent losses, financial disasters, and hypertension? By knowing your faults and how to correct them you can enjoy life more, save money, and, be in tip-top shape. That sounds intriguing, doesn't it?

YOUR MONEY

Money is spent as if you are possessed by a demon — and maybe you are. Your sign is known as the "Compulsive Spender of the Zodiac." You want what you want, when you want it. And, what's more, you get it! There's nothing going to stop you: No obstacle is too great, and no person is big enough.

If you take a moment to pause in front of a store window and see something you like, it's almost impossible for you to resist buying it. If you don't purchase it right then and there, the entire night is spent thinking about it. You can't stand not having it, so the next day it becomes another one of your possessions.

You have a long list of objects that you want to own. As you purchase them, one by one, each is scratched off the list. You tell yourself that when you've bought everything on the list, you will then start to save money. However, you are an individual who has never-ending desires; therefore you will work hard to get the cash to pay for your insatiable longings.

Your dollars are spent on those you deeply care about. (The late Scorpio Richard Burton spent a fortune at an auction to purchase a huge diamond for Elizabeth Taylor.) If a person ever gave away your gift, you'd never buy anything for him/her again. When you give money, you also give instructions how it should be spent. You are generous with those whose company you enjoy. There is no expense spared when you're out for a night on the town.

Your bank account could suffer the strains of your extravagance. But you just say, "There's more where that came from." Your love of money is openly admitted. You are never distracted from the path you've chosen to get your heart's delight.

You know what those greenbacks can do for you. They are your power to control all situations and people. You are not against buying others and are a firm believer that everyone has his price.

Luxuries and affluence are obsessively desired. If you want to impress someone for business reasons, you may flaunt your riches. You do not keep up with the

Jones'; you outdo them. There is a driving force within you that compels you, one way or another, to obtain as much of the world's wealth as you humanly can. This can become your preoccupation throughout your lifetime. It's easy for you to amass enormous sums of money as did the late J. Paul Getty who had Scorpio *dominant* and was considered "the world's richest man."

Both female and male Scorpios can't help squandering their dough. A hobby can have them so intensely wrapped up that they will spend a fortune on it. And it won't do anyone any good to try to talk them into being a little conservative. A Scorpio is his own person and shuns advice, regardless of how expert his would-be advisor is. There's a positive and negative side to Scorpio and if the positive side is expressed you have a better chance of not winding up in the red.

Your Positive Side

Do you concentrate most of your energy on getting money? Are you a materialist? Do you enjoy finding out ways to obtain a buck? Are you resourceful? Does it pay off? Do you follow your first impression, or intuition, with financial transactions? If so, does this work to your advantage? If you answered the preceding questions with a "yes," you are using the harmonious traits you are known for and, as a result, prosperity can be more easily attracted.

Are you always sure you'll come out a winner? You take a risk without batting an eyelash because you know that your never-failing fund of ideas guarantees a handsome payoff. In fact, it's almost as if you were involved in a financial power-game.

Few people know what you are thinking because you are so secretive. If they could only see you while you are intensely engaged in drawing up plans which you hope will bring you the financial freedom desired! Whatever project is undertaken, it is thought about down to the very last detail. And each step along the way is carried out with such a concentration of energy that everything else in life is blocked out.

You are self-assured in your ability and judgment to move in the right direction. Your immediate and direct objective is to get the best and fastest results. A way will be discovered come hell or high water. You plunge in with such force that others are amazed at your strength and breathless at the money you gain.

Your impulsiveness may lead you into dangerous paths. But you have the courage to take a chance on an idea and the persistence to see it through. The means used may appear reckless, and to a certain extent they are, but you manage somehow to come out having made a killing which makes you grin all the way to the bank.

The more difficult the task, the greater the challenge. Nothing frightens you. In fact, the threat of opposition spurs you on. The route chosen is one with difficulties along the way. You don't ever quit; defeat is a word that you don't understand or acknowledge. This relentless attitude helps you on your climb to the top. And the money that awaits you is akin to the pot of gold at the end of the rainbow.

If it's something you believe in, you will invest all of your money in your dream. If there's someone you want to deal with in business, that individual is investigated before any contact is made. The cost of the inquiry may be high, but it's considered as a "must" item on your budget.

When it comes to financial transactions you are very exacting and not an easy person to deal with. You do not make allowances for anyone's weakness. Your inflexible strength of will and confidence make you demand what you know is rightfully yours. And dare anyone say it isn't!

You're constantly testing people by saying things just to get an individual's reaction. This may be done at a party or by your taking someone out to lunch or dinner. All information is bought subtly. And all it costs is the price of a good meal. The questions you ask are well planned and have a definite purpose unknown to your guest. The answers received are filed in your mental cabinet to be used at a later date when the time is ripe. Usually these tête-à-tête gatherings reward you in the long run because you seldom lose a buck from any cleverly disguised interview.

You're considered a rather lucky gambler, not only in business but with making a football wager, playing the Lottery, going to a gambling casino, or playing cards in the privacy of your own home. You have that famous poker face that can bluff so well that you wind up with most of the cash. Once you become involved with a project or game, you can't jump off the merry-go-round until you've won the brass ring.

Financial problems may arise because of the daring way you spend money to make money. But the door of negativity is kept tightly shut. You won't allow yourself to get in a blue mood for anything. Instead, you immediately find the key to get out.

Those dollars may be gained through a struggle, but you don't mind fighting for high stakes. Your burning desire to fatten your wallet makes you tackle gigantic tasks regardless of the sums involved or the work required. Your motto is that old proverb, "Nothing ventured, nothing gained."

If you attend a computer or machinery convention or exhibit and see something that you believe could be useful, it will be purchased immediately, even if you have to borrow or go into debt because of it. Once you're hooked on something, you can't let it go until it belongs to you.

Your Negative Side

Will you do anything to win a point, regardless of how much it costs you? Are you ruthless when it comes to financial transactions? Does your desire for money interfere with those you are close to? If so, has it caused a divorce or break in the relationship? Is it difficult for you to save a buck because there's always something you want to buy? If someone owes you money, will you relentlessly harass the person into paying you? Do you make your dollars through illegal activities? If so, have you been caught by them? Will you rebel if someone tries to tell you what to do with your money? If you answered the preceding questions with a "yes," you are using the inharmonious traits you are known for and, as a result, it's difficult to attract prosperity.

Are you aware that you go to extremes with the spending of your dough? When you are on your economy kick, you do well with the sacrifices you make. But your downfall comes when you read an ad about an item that attracts you. Quick as a flash, you revert to your compulsive kick of throwing away every dime you just saved.

When you become obsessed with an idea or take up some cause, you'll pour every penny you have into fighting for it. It's possible that you will lead in uprising, but you prefer to work quietly in the background while you get everyone else to do your bidding. The time and effort put into this could detract from your career and family, and make you wind up broke. But when you are gung-ho on something it becomes a matter of life and death to you and money means nothing in the process.

You can rough it until you're back on the road to financial recovery. Drastic measures are taken so you can get back on top quickly. Several jobs are worked simultaneously almost around the clock. You are a human dynamo when it comes to energy and do not relent until you are satisfied with your bank account.

The gambler in you is going to wager everything you have on a risky venture. You do not like to be thwarted and if anyone tries he'll feel the Scorpio sting when you let loose with a few profanities or sarcasm. Your violent anger that seethes inside is expelled when anyone tries to come up against you. You are a bitter enemy and, if attacked, you spend every dime you have on revenge.

The urge to prove a point is so strong that it outweighs practicality. It could be nothing more than your spending a fortune on chemicals to make tests and experiments on some new cancer-destroying drug or throwing money down the drain on some way-out drugless healing method.

Perhaps you'll lose a lot of money on some project that is close to your heart, such as tracking down UFO landing sites. You may pay out salaries to hire statistical researchers. Or perhaps your traveling expenses are high because you spend your entire income on taking trips to the places where these beings from outer space allegedly have been seen.

Your "change the decor" kicks can cost you a pretty penny every so many years. You get to the point that you can't stand to look at the same scenery any longer. And, when that mood strikes, it's so sudden that your household members are all agape as you pick up a chair and say about it, "Out — out — out you go." In a jiffy that chair is gone for good. You don't care whether it's picked up by a stranger in the trash area or dumped in the city garbage.

If your loved ones try to talk you into selling the chair you'll balk. You just want it out of your sight as fast as it can go and you don't care what it costs, nor are you interested in making a buck from it. Tomorrow you'll go down to the store and buy a new chair. Of course, this is just the first item to go; once you've started, your family might as well prepare themselves to see the entire house changed.

Computers or office equipment are purchased so hurriedly that no real thought is given as to how profitable it will be for you. Your desire to possess all the latest models can keep you in a financial bind. It's hard for you to get ahead in business with this never-ending battle of splurging on everything that comes along.

Losses of money come when you are fired from a job because your dictativeness has become overbearing. Your coworkers may live in fear of you because when rubbed the wrong way you flash them one of your penetrating stares that strips them naked.

It's almost impossible for you to build up a monetary reserve. The immense obligations and liabilities are piled up a mile high. You will fly into a rage if someone harasses you for the dough you owe. And yet, if it were turned around, you wouldn't hesitate to pester someone until they paid you back in full.

Substantial sums of money are lost through trying to outwit your competitors, regardless of the expense involved in the process. Losses also occur through creative enterprises, fires, accidents, moving too fast, or being too full of hate. You spend more than you make and should learn to control your impelling desires, especially if a recession occurs.

HOW TO HANDLE YOUR MONEY

Have you ever wondered how you can avoid all those financial slumps you get into? Wouldn't it be great to have money saved for stormy days ahead? Have you ever wondered how you can overcome your compulsive spending habits? Is cash being spent on clothes or objects that are stored in a closet as treasures rather than used?

Do you have high expenses because you own several cars? Are you in debt up to your ears? Wouldn't it be better if you didn't owe anybody a cent? Do your hobbies keep you broke? Wouldn't it be wonderful if you could still enjoy all those things desired, but yet be solvent?

If you answered "yes" to the preceding questions, these are some of the areas you've got to work with and change. Because you are a fixed sign, it'll be difficult for you to break bad habits. But you can do anything once you feel it's essential.

If you can't afford paying cash for something, you should save your money until you can. Stay away from charge accounts; in fact, cut the cards up and throw them out. Don't look in store windows or at catalogues that come in the mail; one glance and you could be a goner. If you don't know what's out there, your pocketbook won't be emptied.

Try to live within your means; don't go overboard on some new hobby. Try to cut down on costs, eliminate waste, and economize. This does not mean you won't have fun, it just means that you will have something to fall back on if times get rough.

Whatever it costs in sweat, mental fatigue, or in rocky relationships, you gladly pay the price so you can obtain the almighty dollar. Your needs must be satisfied first and at all costs: Friends, family, or loved ones are sacrificed and neglected. Employees are driven to work as hard as you, if you are your own boss. If you continue this way you may wind up rich, but alone. So try to find a way to accomplish your tasks more efficiently, perhaps by hiring more employees to take over some of your load, and then you'll have time to be with those who care about you.

Your deep interest in exploring the mysteries of the universe can cost you a pretty penny. Once you get hooked you may devote your entire life trying to solve some big riddle. Instead of paying money out of your pocket, do what the late Scorpio Richard E. Byrd did and raise funds to finance your expedition. To pay some of his debts, the famous explorer wrote books. So if you want, write a book about your ideas; maybe others will join you, thus cutting down on your exploration expenses.

If you want to supplement your income, become a financial or mortgage broker; this is something you can do during your spare hours and with the extra money you can buy those items you feel should belong to you. Or make money on the side by selling *will kits*. You can sell them through the mail, to individuals and fund-raising groups. And with the cash, buy that motorcycle you've got your eye on. If you have artistic talents, paint when you've got time to kill. If you are qualified to do portraits, get some customers to commission you to paint them. However, there may be a snag when it comes to selling your work: You dislike letting go of anything. So if this is your problem just paint for your own enjoyment, unless you learn to change. You could take a photograph of your art work and then you'd be able to look at your work and still make a buck.

To avoid losing a job or business, and consequently money, restrain your temper by applying charm; talk slowly and you'll find you're less inclined to get argumentative. Control your urge to dictate: Give orders, but in a kind and firm manner. When you apply brute force you repel success. If you are placid, not only will you feel inwardly peaceful, but you are more likely to attract prosperity.

Comparison shopping turns you off because it's too time consuming and you don't plan purchases, you buy on impulse. This spur-of-the-moment spending should be curbed because this is what gets you so deeply into debt. Get a family member to make the rounds of the stores, write down prices, and give you the report. The high mark-ups will enrage you. You can't stand to be cheated, and to your way of thinking that's what the store is doing when it charges more for an item than another store does. Once you are aware of the big differences in price, you'll adore this price-comparing. And that will save you lots of money that you can spend on something else, or put away in the bank.

You dislike asking anyone for advice, but why not ask an accountant whether you should splurge on that new computer you are so carried away with? You can't get ahead financially if you become such a tyrant that you are the law and the only one with any knowledge. Why do you think others get paid salaries and make a living? They are there to help, not hinder you. If you can't get their opinion, then before buying anything look over your books to see if you can really afford it, and then try to recall what happened the last time you leaped into the fire.

Start a financial plan that doesn't interfere with your present life-style too much and yet can give you something to fall back on when you are retired or older. Tell yourself, "I *desire*" — the keyword for Scorpio — "to save for me."

To start with, a budget is necessary. The details of it will appeal to you, but the limits it places on your spending will turn you off. You must have your own dough to do with as you please. It's your ticket to a paradise that puts you in command. So by having a budget, not only will you handle your own money, but you'll have more of it to handle.

On a piece of paper list how much you make, how much is needed for the basic necessities (rent, utilities, telephone), food, medical, dental, and transportation (including car insurance but not the car payments). Figure out how much goes out on your wardrobe, dining out, recreation, entertainment, and gifts purchased at Christmas and other occasions during the entire year: These are the areas you can cut down on in order to save a few bucks and/or to invest them wisely. Put aside seven percent of your earnings or more in savings or investments.

Write down how much you pay out in loans, credit cards, charge or revolving accounts. To save money on the interest, pay them off quickly. Outline in red ink your desires to save money. Look them over *every day* and when you get an urge to spend, do it only according to your budget.

Under recreation expenses in your budget, include the money that goes out for gambling. Never bet more than you might spend on some other form of recreation such as going away for a weekend to a ski lodge or renting a boat and going sailing. Instead of thinking about how much you want to win, think about how much you can afford to lose. And quit when you've played all the money your budget allows for. This is the most difficult task for your sign to do because you are "the compulsive-professional gambler of the zodiac."

Don't go overboard with entertainment expenses. Keep your allowance down to a minimum; watch your hobby expenditures closely. Rent whenever applicable. Go to the museums, art galleries, and other inexpensive places. Because you are a Water sign you like to swim, water-ski, scuba dive, shoot the rapids, and ride the surf on a surfboard. But don't spend all of your money going to faraway and expensive places.

Other sports that appeal to your sign are hunting, snowshoeing, and baseball. Keep gun expenses down: You could easily become an avid gun collector and that's an expensive hobby. Play some poker, Monopoly, and backgammon, but watch those bets. Competitive sports like bowling, tennis, golfing, fencing, judo, and karate could be rather inexpensive and keep you motivated to stay on your budget.

Make money through entering tournaments; turn professional or teach if you excel in a sport. Because you are disciplined, persistent, and must be the best in everything, you could drive yourself into becoming a champion. Scorpios Roy

Campanella, Billie Jean King, Stan Musial, and Ted Williams didn't fare so badly, did they?

YOUR INVESTMENTS

You can benefit by setting aside money now so your future will be secure. Or perhaps you prefer investing in something other than a business. However, before you go leaping into any undertaking, it would be to your advantage to understand your assets and shortcomings, thereby avoiding pitfalls.

Your Positive Side

A "yes" answer to any of the following questions indicates that you are expressing harmonious Scorpio traits, thus enhancing your chances to gain prosperity: Is investing an irresistible urge that pays off? Are quick gains preferable to long-term ones? If so, have you been successful? Do you spend time to investigate a corporation thoroughly before shelling out any money? Do you put all your eggs in one basket? If so, are you well compensated? If you don't have the cash, will you find a way to get it just so you can invest in something?

Will you buy, if possible, all existing shares of stock so you can be in control? The late J. Paul Getty did. (The sign Scorpio was *dominant* in his horoscope.) It took him twenty years to buy out everyone so he could be in control. He planned his strategy years in advance and persistently waited until he won out. Like Getty, the more stock you have, the more you want to own. You are never satisfied with little; you've got to have a lot.

Stocks are evaluated, graphs and diagrams drawn up, everything is analyzed. Then the next move is to research the tactic which can bring you the most gains. Once this is discovered, a risk is taken without batting an eyelash as you plunge in. Often it's your intuition that gives you the go-ahead signal. Speculating is an exhilarating experience for you, especially when you come out on top. Action is desired with investments; that's why you select those that appear to be movers.

When a new company starts to go public and issue stock and that company manufactures a product that you believe in, you will demonstrate your faith in the enterprise by backing it all the way when you purchase enormous shares of its stock. Furthermore, your acquaintances and friends will be told to buy it while it's hot. And when they do and the price of the stock escalates to a profitable price for you to sell, you will.

If there's a piece of property you want, you don't hesitate to seize the opportunity to purchase it. This is one area that you are inconsistent in: You are likely to improve it and sell it at a high profit a year later, or you may hang on to it forever. Either way you move, it always seems to be auspicious for you.

People who try to discourage you from getting involved in risky ventures are amazed at how you will stick to your guns and carry out your plans. Whenever they say "can't," you say "will" and dare them interfere with your method of operation. You will do everything in your power to prove that your decision is the right one. And it usually is.

Works of art, like people, are sized up instantly by you. Those penetrating eyes of yours are put to work to spot phony paintings. You make the rounds among the flea market, thrift shop, and auction house. If there's a bazaar in town, you'll be there, too. An auction room is packed with excitement for you. Your enthusiasm to own a painting is seen by the way you bid. It may appear to others that you are possessed by some spirit, but all you can think about is, "I *must own* that treasure."

Your Negative Side

A "yes" answer to the following questions indicates that you are expressing the inharmonious Scorpio traits, thus lessening your chances to gain prosperity: Is the money received from interest or dividend payments lavishly spent rather than reinvested? Do you pressure others to invest so your holdings will be increased in value? Do you become possessive with investments, thus attracting losses?

Is money lost because you are in and out of everything too quickly? Do you take wild chances now and worry about the outcome later? Do your compulsive buying habits cause losses? Have you been monetarily disappointed with your short-term investments? Did you go into the hole because you put all of your money into one thing?

Are you aware that there's never an end to what you want with investments? Your demanding nature makes it impossible to satisfy your needs. When mistakes are made they are remembered, and you try a different approach the next time around. Whatever you do, you do with all of your might. Nothing is plunged into halfway. Your one-track mind makes you moody around loved ones. Your investments are kept secret, but if they knew about them they'd swear you were on a destructive kick.

Of course if you are a stamp collector, your family won't be seeing much of you because you may require privacy as you study each stamp and place it neatly in the book. Your obsession with philately can keep you broke because you want to own every single stamp in the world. When you look in a stamp book and see an empty space where a particular stamp is supposed to go, you may suddenly have an urge to own it just so it can be placed over its picture. Furthermore, you'll find a means to buy it, regardless of how expensive it may be. You could get so wrapped up in this hobby that you will ignore a business and everything else around you.

Commodity futures are something that turns you on with an excitement that is unequaled. You may buy a futures contract for two thousand dollars through your stockbroker for delivery of Government Mortgage Association certificates worth one hundred thousand dollars in, say, twelve months. If mortgage rates fall one percent during that period, the certificate's price would rise three and one-half times the investment (seven thousand dollars). So the killing in this fascinates you, but when you guess wrong and the interest rates only rise a mere three-tenths percent, you are wiped out, consequently losing your two thousand dollar investment. But you don't care, it's the possibility of a big bundle that makes you willing to risk a mere two thousand dollars.

Short selling in the commodity futures and options market is something you find extremely stimulating. You get all keyed up thinking your stock is going to go down in price by a specified date. As each day passes you become so excited that you can hardly stand it. The uncertainty and expectation of a huge profit is more thrilling to you than a car ride in a drag race. When the stock's price goes up, you lose all the money, bonds, stocks, or personal possessions you had put up in the margin account. And do you think that you are going to be cured after that? You're right, you aren't. You'll get another stake and be back for more fun and games. "And maybe this next time," you tell yourself, "I'll make enough to make up for previous losses and then some." Of course, this attitude isn't going to help you make a fortune.

WHAT SHOULD YOU INVEST IN?

Try to avoid taking too many chances with speculative ventures. Because you like quick returns on your money, follow a short-term policy with as many investments as is possible. Be out of everything within thirty, sixty, or ninety days, six months, or a year.

Buy short term Treasury bills or notes and keep rolling them over. Invest in municipal bonds and when they mature (in a year's time, if you get those kind), buy more. Purchase certificates of deposit from your bank and as they become due, continue to buy more. Invest in commercial paper (corporations that need to raise money float their notes and pay you back in thirty days if they are doing well) — but remember, it's risky because if a company isn't faring well and goes bankrupt, you'll be out your money.

If in the past you've gained through speculation, then continue along these lines; however, if the reverse holds true, stay away from speculation because you are expressing the Scorpio traits on their negative side and are likely to get a repeat performance. Abide by this rule with margin accounts and the other risky areas such as commodity futures, options, and investment notes (thrift certificates), etc.

You may be interested in purchasing shares of REIT's, which are traded on the stock market. These funds are partnerships that invest in pools of income-producing property. The partnerships are free to sell and realize gains on properties that have appreciated in value. They are risky and liquid; they leave the management to others; you're just buying the paper.

If you want to be practical (which you can be), it might be advisable for you to invest in some sure things. The fixed-income funds (money market funds, municipal bond funds, and municipal bond unit-investment trusts) make you feel safe. Ginnie Mae (Government National Mortgage Association) unit investment trusts are based on the most conservative strategy. In effect, they offer you a share in a pool of residential mortgages guaranteed by the government. The government puts its backing behind certificates sold to investors by securities dealers to raise funds for mortgage lenders such as banks and savings and loan associations.

Mutual funds are appealing to your sign, especially the high-yield bond ones and all insurance company mutual funds. Of course, the high-yield bond funds are not for the fainthearted; they are for gutsy people like you. They consist of low-rated or even unrated corporate bonds — the kind of securities usually labeled "junk bonds." They are risky.

Bonds and index funds are other investment areas you may consider. The short-term corporate bonds appeal to your "hurry, hurry" mood. The index funds are designed to move along with market indicators like Standard & Poor's five hundred stock index. They are based on the theory that matching the market averages will produce better long-run performance than the efforts of money managers. That's something for a Scorpio to think about.

In the collectibles you like Oriental rugs, furniture, and vases as well as sculpture, paintings, stamps, and historical documents. Or perhaps you saved or inherited a Captain Midnight decoder, offered as a radio premium in 1941 for a few Ovaltine labels and a three-cent stamp, which recently sold for seventy-five dollars? In the contemporary print you prefer the engraving and etching type which is called the intaglio process.

Because you have an insatiable appetite, perhaps you'd like to invest in a fast-food franchise? Or you may go into a cable-television franchise. Whatever it is that you buy, you will own a chain of them before you're through investing.

To offset your chances of being in a poor position if a recession occurs, and due to your speculative nature, you should consider investing in some form of annuity: fixed-income refund annuity, fixed-rate annuity, or tax-deferred annuity. Or perhaps you'd like an endowment retirement policy?

Perhaps you'd like to invest in the gem your sign rules — the topaz. Or what about the stones ruled by Scorpio? — bloodstones, lodestone, vermilion, and carnelian. Buy shares in this jewel or these stones, purchase your own mine, or go into them as a business.

In the foreign-bond market your sign is attracted to the Scorpio-ruled countries of Belgium, Brazil, or Hungary. Perhaps you'd like to invest in Brazil's foreign-currency market?

You may not have time to keep abreast of the trends and what's happening in the world, but if you do you are one step ahead when it comes to investing wisely. If you decide to seek the advice of a broker, perhaps one of these signs is for you.

A broker who thinks along the same lines as you may be desirable. Therefore deal with another Scorpio, Aries, Gemini, Leo, Sagittarius, Aquarius, or Pisces. These signs will encourage those calculated risks that you must be aware of. They, like you, take chances. So from a strictly financial standpoint, they may not be the best signs for you to listen to or be involved with.

You really need a broker who is practical and able to provide the balance you so sorely need. Therefore, consider Capricorn, Taurus, and Virgo. They are the best suited for safe and sound investments. Their slowness may bug you, but deep down you'll appreciate their wanting to do the right thing by you.

Cancer and Libra may appeal to you because they are interested in both safe and risky investments. However, they may be too indecisive for you. If you are lucky, you might find a broker who is an Aries, Aquarius, Gemini, Leo, Sagittarius, or a Pisces, or another Scorpio Sun sign and this individual *may also have* Taurus, Virgo, or Capricorn as a *dominant* sign in his/her horoscope. If this occurs you'll have the best of two worlds: One who is inclined to speculate but who uses sound judgment.

Astrology can guide you in the type of bonds your sign should consider investing in. In the municipal-bond area there are special tax bonds, which are payable from some specific source of revenue such as a single tax or series of taxes which are Scorpio-ruled bonds. Other municipals are the tax-exempt revenue bonds: For your sign it's the one that deals with drainage and sewerage systems. Iron and steel companies are likewise attractive to you.

Because everything in life has an astrological correspondence each type of corporate bond, stock, or commodity has a sign/planet that rules it. Therefore, under the Scorpio/Pluto influence, invest in manufacturing corporations that produce radio, TV, CD's, video discs/tapes, or cassette tapes, tape recording machines, transistors, phonograph records, hi-fi or stereo equipment, walkie-talkies, intercoms, cables, microwaves, X-rays, radioactive materials, plutonium, chemicals, or caskets.

Other Scorpio/Pluto-ruled areas are firms that deal with medical health programs or the medical field: research companies that deal in medicine and/or cures for disease; medical electronics, nuclear medicine, makers of medical devices, or medical supply companies. Or those companies which are involved with radar, atomic energy, or nuclear power projects and plants. Or firms that manufacture equipment for undersea or one that does research under the ocean, drills underneath, or one that uses experimental ocean farming labs, underground equipment like putting down cable, pipelines, sewers, submarines, or pork bellies in the commodity futures market might appeal to you.

Also, you may find these Scorpio/Pluto-ruled areas a delight: stock in companies that deal with detective agencies, missing persons businesses, liquor, credit, insurance, mortgages, brokerage firms, savings and loan associations, tax preparers, operators of barge fleets, missiles, communications equipment for cable television and satellites, earth stations, and stimulating soft drink beverages that contain caffeine.

HOW TO HANDLE YOUR INVESTMENTS

You should seek safe and sure areas rather than the speculative ventures you favor. There are large gains to be made in many sure things and, in the process, your pocketbook won't suffer. Be leery of jumping into a new project; get the facts and statistics and study them before investing. Think about the possible losses that could occur.

Over-the-counter stocks, new issues, and stocks in general appeal to the gambler in you. Also commodity futures with Treasury bills and notes futures as well as speculating on dollar fluctuations in currency futures. They are all very risky with margin calls; so take care you don't spend more than you can afford to lose.

A margin account allows you that chance you need to make those enormous sums of money that you desire. But if you put your home up for chattel, you could lose it on one wrong move. You may become so preoccupied with the desire to make riches overnight that you fail to see all the disadvantages of such an action.

If you analyze every step before it's taken, it can save you headaches and debts later. Find out how much you can afford to lose; ask an accountant. Perhaps you'll want to invest in blue-chip stocks and set aside some gambling money for your real risk-taking investments. You don't like listening to anyone, but you should pay attention to the accountant or investment counselor. Perhaps you'll learn something valuable that might help you gain more money than you had anticipated.

Curb your impatience in all investment areas. Don't leap in and out; consistent effort should be sought if you wish to stay ahead of the game. You really do need something you can't convert too quickly into cash because you'll spend it. However, it's best to be as liquid as possible with bonds, stocks, cash-value life insurance, or even a pension.

A savings account is too tempting for you to touch. Money would be withdrawn when the urge strikes. If you do want to have a savings account, use several banks that are not too handy for you to get to.

Buy as many long-term durables, tools, raw materials, replacement parts, etc., as you can, even if you have to buy them retail. Then, if a bad period comes and prices are higher, you can make a profit with your goods. You could even use them for bartering if need be.

Are you a winner or loser? It not only depends upon your Sun sign and how you use it, but also on the influence of Jupiter and Saturn. Jupiter attracts a gain, whereas Saturn attracts a loss. Everyone has these planets in his/her horoscope. But their influence depends upon whether their harmonious or inharmonious side is expressed at the moment a decision is made.

Under the influence of the positive side of Saturn, you are practical, conservative, cautious, serious, contemplative, and make a move only when you are sure the time is ripe. Long-range investments are favored. You use sound judgment, and thus can buy to advantage.

Under the influence of the negative side of Saturn you are pessimistic and cry poverty; you worry, gripe, complain, and have the blues. You are slow because you are afraid of making the wrong move, and thus can attract losses. You lack confidence and chances are if you purchase anything, it could be a real downer.

Whenever you are depressed and feel the Saturn negative traits, avoid investing in anything, because your Saturn is being stimulated in your horoscope at that moment (this could last an hour, a day, a week, a month, a year, or more). If you do invest when this inharmonious energy is being expressed, you are likely to attract a loss.

Under the influence of the positive side of Jupiter you are confident, optimistic, cheerful, easygoing, honest, understanding, happy, and generous. Speculation is favored and brings success. You use sound judgment and can sell to an advantage, take options, buy on margin, and do well all around.

Under the influence of the negative side of Jupiter you are overly confident, too optimistic, wasteful, ostentatious, extravagant, and refuse to take into account prices, expenditures, or the views of others. You are in the mood to do everything to excess. At a party you'd be on center stage making everyone laugh. If you sell an investment when you are in this frame of mind you won't get the price it's worth; your judgment will be off.

Whenever you discover you are using the negative side of Jupiter, don't take a chance with the stock market or any other form of investment. Lie low and wait until the positive side of Jupiter is being expressed, then sell. It'll be worth the wait.

In astrology *buying* is ruled by Saturn and *selling* by Jupiter. Every time you buy under a harmonious Saturn aspect your purchase will be a bargain, a good deal, or investment. Every time you sell under a harmonious Jupiter aspect your sale will be a considerable gain. The moment these planets are activated in your horoscope are determined by your time, place, day, month, and year of birth. But you don't need a horoscope to know when you are in a depressed state or happy mood. By being aware of your frame of mind, you'll know how to invest wisely. The moment the negative side of Jupiter, Saturn, or Scorpio is expressed, that's the time to watch out for losses; the reverse if true when their positive side is expressed.

Now that you are armed with this information you can invest wisely and be ready for whatever the world economy brings. However, you are one step further ahead than the majority of people because by using this positive energy you can improve your chances to be wealthy.

CHAPTER NINE

Sagittarius — Money and Investments

Those born from November 22 through December 21 have the Sun in the sign Sagittarius. Every sign of the zodiac corresponds to a particular type of prosperity; it's what you do and how you use it that determines whether you'll be successful or not.

Do you want to wind up in a mess because of your extravagant spending habits? Instead, wouldn't it be better if you could prevent losses, shortages, and hardships? By knowing your faults and how to correct them you can enjoy life more, save money, and, be in tip-top shape. And that's well worth making a few changes for, isn't it?

YOUR MONEY

Money disappears as fast as it comes in. Your sign is known as the "Extravagant Spender of the Zodiac." You have an "easy come, easy go" attitude. If you don't have a dime in your pocket for tomorrow, you really don't care because you know that you'll be saved at the last moment. And you usually are.

Anyone going shopping with you needs roller skates. When you pass counters in a store, you glance quickly at the merchandise. If something catches your eye it's immediately grabbed and purchased without a second look, and without worry over the cost.

You go on shopping sprees and usually don't limit your buying to one dress or pair of pants: It's got to be five or six. You have expensive tastes and buy what you like rather than what you can afford. Your generosity shows every day in some way. Your friends and loved ones are given so many presents you spoil them rotten.

Money is spent on sports, travel, and fun, and donated to a church or charity, or to a poor beggar on the street. You are also known as the "Philanthropist of the Zodiac." Good deeds are done for others without thought of recompense. You give — give — give more than any other sign; not only of your money, but of your time and talent, like Sagittarians Ossie Davis and the late Frank Sinatra. On one occasion, when I was in the company of Frank Sinatra, he gave a one-hundred dollar bill to a little old man who sells newspapers in the street. Frank never took one paper.

The fancy restaurants are attended: You stuff yourself on rich, gourmet food and drink the finest of wines. No wonder you have a weight problem. And you don't mind picking up the tab for a whole group of people, as Mr. Sinatra did.

The late Ava Gardner once told me, "Sagittarius is the luckiest sign of the Zodiac." And she's right. It's because you have faith that all will work out for the best. Your eternal optimism makes you send out positive thoughts and whatever is sent out is what is returned. Some wealthy Sagittarians were Andrew Carnegie,

J. Paul Getty, who was called the richest man in the world, and the Aga Khan, who was supposed to be worth his weight in gold.

There's a positive and negative side of Sagittarius and if the positive side is expressed you have a better chance of winding up on top of the heap, as millionaires Robert Woodruff and Philip K. Wrigley did.

Your Positive Side

Do you tirelessly search for new areas to make a buck? If so, do you find them? Is money earned by quickness of decision and action? Have you gained financially because you expanded a business? Do you feel the sky's the limit as to what you can earn in your lifetime? have your enthusiastic ideas paid off at the bank? If you answered the preceding questions with a "yes," you are using the harmonious traits you are known for and, as a result, prosperity can be more easily attracted.

Are you aware that your share-the-wealth attitude makes your money return threefold? When you encourage and assist others to reap profits from the cash you give (not lend) to them, someday, in some way, that wonderful humanitarian endeavor will pay off with enormous sums falling right into your lap. But that thought doesn't enter your mind; all you care about is that your pal should make a big bundle.

Often financial gains come because you are guided by your feelings. Call it intuition, ESP, or whatever — but when it hits, you get so carried away with your plans that everyone around you gets caught up in the whirl. And there's no mountain too high for you to climb, nor shore too far to travel, because you are going to make it all the way to the top.

And once those dollars come flowing in, you will risk them in bigger game. You are never content to sit on your behind and do nothing; your restless nature won't allow that. So it's on to one venture after another and your zeal and vivaciousness show regardless of what money-making scheme you become involved in.

You never look back. That arrow (ruled by your sign) is always pointed upward. It's only the future and the promises it holds that you are interest in: new worlds, new people, new gains, new truths. Yes, you are a seeker and will find that which will prove financially as well as spiritually rewarding.

Your pals are numerous and increase daily. A friendly smile draws others to you. You spread good cheer to all those who are fortunate enough to be in your company. Laughter is contagious. Is it any wonder that those who know you want to be around you all of the time? You are in touch with all the right people. So when a favor is needed you contact them. Through their good will and connections a deal is consummated. And those greenbacks come flowing in as if they were falling from out of the sky.

Your impulsiveness takes you down many fascinating lanes and byways. To you *all* paths are paved with gold. Is that because you are wearing those rose-colored glasses again? Or is it because you believe that an individual can get anything he/she wants if he/she has faith and confidence? It's a little bit of both: but it's your belief in God that makes you strive onward and upward to reach the pinnacle of success that you know is waiting for you, if only you give it a try.

You're a great sports fan as well as player. But you're also a gambler and spend a lot of cash on the horse races (your sign is represented by a centaur — half man, half horse). You like to make large bets and get emotionally involved as the horse comes around the bend. And when you win you jump up and down with such joy and excitement that it's hard to quiet you. That wad of money you won may be equally divided between your buddies, a poor family, and the bank. You say, "There's more where that came from," and there always is.

You'll take a chance on whatever you believe in. In fact, you'll risk every dime you have. Generally you can sense if a business opportunity is going to pay off. You think in terms of billions and millions rather than thousands of dollars. Everything you touch is done on a large scale — remember the late Sagittarian Walt Disney with his fabulous Disneyland?

Everything that could possibly be in an office is in yours. It's brimful of everything you may or may not need. You like to be well prepared in case of an emergency. Money is spent readily on all the latest computers or machinery. You buy the most expensive brand because you believe that if you pay for the best, that's what you'll get. It's quality that you go for regardless of whether the expenditure is for business or for personal reasons.

A financial problem may arise, which is not surprising with the way you go on spending escapades. But it's dismissed about a minute later. You have more important things to do with your time than to be concerned over a few bucks. Because you don't give it negative attention, it soon disappears.

Your Negative Side

Do you take chances with money and gamble on something you believe in? If so, do you sometimes take a dive? Do you laugh your way through one financial disaster after another? Does your optimism blind you to the realities of the financial world? Does failure result? if you answered the preceding questions with a "yes," you are using the inharmonious traits you are known for and, as a result, it's difficult to attract prosperity.

Do you spend money before it arrives? Are your dollars lost because you decided and acted too quickly? Did expanding in business cost you a pretty penny? If so, was it a poor move? Do you have a complete disregard for the value of a dollar? Are you overly confident with all financial transactions?

Are you guided by your feelings in business deals? Generally you allow yourself to be so carried away by your instincts that you don't take time to analyze anything or listen to reason if somebody gives you advice. And when those bucks go down the drain, you wonder how you ever could have been so stupid.

You allow others to impose on your generosity because you're a good sport and don't mind parting with a dime. But this becomes a pattern because word gets around that you are a fool, and so you get used time and again. It does disturb you and with each occurrence you say, "I've learned my lesson. This will never happen again." But, unfortunately for your pocketbook, this isn't the case and may never be unless you change your ways.

A con artist sees you coming a mile away. Because you are honest and never suspect that others are dishonest, you trust them wholeheartedly with every penny you own. You are likely to part with some dollars on some enormous scheme that's going to make you rich overnight.

You are a prankster from the word go. The price you pay for a laugh is costly to you as well as others. "It's all in fun," said the late Frank Sinatra as he cut up the necktie of his pal Joe E. Lewis, and threw his jacket out the window down into the river. Oh, the next day Frank bought Joe E. several new neckties. Or what about the coffee shop Frank and his buddies destroyed for a hilarious and frolicking time? So the restaurant owner got reimbursed double for what everything was worth. (All of these antics I witnessed when in the company of the late Frank Sinatra.)

Your unwise impulses can keep your bank account down to zero. As a rule you are in a hurry and don't take the time to do any comparison shopping. If it's a new watch you want, you grab one, two, or three that you like. If it's new office equipment, you act just as quickly, only you restrict your purchase to one item. Later you may discover that you were overcharged. What's your reaction? "Oh, well, I guess the seller needed the money more than me. I'm glad I helped him out."

You look forward with great eagerness to a day at the track. The excitement of it all races through your blood. You are a high roller and will splurge your whole paycheck on one horse, if you believe in that filly. You go home broke, but you have enjoyed yourself and that's all that counts, isn't it? But your problem is that this happens several times a month so you are never able to get out of a financial rut.

Your living quarters are luxurious. The rent is enormous. You live high on the hog and enjoy every indulgent moment of it. If a home has only the bare necessities, you get depressed. To make sure your abode isn't like this you cover the walls with paintings, mirrors, sconces, etc. When you are through there isn't much space left between things. Because you buy expensive furniture, accessories, and everything else, you are head over heels in debt.

A lot of dough is shelled out for all those hobbies you take up and discard. One month you are into stamp collecting because it satisfies your wanderlust. However, you're too impatient to take the time to put them neatly in place. Instead they are stuck in so fast that you ruin a stamp's value. The next month you've decided to take up photography; expensive equipment is bought and used for a short period and left forgotten.

Then, after one tennis lesson, you're all gung-ho, so, you have to buy several complete tennis outfits. Why? Because you can't play if you aren't dressed for the occasion! And what about those ski clothes now that you've taken that up during the winter months? And so it goes with your pocketbook: one expenditure after another.

Because those foreign lands beckon, you must go skiing in the Alps. So off you go, not counting the cost of your long holiday weekend. Your summer vacations are spent hopping from one country to another. You see them quickly — one or two days in each exotic locale. How expensive are these trips? They cost you everything you had saved for that rainy day.

Spending more than you make is a big problem of yours. You should learn how to handle your money in case a recession occurs.

HOW TO HANDLE YOUR MONEY

Wouldn't you like to avoid those few moments of depression when you worry about where your next meal is coming from? Have you ever thought that you could prevent this from occurring? Are you spending every dime you have on fun and pleasure? Wouldn't it be great if you could have a nest egg to fall back on when those emergencies strike — or what about for your retirement years?

Are you broke most of the time just because you have high living expenses? Do your reckless and wild decisions put you into a hole financially? Wouldn't it be great if you didn't have any debts? Does your cash go out on frivolities?

If you answered "yes" to the preceding questions these are some of the areas you've got to work with and change. You are an adaptable person so you could get rid of your old bad spending habits and develop good new ones. It's going to be strange for you to save, rather than splurge. But it'll be easy once you become accustomed to it.

You should save your money until you can afford the item desired, rather than spending money you really don't have. Cut up and throw out all charge cards: They make it too easy for you to go into debt because you know that the funds are available for you to use at any time. And when you go shopping, even though you think it's for one outfit, it never ends up that way. You have difficulty controlling your impulses.

The moment the urge hits to untie your purse strings, you should immediately think about what happened the last time you opened your pocketbook and blew every cent you had on something you later gave away to a pal. Generally you never remember, or look back to the past, so if you want to avoid future money problems, you must learn to recall the days of yore.

It's going to be difficult for you to live within your means, but it's a necessity if you are going to wind up with a sizable bank account.

You can still throw away some of your dollars, but not all of them. If you can put aside a few dimes and nickels you may be surprised at how they add up to larger amounts. Get a piggy bank that you can't break open and put all of your change in it. When it's full, use this cash to scatter to the winds on some frivolous notion.

Think twice the next time you're in the mood to shoot your whole wad on some horse. Bet only a small amount. Never gamble with money you can't afford to lose. If you pour everything into this one area, you'll continue to be in hock up to your ears. Your dough should be spread around: some in the bank, investments, etc. Set aside a gambling allowance; *never* touch a cent above it — once you do, you're a goner!

You are extremely giving with whatever you have in your wallet. Often your generosity is unappreciated by a buddy. Apply intelligence and analyze exactly what you are doing and whether you are making your funds a crutch for the other party. You don't have to buy your friends because everyone enjoys your companionship. You won't lose a genuine pal, if you say no to his/her request for a handout. Your loved ones will still care for you if you don't buy them gifts all the time. When you spoil them, they take you for granted. Surprise them, now and then, and watch how much nicer and happier they are when the presents are not given as frequently.

Before you leap into buying the first sumptuous home you see, ask yourself whether you will be able to keep up with the mortgage payments, furnish it lavishly (how else would you do it?), and still be able to have enough money to squander on the riotous living you feel you must indulge in. If you go ahead, expect to be in a financial bind for the rest of your life — unless you sell it, increase your income, or make some sort of change in your life-style. If you decide against it, purchase a duplex and live in one part and rent the other. That way the rent you earn could pay for the monthly installment payments on your mortgage. And you'd have a few bucks to dissipate on a fling.

When buying a new computer or any equipment in business, check out the details of the machinery. Don't go according to its fancy price, but find out how it performs. Call a few of your competitors (with you they are pals because you don't believe in being competitive — you have a share-the-wealth attitude, remember?) and ask them if they've had any experience with a particular brand and get their opinion. Then talk it over with an accountant and see whether your budget allows you to purchase it.

When business opportunities arise, don't leap in without first having all the pros and cons weighed by an accountant. Plan and analyze a method of action rather than blindly relying upon chance that all will turn out well.

Keep a record of every expenditure you make, even if it's just a Popsicle. Review your outlays of cash. Use care with finances and try to avoid extravagant display. Being lavish or wasteful isn't practical, and the new budget you are going to have doesn't include room for pouring money down the drain.

Because you are the type who always looks ahead, start a financial plan that will let you enjoy yourself now and when you are older or retired. A budget is a necessity, even though it goes against your grain. Restrict some of your expenses now and dream about all that money you'll have later on.

Write down your earnings, how much you need for rent, telephone, utilities, medical, dental, and transportation (include car insurance but not payments). Figure your clothing disbursements, food bills, entertainment, recreation, and gifts bought throughout the year and any other miscellaneous items you can think of —

these are the areas you can cut down on in order to save money and/or invest it wisely. Put aside seven percent of your earnings, or more, in savings or investments.

List the money you pay out in loans, credit cards, or charge accounts. Pay them off as fast as you can; you'll save a lot of interest — possibly enough to buy a small trinket with. Set aside a small (and I do mean small) amount for gambling, although you really should lump this into your recreation expense account.

Don't go overboard with entertainment expense. Use moderation whenever possible. Go to inexpensive places. Try free concerts or those that don't cost much. Don't go to the movies or the theater every night of the week: Go less often. The same applies for those sporting events you love. Don't pick up the tab, unless you can afford to; go Dutch treat with your buddies.

Keep your hobby expenditures down; rent whenever feasible. Don't pay through the nose for something you could have rented. Indulge in the sports you love: skiing, horseback riding, tennis, quoits, softball, baseball, archery, and basketball. Hike in a forest or woods, climb a mountain, go camping, jump rope, roller skate, or try the skateboard.

Keep your weight down with some gymnastics, calisthenics, or bicycling, or go to a disco dance or roller disco. Play Ping-Pong, Monopoly, throw darts, and pitch horseshoes — all ruled by your sign. So you see, you can still have a good time without a huge outlay of cash.

Earn extra income by entering tournaments or contests, or by engaging in wholesale trade, especially of Bibles (ruled by your sign). Those spare moments could be used beneficially rather than wasted.

Look at your budget every day so you don't forget about it; you're the type who will. And the hardest part for you is *to stick with the budget.* Get your friends to go on one, too; then it'll be easier for you to abide by it. If you want wealth, it must come through systematic planning, sacrificing, and saving. And with wealth, you won't have to worry about a recession.

YOUR INVESTMENTS

You can benefit by setting aside money now so your future will be secure. Or perhaps you prefer investing in something other than a business. However, before you go leaping into any undertaking, it would be to your advantage to understand your assets and shortcomings, thereby avoiding pitfalls.

Your Positive Side

A "yes" answer to any of the following questions indicates that you are expressing harmonious Sagittarius traits, thus enhancing your chances to gain prosperity. Do you have unbounding faith in your good luck with investments? Have you always been right? Will you take chances and gamble on something you believe in? If so, do you come out ahead? Have you been able to accurately foresee stock market trends? Is money gained through quick decisions and actions in investment areas? Do you get carried away with an investment and talk your friends into jumping in, too?

Are you aware that your lucky streaks with the stock market and other investments come through your being guided by your instincts? Your highly intuitive nature impels you to take a risk so a huge profit will be made. Also, a lot of your good fortune comes through the goodwill of others. You're on the inside track because you have the right contacts and pay attention to those tips you get.

You absolutely adore speculation and want to clean up, making millions overnight. Everything has to have a short-term maturation because you are in a hurry to make large gains right away. You are far too impatient to wait around for years for long-term maturation to pay off.

If your investments aren't moving fast enough for you, you'll sell them and get into something that is escalating. You're the type who buys a stock today and three days later, when it's gone up a few points, gets out and purchases something new only to sell it the moment it goes up enough to satisfy you.

Because you want everyone to make a buck, the moment you hear about a terrific investment, you excitedly tell all your friends that it'll make them rich. Your enthusiasm is so contagious that everyone jumps on the bandwagon. You're riding up front with the most money on the line. And when the urge to sell strikes, you encourage your buddies to do the same. Luckily, you all profit by your foresight.

You enjoy going to the auction with a group of pals. It's easy for you to get carried away with something you like. Naturally you are going to pay through the nose when you bid an exorbitant amount for a rare book to add to your already vast collection.

The commodity futures market is a game of chance that turns you on, every stimulating and nerve-wracking moment of it. You enjoy the risk as the prices fluctuate hourly. Your flexibility is exercised to the limit. You delight in predicting when the stock is going to go down in price. And, when it does, that big pile of money gained is right up your alley. And to think you only had to put up a fifteen percent deposit on a margin account to get back such a large return!

Your Negative Side

A "yes" answer to the following questions indicates that you are expressing the inharmonious Sagittarius traits, thus lessening your chances to gain prosperity: Are you overly confident of the gains you are going to make through your investments? Did you take a dive because you took a chance on something you believed in? Is money lost because you jump in too fast?

Do you have difficulty meeting those margin calls? Have you been wiped out because you didn't? Are you guided by your feelings with investments? As a result, do you wind up behind the eight ball? Do you buy something at an auction only to sell it later at a discount just because you grew tired of it? Will you sell property you own to the first buyer, and at a loss, because you've lost interest in it?

Are you aware that you continue to make the same mistakes because you never learn your lesson? You tend to live for tomorrow, therefore what the market is doing for today is not considered; nor do you think about what it did last week when you almost lost your shirt. You plunge in with the thought of winning the goose that lays the golden egg; however, the eggs turn out rotten. And what do you say to that? — "I don't care!"

Your restless nature gets you into financial hot water in the investment arena. This desire for change, because you're bored and feel you're in a rut, makes you compensate by doing something wild and crazy. So what do you do? It's anyone's guess — but when these moods strike, your money is likely to be scattered to the winds. And, what's more, you won't even try to catch a fifty-dollar bill as it flies through the air. Why? Because you are too busy borrowing some loot to put down on a piece of land you heard about somewhere in the middle of the desert.

And then there's the silver mine you decided to invest in. What happened to it a year later? You decided you couldn't be bothered making any more trips to dig a few pieces of silver out. After all, it took a year to get an ounce, so perhaps you'd been given a bum steer. So you gave it to that old man you felt sorry for because he had been prospecting for gold and wasn't doing so well.

You tend, because you are honest, to believe in other people so much that your gullibility puts you into the red. That mail-order business you thought was going to make you rich turned out to be nothing more than a fraud. Your merchandise was never shipped after you paid for it. And when you had it investigated, the place had folded and the man operating it had skipped with your money. "Oh, well" you say, "I can't win them all."

And what about the horse you bought when you thought you'd enter the racing business? After all the upkeep expense and training that went into your pet project, the filly lagged behind and came in last at the race. There went your betting money and great potential income. So instead of selling the horse, you gave it to some kid. At the rate you're going you could end up behind the eight ball.

WHAT SHOULD YOU INVEST IN?

If you want to make a profit you should stay clear of too many speculative ventures. To compensate and keep you in your usual cheerful mood, your best bet is to follow a short-term policy in the investment field. Then you can see your money working for you when the returns come rolling in. Therefore, be in and out of everything within thirty, sixty, or ninety days or in some cases within twelve months.

Purchase a house and sell it a year later. Buy ninety-day Treasury bills or notes and keep rolling them over. Invest in municipal or corporate bonds that mature in a year. Purchase six-month certificates of deposit from your bank.

Perhaps a contemporary print made from a woodcut would appeal to you as a collectible. Or invest in commercial paper (these are thirty- to ninety-day unsecured notes sold by major corporations who want to raise money — they are risky).

Investment notes, also called thrift certificates, vary in risk and are not insured, but give some high yields. They are issued by finance companies.

What about a stock and bond fund? They can be risky but emphasize capital gains. High-yield bond funds are low or unrated corporate bonds — the kind of securities usually called "junk bonds" — risky, but you like that. And there is diversity (another feature that appeals to your desire for change) in a big fund's portfolio. Or to keep you occupied switching back and forth, try a no-load bear or bull fund in the mutual fund department. You will be encouraged to switch your assets back and forth, at no charge. You should go for that!

Foreign currency futures are your "baby" because they are so changeable and can make you enormous profits. But you must guard against getting too carried away with the amount of chattel put up. If in the past you've gained through this, or any other form of speculation, then continue along these lines; however, if the reverse holds true, stay away from this because you are expressing the Sagittarius traits on their negative side and are likely to get a repeat performance. Also, abide by this rule with margin accounts.

If you can't afford to take a risk in foreign-currency futures (and you shouldn't unless you can afford to lose whatever you pledge), or to open an overseas savings account, or to invest in Eurodollars, then try foreign currency traveler's checks. They are good for the novice dealing in relatively small amounts of money because they are inexpensive, convenient, and nearly as liquid as cash. Plus, there is no time limit on redemption with the Swiss ones. If you are planning a trip to Switzerland to ski the Alps, buy the Swiss currency traveler's checks. When you return home you may get more dollars back for leftover checks than you originally paid for them because the dollars decreased while you were away (from the time you bought them to your return date). Unless you want to hang on to them as an investment.

Make use of your friendly personality by collecting autographs of celebrities from the fields of sports, movies, music, stage, television, politics. Sell them later at a profit. Invest in art and tapestries as the late Sagittarian J. Paul Getty did. Or collect rare books: One four-volume set of books sold for $396,000. Perhaps you'll get lucky and buy something cheap that later turns out to be priceless! Invest in a sports team or contribute to the Olympic team.

Perhaps you'd like to invest in the gems your sign rules — red garnet, jade, and turquoise? Or do you prefer the Sagittarian stones which are mixed with red and green? Buy shares in these jewels or stones, purchase your own mine, or go into them as a business.

Options funds can be risky, but you can achieve greater income return with less price volatility. These funds sell call options on stocks they own. Or for safety, why not try government funds: They are for six and nine months and are backed by the government.

To offset your chances of being in a poor position as inflation rises, and due to your speculative nature, invest in some form of annuity which is designed to provide future security. Deferred annuities may appeal to you if you are in a high tax bracket. Or, because you have wanderlust for foreign lands, try the deferred Swiss franc annuity.

In the foreign-bond market, your sign could be attracted to the Sagittarius-ruled country of Venezuela. Or does Venezuela's currency appeal to you? If so, invest in it.

You don't always have time to keep abreast of world affairs which would be helpful when involved with investing. Perhaps it would be to your advantage to seek the advice of an expert in the commodity or stock market field, or an all-around investment counselor may suffice.

A broker who thinks along the same lines as you may be desirable. Therefore, deal with another Sagittarius, Aries, Gemini, Leo, Scorpio, Aquarius, or Pisces. These signs, however, will encourage those calculated risks that you must beware of. They, like you, take chances. So from a strictly financial standpoint they may not be the best signs for you to listen to or be involved with.

You really need a broker who is analytical, practical, and able to provide the balance you so sorely need. Therefore, consider Capricorn, Taurus, and Virgo. They are the best suited for safe and sound investments. However, don't be surprised if you disagree with them. Their slowness may bug you. But it's good for you to slow down once in a while. By the way, Cancer and Libra are too indecisive for you and that might just drive you up the wall.

If you are lucky you might find a broker who is an Aries or a Gemini, a Leo, a Scorpio, another Sagittarius, an Aquarius, or a Pisces Sun sign and this individual *may also have* Capricorn, Taurus, or Virgo as a *dominant* sign in his/her horoscope. If this occurs you'll have the best of two worlds: One who is inclined to speculate but who uses sound judgment.

Astrology can guide you in the type of bonds your sign should consider investing in. Therefore, be on the alert for the Sagittarius/Jupiter-ruled municipal bonds that deal with colleges and universities, as well as firms that deal with cable, broadcasting, shipping, the courts, or the government.

Because everything in life has an astrological correspondence, each type of corporate bond, stock, or commodity has a sign/planet that rules it. Therefore, under the Sagittarius/Jupiter influence invest in manufacturing corporations that produce gourmet food, spices, condiments, mustard, curry, butter, peanut butter, soybeans, corn, cable, or tin cans.

If these areas don't capture your interest try companies that produce corsets, exhibit stands, Bibles, luggage, tin, aluminum foil, golf balls, tennis rackets, jogging shoes, and other sports equipment. Or try stocks or bonds that deal with travel, publishing, advertising, broadcasting stations, international communications, satellites, telegraph, shipping, mercantile-importing/exporting, or overseas shares on the foreign stock exchange.

Other Sagittarius/Jupiter-ruled stock-and-bond areas are financial institutions (like banks — domestic or foreign), merchandising in general, religious items, sales corporations, promotion agencies, horses, breeding farms/stables, or items for horses and race tracks, or firms that give services for lawyers, the courts, government, or international market-commerce/trade.

The Sagittarius/Jupiter-ruled commodity futures areas are all the fats and oils; oil of coconut, corn, cottonseed, linseed, palm, peanut, soybean, grease, lard, butter, and tallow (bleachable, edible), as well as corn, coconut, and peanuts themselves. Also ruled by your sign and Jupiter are the foreign currency futures and interest futures.

HOW TO HANDLE YOUR INVESTMENTS

Conservative investments are frowned on by you, but they should be sought in preference to the many risky ventures that you favor. You can still make money from sure things; perhaps not as much as from the speculative ones, but over a period of time you will be in better shape for the higher cost of living in case a recession occurs.

Be leery of new projects, but satisfy your gambling nature with some new-issue and over-the-counter stocks. About other investments that you are unsure of, ask an accountant, lawyer, or investment counselor. Before investing, stop and think of the possible consequences in case a loss should occur: Ask yourself if you can afford to lose the money you want to invest.

Stay away from the so-called London options because you may be defrauded or lose everything if you don't guess right. When buying your sign's gemstone — the turquoise — be careful of those that are not genuine: Some are mixed with plastic and are dyed stones. For a fee the Gemological Institute of America will certify genuine turquoise.

When purchasing contemporary prints in the collectibles, do not buy anything that is not signed individually by the artist, nor anything that says "signed in stone." Have a dealer guarantee the authenticity of his prints in writing. Take the time to do this rather than rushing in and out of a gallery.

Try to stay clear of margin accounts. Don't buy something unless you can afford to pay for it. Excessive debts should be eliminated, especially with rising prices. Reinvest your stock dividend checks rather than living it up and having a ball with your profits.

Short-term bonds are generally considered the safest but lowest yielding. Long-term bonds are the riskiest and highest yielding. Curb your impatience in all investment areas. Consistent effort should be sought if you wish to reap financial rewards. And you do!

If you buy silver, take delivery; avoid silver futures because of the volatility and lack of liquidity — silver and gold are not really your "lucky thing." When you are investing in non-income producing assets such as real estate which doesn't produce spendable money, then you should also strive to accumulate an equal amount of liquid assets. This liquidity can be in the form of bonds, cash, stocks, cash-value life insurance, or even a pension.

Are you a winner or loser? It not only depends upon your Sun sign and how you use it, but also on the influence of Jupiter and Saturn. Jupiter attracts a gain, whereas Saturn attracts a loss. Everyone has these planets in his/her horoscope. But their influence depends upon whether their harmonious or inharmonious side is expressed at the moment a decision is made.

Under the influence of the positive side of Saturn, you are practical, conservative, cautious, serious, contemplative, and make a move only when you are sure the time is ripe. Long-range investments are favored. You use sound judgment, and thus can buy to advantage.

Under the influence of the negative side of Saturn you are pessimistic and cry poverty; you worry, gripe, complain, and have the blues. You are slow because you are afraid of making the wrong move, and thus can attract losses. You lack confidence and chances are if you purchase anything, it could be a real downer.

Whenever you are depressed and feel the Saturn negative traits, avoid investing in anything, because your Saturn is being stimulated in your horoscope at that moment (this could last an hour, a day, a week, a month, a year, or more). If you do invest when this inharmonious energy is being expressed, you are likely to attract a loss.

Under the influence of the positive side of Jupiter you are confident, optimistic, cheerful, easygoing, honest, understanding, happy, and generous. Speculation is favored and brings success. You use sound judgment and can sell to an advantage, take options, buy on margin, and do well all around.

Under the influence of the negative side of Jupiter you are overly confident, too optimistic, wasteful, ostentatious, extravagant, and refuse to take into account prices, expenditures, or the views of others. You are in the mood to do everything to excess. At a party you'd be on center stage making everyone laugh. If you sell an investment when you are in this frame of mind you won't get the price it's worth; your judgment will be off.

Whenever you discover you are using the negative side of Jupiter, don't take a chance with the stock market or any other form of investment. Lie low and wait until the positive side of Jupiter is being expressed, then sell. It'll be worth the wait.

In astrology *buying* is ruled by Saturn and *selling* by Jupiter. Every time you buy under a harmonious Saturn aspect your purchase will be a bargain, a good deal, or investment. Every time you sell under a harmonious Jupiter aspect your sale will be a considerable gain. The moment these planets are activated in your horoscope are determined by your time, place, day, month, and year of birth. But you don't need a horoscope to know when you are in a depressed state or happy mood. By being aware of your frame of mind, you'll know how to invest wisely. The moment the negative side of Jupiter, Saturn, or Sagittarius is expressed, that's the time to watch out for losses; the reverse is true when their positive side is expressed.

Now that you are armed with this information you can invest wisely and be ready for whatever the world economy brings. However, you are one step further ahead than the majority of people because by using this positive energy you can improve your chances to be wealthy.

CHAPTER TEN

Capricorn - Money and Investments

Those born from December 22 through January 19 have the Sun in the sign Capricorn. Every sign of the zodiac corresponds to a particular type of prosperity; it's what you do and how you use it that determines whether you'll be successful or not.

You'd like to wind up ahead of the game, wouldn't you? However, you tend to be overly cautious to the point of attracting losses. Instead, wouldn't it be better if you could prevent them, as well as hardships and negative thinking? By knowing your faults and how to correct them you can enjoy life more, save money, and, be in tip-top shape. And you find that appealing, don't you?

YOUR MONEY

You hang on to money tightly. It's as if you are afraid that it's going to slip out of your hands. Your sign is known as the "Conservative Sign of the Zodiac." Because you are fearful of poverty, you will do everything in your power to prevent its touching you. People might jest with you and say that you remind them of Ebenezer Scrooge from Charles Dickens's *Christmas Carol.* You may reply, "I'm just being practical."

When you go to a shop you move slowly, look over every item inside and out, touch it for durability, and jot down the price. Nothing is bought until you've compared prices in all the stores. You are a born bargain hunter and wait for special sale days to be announced. But you won't buy anything that's cheap unless it is made to last a long time.

If you have the right contacts, you will buy everything wholesale. Anything to save a penny. You are a necessity-minded spender. Nothing is purchased unless it is needed and can be useful. You have a horror of waste and can't stand to see someone spend foolishly. Your loved ones, friends, and children are *not* spoiled. Presents are given only on traditional dates such as birthdays, Christmas, and weddings, and even then it's because it's your duty to do so. However, in business, if it will bring a future gain, you are likely to buy gifts generously and whenever you deem necessary.

You don't like to part with anything: money, clothes, objects, all are saved. The old styles will return and you won't have to spend a dime to be right up with the latest fashion. The objects that you keep may be used in some way or another: You might save an earring or a shiny button and some old scraps of lace material and decorate your Christmas tree with them.

There's a motive behind your social activities. You want to meet people who can be useful to you in some way or another. Perhaps a particular individual could introduce you to someone important in your scheme of things. Those you take out are wined and dined in expensive restaurants. You like to impress people. The bill is scrutinized carefully because you don't trust anyone's arithmetic and because you dislike being cheated. And if it's a penny off, you'll mention it quietly. It's not the money that counts, it's the principle.

The desire to be safe and secure makes you drive yourself to the top of the ladder. You are extremely security conscious and will toil for the material rewards that are your ultimate goal in life. Along the way you will see to it that you receive the recognition craved.

You can amass a fortune, as the late Capricorn Aristotle Onassis did. If you lose it all, you'll try again and succeed. There's a positive and negative side of Capricorn, and if the positive side is expressed you have a better chance of staying on top financially.

Your Positive Side

Does your patience pay off with financial deals? Are you thrifty? Can you be counted on to hold up your end of a deal? Through applying your excellent reasoning abilities, have you been able to avoid monetary disasters? Do you quietly listen to the conversations of others, retain the knowledge, and later use it to make a buck? If you answered the preceding questions with a "yes," you are using the harmonious traits you are known for, and as a result, prosperity can be more easily attracted.

Will you refuse to budge if someone tries to talk you into investing in a get-rich-quick scheme? You are leery of anything that sounds too easy because you've had to work arduously for everything you've gained. Any con, swindle, fraud, or phony deal that comes along, you can spot immediately. You'll never be anyone's fool caught up in a web of deception.

You are an opportunist who will not let anything good pass by. But because you have a cautious nature, you will take your time before getting involved. If a substantial profit can't be gained, you won't even bother with it. You are the type of person who always seems to be in the right place at the right time. Perhaps it's because your sign rules "old father time."

The mountain goat is the animal that represents Capricorn. You can be as stubborn and persistent as the goat is when he tries to climb to the top of the mountain. It's a slow process to get there, but along the way nothing is overlooked. Every advantage is seized. If you fall down a step, that won't deter you from continuing to reach the top level. While going up the mountain, you make sacrifices, deny yourself pleasures, undergo long hours of hard labor, and all the time there is but one single thought on your mind — *success!* And it's usually yours!

You are the most ambitious sign of the zodiac and money comes pouring in because you put action behind those brilliant dreams. Your thoughts and ideas are lofty. Perhaps you think like Capricorn Diane Von Furstenberg. One day while walking down the street she asked Pearl Bedell, "Do you see that skyscraper? Someday I'll own one like that." And with that, Aries Pearl quipped back, "Someday I'll have an office in that building." It wouldn't surprise me if Diane buys the building some day. She is one of the most dynamic women of our times; she has achieved so much for one so young. I believe she makes a marvelous example that others should try to follow.

Money is gained because you use foresight in everything. The newest techniques and developments in your field are explored. Performance, efficiency, durability, and price are considered before you make a move. You won't purchase anything unless you can afford it.

Your ability to economize, cut down on costs, and inaugurate cost-saving methods, especially through reorganization, astounds those not acquainted with your methods. But profits result. On one occasion J. Paul Getty, who had Capricorn as one of his *dominant* signs (his ascendant, rising sign), decided to have a night inspection of wastepaper baskets in the huge skyscraper building he owned. He discovered that pencils, erasers, and other supplies were thrown out when they were still usable. New office supply rules at Getty Oil were put into effect which resulted in his saving five thousand dollars a year.

If you go on an interview and are offered a job that doesn't pay well you won't accept it if you have money saved in the bank. However, if you don't have a dime put away in a nest egg, you will take the position if it has good possibilities for advancement. If you do accept this low-paying salary, you'll work another job on the side and save every cent earned from these two sources of income. And then, when you've got enough greenbacks stashed away, you will be ready to bargain for a raise. Your ability to negotiate contracts and deals is one of your greatest talents.

Your sagacity might pay off as it did with the late Capricorn Helena Rubinstein when she built an empire and gained a fortune in the cosmetics industry. You are one who plans for the future and saves for stormy days ahead. You'd rather accumulate money than spend it. Though you are known to have your wild moments of extravagance, they don't last long because you bounce right back to being conservative.

You can account for every penny you have whether you are drunk or sober. The care of those dollars and cents is subconsciously ingrained. If you have one drink too many you can still handle yourself to wheel and deal in any financial matter. And the gains are just as fabulous as they are when you are not inebriated. It's that famous Capricorn know-how that makes you so successful.

Your Negative Side

Do you have an inferiority complex about your ability to make money? Are you constantly crying poverty? Do you feel you're limited in the amount of cash you can make and save? Have you lost a buck because you waited too long to take action?

Do you hunt for a bargain that consumes valuable time that could be spent in making dough? Have you many restrictions imposed upon you in relation to finances? Do you lose dollars because you are distrustful of everyone, thinking that they are going to take advantage of you? If you answered the preceding questions with a "yes," you are using the inharmonious traits you are known for, and as a result, it's difficult to attract prosperity.

Do you continually worry about money? You are so vastly concerned about every penny you have that you are afraid those greenbacks will stop coming in, or that someone is going to cheat you out of a buck. As a result of this negative attitude you not only lose a few nights' sleep, but golden opportunities are ignored.

You are a miser and hoard everything. It goes against your grain to keep you dough in circulation. Your fear of abject poverty makes you so miserable that others shun your company and then you wonder why you are alone and without many friends.

Your greed can be your downfall. Trickery may be employed to buy a business, property, or anything else you want. If there's a particular building you want to purchase and it's not for sale, you may have the owner's past investigated. Those skeletons in the closet are used to force the man into selling to you at your cheap price. But someday you may lose it all when someone pulls the same trick on you.

You could be the type who wants something for nothing. Perhaps there's a particular Broadway show you want to see but tickets are unavailable, or you don't want to shell out any bread, so you make use of an acquaintance who has a press pass. You call the theater and tell them you're a reporter from out of state who wants to review the show. The pass is hurriedly flashed, and you've seen a free show with orchestra seats to boot! But if the pass is scrutinized you could wind up in trouble for impersonation and be unjustly charged with theft. Of course, your pal will bail you out, but it may cost you a pretty penny.

If you are a really ruthless Capricorn, you could land in jail, especially if you get involved in some illegal activity. Opportunities are seized regardless of the nature of the business. Your fear of debt, and your ambition to have oodles of money, make you appear humble just so you can gain your ends.

People are used as stepping stones. The moment they are no longer of use to you they are discarded as if they were trash. For example, if you are looking for a backer to invest enormous sums of cash in a project of yours, you will use everyone you know to introduce you to one person after another until you find the party who will put up the desired money. And once found, those who helped you are forgotten. And when losses occur, and you are in need, you have the nerve to reacquaint yourself with all of those you turned your back on. And what do they do? They drop you like a ton of bricks! And you can't understand why!

You may be the type of Capricorn who makes a bundle of money only to spend it in drinking and riotous living, as the late legendary Capricorn Elvis Presley did. If you've done this and ended up broke, your poverty probably didn't last long because you can pull yourself up and try again. Often Capricorns repeat this several times during their lifetime.

Perhaps you've worked hard all of your life and saved your pennies by not enjoying the pleasures of life. You wonder why you haven't made it big. If you hang on to your money so tightly that you don't even trust a bank, you could lose out because you don't have your money working for you — it's lying dormant. Or it could be stolen if you've hidden it under the mattress or anything else in the house. If you gripe and complain about your lot in life, and are scared to take advantage of opportunities, you can remain a prisoner of your own greed and self-ishness.

If you marry for security, you'll push your husband to earn a larger income. You could manipulate and control the purse strings, especially if he's the spend-thrift type. If you become too cold blooded and money hungry, he could become so disillusioned that he divorces you; your alimony payment may be small. Or perhaps he stays with you and both of you lead an unhappy existence and, when he dies, you discover that you're in financial hot water because you've been left out of the will!

Dollars are lost because you're fearful or because you assume the heavy burdens and responsibilities of other people. You need to change your attitude to attract money and happiness into your life. Also, you should learn how to avoid monetary losses so you'll be prepared in case a recession occurs.

HOW TO HANDLE YOUR MONEY

Don't you think it would be great if you could laugh more often and give some life to a party instead of being so depressed about finances that you dampen everything? Doesn't it bother you a little to use people and wind up alone, without friends? Wouldn't it be better if you could still take advantage of others, but in such a way that they like you and you end up being surrounded by your pals?

Doesn't it bother you that you lose out on deals because you're overly cau-tious? Does your refusal to budge on a big money commitment cause a loss? Don't you think it would be to your benefit if you could learn to be more adaptable?

If you answered "yes" to the preceding questions, these are the areas you've got to work with and change. This will be an extremely arduous task because you are so stubborn that it will take extra work on your part. But nothing is impossible. You can do anything once you've made up your mind to it.

It's important that you remember that negative thoughts attract negative conditions. Every time you get depressed, sing the blues, and worry about money, those thoughts bounce back and make it difficult for you to attract money. Nega-tiveness repels success; positiveness attracts success.

When you get down in the dumps, take on more work and responsibilities. Be so busy that you don't have time on your hands to think — and watch those doldrums disappear. Take on an extra job or go to school and further your educa-tion so you can improve your position in life.

You are your own worst enemy, especially when you gripe and complain about how you suffer and have had it rougher than most people. Have you ever stopped to think that you've brought it upon yourself? Your desire for security makes you sacrifice in a relationship just so you can be financially solvent. And you may have to deprive yourself of something because avarice is your God. Did you know that others have a rough time, too? Only they don't talk about it, they try to make the best of all situations; an attitude you could learn from. Go out, smile, abandon your fears, and start to enjoy being part of the human race.

Don't be so cowardly that you stay in a rut all of your life making the same money, on the same job. Take a few nights a week to go to a special trade school. And once you've got a diploma, be gutsy and get a job in this new field. If you lack confidence, others will smell it, and you'll never get ahead.

If you want to make an extra buck, why not work in your spare moments in something that pays well? There are jobs in wholesaling by mail. Learn custom framing and do some for your acquaintances (for money, of course). If you're a good climber, make extra money scaling buildings for promotional tours. Hold garage sales or organize rummage sales for others, getting a fee for your services. You're good at chiseling wood and carpentry: Get involved in marketing home-crafted products.

If you're having a financial struggle, cut grocery bills by more than fifty percent by being a "refunder." Take advantage of the paltry cash refund and merchandise offers on food and home products. When they are added up, there are from eight hundred to one thousand available offers being made from just about every home product and food manufacturer. There are fine china, silverware sets, and even mink capes in these offers. That should really brighten your day. Watch the newspapers for grocery advertisements, flip some box tops, and plan your meals round them. You'll get variety, which is something a Capricorn needs and doesn't often get.

One of your greatest assets is your diplomacy. You can turn on charm, when you want something. But what about doing it all of the time? Instead of coldly dropping people because they are no longer of any use to you, continue to be friendly with them. Who knows, they may surprise you and give you a hot tip that could make you a lot of money.

Be more flexible and resist being so stubborn. Give an inch and maybe you'll get two. Learn to take chances; sometimes one has to take a risk to get ahead. After all, isn't life a gamble? Your over-cautiousness can hold you back from business transactions that could be profitable. If uncertain of offers, don't wait forever and a day to make your decision, consult an accountant and get his advice. Such an action could be to your advantage because it may make you move faster and not lose out on the deal.

If you don't have a budget, start one now. Write down your income, how much you need for the basic necessities (rent, utilities, telephone), food, medical, dental, life insurance, and transportation to and from work (including car insurance, but not payments). Figure out how much is spent on clothing, eating out, entertainment, recreation, and gifts bought throughout the year — these are the areas you can cut down on in order to save money and/or invest wisely. Figure to put aside seven percent of your earnings, or more, in savings or investments.

You probably don't have too many financial debts, unless you're the big-spending Capricorn — but if you do, list them and pay them off as fast as possible. Just think of all that interest you can save. The fact that it's costing you a pretty penny should make you wise up fast. If you have credit cards (most of you do, to impress others you deal with) cut up and throw out personal ones; with the business ones, pay the total sum when the bill arrives each month, thereby avoiding finance charges.

Don't keep your entertainment expenses down so low that life becomes dull. Go to free concerts, exhibits, the flea market, or to inexpensive shows and movies, and take in a few museums. Perhaps some square dancing could keep you in good shape. Or if you really want to let your hair down and be a wild Capricorn goat, go to a discotheque. Dance and let go of your inhibitions. The fun of it will improve your disposition and make your existence that much more bearable.

Go skiing, mountain climbing, rock hunting in the desert, hiking in the woods, or walking down a country lane. Play some golf, Ping-Pong, Monopoly (you'll probably own all of the hotels and collect rent from those who stop on your property). For your quiet moods, try some chess. You are great at maneuvering and strategy playing, and so should beat your opponent. Try your hand at shuffleboard or croquet — other Capricorn-ruled games. And they are all so inexpensive! Of course, golf might be the exception, unless you decide to buy an all-ivory chess set (ivory is ruled by your sign).

Outline in red ink your desires to save money, and underline in green ink your desires to have a good time (inexpensively, of course). Spend only according to your budget. Declare to yourself all the good things you want in life. Forget poverty, failure, and want and think only of financial freedom, success, and satisfaction. If you want wealth, vividly imagine it, ardently desire it, sincerely believe it will come to fruition, and enthusiastically act upon it and watch it come to pass.

YOUR INVESTMENTS

You can benefit by setting aside money now so your future will be secure. Or perhaps you prefer investing in something other than a business. However, before you go leaping into any undertaking, it would be to your advantage to understand your assets and shortcomings, thereby avoiding pitfalls.

Your Positive Side

A "yes" answer to any of the following questions indicates that you are expressing harmonious Capricorn traits, thus enhancing your chances to gain prosperity. Do you have your own system which is employed in all of your investment procedures? If so, does this always work to your advantage? Have you been able to correctly judge, through foresight, that a particular piece of land will be valuable in later years? If so, has this ability also proved profitable with stock, bond, and warrant purchases? Does your patience pay off with investments? Are you cautious in all areas of investing? If so, has this been beneficial?

Are you aware that you're a conservative investor? Risks are shunned; you want something that is safe and sure. When interest rates rise, you switch from long-term bond investments to short term; when the rates drop you switch back to short-term maturation. Your timing is so perfect that either way, you gain.

Those who know you swear that you have eyes in the back of your head. You seldom miss a thing. A hot tip is analyzed and if you think you can make a buck from it, you seize the opportunity to do so. If an investment is not moving the way you've calculated it should, you don't waste any time in getting out before a loss occurs. Usually your sagaciousness pays off time and again.

You come alive at a flea market because you enjoy bargaining. You're a natural-born negotiator and usually get the best deal. At an auction the faces of your competitors are studied as they make their bids. You patiently wait for the right moment before bidding. If you can't buy at the price you want and think it's worth, you'll let it go to someone else. You believe "a penny saved is a penny earned."

Your sound judgment brings the dough in when you buy warrants. Because you've got the patience to wait years for something to bear fruit, the warrants you hold bring you enormous profits when, later, the stock is much higher than what your warrant cost. As an example, you might have paid a dollar for something that is worth fifty dollars in a few years or less. Your friends may call you a prophet when this occurs, but you were born with an innate ability to fore-glimpse future business trends; seldom do you err.

Because you are an Earth sign you believe that anything connected with the earth has solidity; its value will appreciate in the coming years. Perhaps you are like the late Capricorn Howard Hughes who had enormous holdings in land. Generally prudence is your guide.

You are the type who can rent an unfurnished apartment, decorate it, sublease it at a higher price than you are paying on the lease, and live off the profits. Perhaps you have thirty different apartments in the big city that you collect rent on without owning the apartment. At this rate, it won't be long before you buy your own building!

Your Negative Side

A "yes" answer to the following questions indicates that you are expressing the inharmonious Capricorn traits, thus lessening your chances to gain prosperity: Do you hoard investments? Are you acquisitive to a fault? Were you reluctant to get involved in a real estate trade which resulted in missing a good opportunity? Did you lose money because you waited too long to take action?

Has your preference for solid assets over liquid ones cost you a pretty penny in the past? Does investing in stock keep you awake nights when the stock takes a low dive? If so, are you upset with yourself because you didn't listen to someone's advice to sell when you could have profited? Have you worked hard, scrimped and saved every dime you could, only to lose the whole bulk of it because you failed to move fast enough with it?

Are you aware that you learn bitter lessons from your past errors? You probably are; in fact, they are so deeply embedded with pain that just the thought of investing again has you scared to death. You are a poor loser and why shouldn't you be? Your money was accumulated through depriving yourself of food, clothes, fun, love, and by living practically in abject poverty. The sacrifices made would do most people in. But you're as strong as that mountain goat that rules your sign. And you keep coming back for more. The negative experience of loss is not as powerful as your greed; therefore, after you've suffered for as long as you deem necessary, and saved up your dough again, you will once more try your luck at making a buck in the stock market.

Some of you Capricorns become so wrapped up in a project that you fail to see anything except what you want to see. Perhaps you've done what Howard Hughes did — built a flying goose that laid an egg. This enormous airplane cost him a fortune to build and could hardly get off the ground; he didn't reap a dime of profit from it.

You could be attracted to "put" calls and short selling in the options market because you tend to have a pessimistic outlook on the world. You believe that a depression is likely to occur at any moment because the unemployment and rising costs have worsened. Therefore you believe that a particular stock will go way down, and if you buy a "put" call and sell short, you can make a fat profit the moment it goes down to the price you specified. However, when the stock escalates way up, you lose at least a hundred dollars for every dollar it rises, as well as the fifty percent of the stock's price you put up as margin. So you are wiped out!

Because you are too stingy to pay for expensive contemporary prints and because it goes against your grain to venture into a field you're not familiar with, you can be gypped if you buy a lithograph that's signed "in stone." Of course, when you see those words, you believe you've struck it rich with a masterpiece. So you buy it without telling the gallery dealer your discovery. Later, when you try to sell it to an auction house, you are informed it's a reproduction because it's not signed or numbered by the artist. So your inflationary hedge is worthless.

WHAT SHOULD YOU INVEST IN?

Conservative ventures are preferred; invest in short- and long-term areas, depending upon how the inflation rate is going. Ask an investment counselor if you're too busy to keep track of it.

Because of your safe feeling with the solid and cold earth, invest in real estate. You enjoy taking something old and improving upon it; renovation and rehabilitation are ruled by your sign. Therefore, buy old houses, improve them, and sell them a year later at a profit. Or rent them, if you want to be a landlord — and what Capricorn doesn't?

Purchase equity trust REIT's on the stock exchange. They are paper which you buy, representing ownership shares in one type of property or another. Because you are a business sign, you'd probably be more interested in the skyscraper office buildings and shopping centers and malls than in the condominiums or private houses that you can buy REIT shares in.

Try index funds, which are funds designed to move along with market indicators — like Standard & Poor's 500 stock index — and which have been largely the preserve of pension funds and other large accounts. Indexing is based on the theory that matching the market averages will produce better long-run performances than the efforts of money managers. That is a typical Capricorn way of thinking.

The guaranteed fixed-income funds make it easy for you to go to sleep at night. They consist of the money market funds, municipal-bond funds, and municipal-bond-unit-investment trusts. As an example, the money market funds invest in large-denomination bank certificates or deposit corporations' short-term debts and government securities. Therefore you can see why your rest won't be disturbed with a fixed-income fund.

Closed-end funds appeal to you because they emphasize growth and/or stability. If you want a safe investment (and you do), try government funds, which are short-term (six and nine months) bills and notes and are issued by different agencies of the government. Treasury bills and notes also are reliable and may be short term (some are twenty-six weeks, others ninety days).

Convertible bonds may make you feel that you've made a smart buy in a confusing market. Because they pay fixed interest instead of variable dividends, yields are more predictable than those on stocks. The safety of these bonds should restrain you from worrying.

Bank certificates of deposit are sound and the short-term ones (six months or one year) may be desired because they pay high interest rates. Buying a "put" option may be the most conservative strategy to use when you expect a stock to drop in price. Just stay out of the short selling and margin account and you won't be in such a risk-taking position.

You're known as a real collector from the word go. Once you have your hands on something, you dislike letting go. Early in life you may start out with inexpensive objects and, as your income increases, so do your expenditures on the collectibles. Because you love history, historical documents can be your "bag." Also, you like art, sculpture, tapestries, Oriental rugs, stamps, coins, and anything that is old. Because you're so time conscious, you'd enjoy owning an antique grandfather's clock. The type of contemporary prints ruled by your sign are the woodcuts and lithographs.

Perhaps you'd like to invest in the gems your sign rules — onyx, jet, and sardonyx? Buy shares in them, purchase your own mine, or go into them as a business. Go on a prospecting trip and search for valuable minerals, rocks and ores — all Capricorn-ruled. Products that are mined from the earth appeal to you. Ash-colored stones, or black minerals such as coal, could be your "baby." Lead, zinc, pewter, masonite, cement, as well as the junk and scrap-metal industry all come under the Capricorn banner. Perhaps you'd like to buy shares in them, or have your own mine or business.

To give you that comfy feeling so necessary to chase the Capricorn blues away, invest in a financial program designed to provide future security. If you are eligible, a Keogh or IRA retirement plan may be just what you are looking for. If you're not eligible for either one of those plans, perhaps annuities or deferred annuities are worth looking into — deferred annuities may be desirable if you want the opportunity to realize attractive appreciation potential without the burden of immediate taxation.

In the foreign-bond market you could be attracted to Finland or England, both ruled by Capricorn. Perhaps you'd like to invest in one of these countries' foreign-currency. You do keep abreast of world affairs; therefore you are one step ahead when it comes to investing wisely. If you are too busy making all that money to invest, perhaps, you'd like to take a few minutes to consult with an expert.

A broker that thinks along the same lines as you may be desirable. Therefore deal with another Capricorn, Taurus, or Virgo. These signs are the best suited for safe and sound investments. Cancer and Libra may help you with balance because they weigh the pros and cons of everything. At least you'll get both sides of the coin with them. However, if they are too indecisive, this might annoy you.

An Aries, Aquarius, Gemini, Leo, Scorpio, Sagittarius, or Pisces may scare you with one of their risky moves. They will encourage you to speculate because they like to take chances and go in for that big killing. From a financial standpoint they move too fast for you and may not be the best signs for you to listen to, or be involved with.

Perhaps the broker you choose is born under one of the preceding signs (the speculators); however, this person follows a solid, safe, and sagacious investment procedure. This individual takes this approach, which is opposite his/her Sun-sign traits, because he/she probably has Taurus, Virgo, or Capricorn as a *dominant* sign in his/her horoscope. If this occurs, you're in fairly good hands.

Astrology can guide you as to the type of bonds your sign should consider investing in. Therefore, be on the alert for the Capricorn/Saturn-ruled municipals, including tax-exempt bonds, that deal with minerals, mines, agriculture, land, real estate, toll roads, streets and highways, tunnels, county improvement, and pollution control.

Because everything in life has an astrological correspondence, each type of corporate bond, stock, or commodity has a sign/planet that rules it. Therefore, under the Capricorn/Saturn influence invest in manufacturing corporations that produce burglar alarm systems, clocks, watches, hourglasses, farm implements and machinery, tire retreaders, paint, and coatings.

If these don't whet your appetite, try other Capricorn/Saturn rulerships such as coal mining and waste-control equipment, pollution-control devices, water-cooling towers, real estate and property developers, ice removers, do-it-yourself kits, frames, warehouses, items for the aged, retirement and leisure homes for the elderly.

Other bonds and stocks ruled by your sign and Saturn deal with ivory, cement, glue, masonite, lumber, timber, plywood, farming, agriculture, irrigation and flood control projects, products from the earth — rocks, stones, tar, zinc, coal, lead, pewter, nickel, ores, minerals, mining companies, junk and scrap metal industry, vanadium, strategic metals (cobalt, cadmium), especially those companies that put down underground cable or equipment, pipelines, and firms which deal with conservation and natural resources or buy stock in utility companies which use coal.

In the commodity futures market, Capricorn/Saturn-ruled areas are: Nickel, millet, wheat, grain, oats, rye, barley, soybeans, alfalfa pellets, Brewer's grains, bonemeal, feeds. If you don't want to get involved in the futures market, then buy stock in companies that deal with (process) these products. Your sign rules the old established companies and blue chips, so when purchasing any type of stock, perhaps that's where you're happiest.

HOW TO HANDLE YOUR INVESTMENTS

Because you are a conservative investor you really don't tend to have as many losses as you would have if you were an out-and-out speculator. But if the "bug" hits, stay away from margin accounts and commodity futures because they could wipe you out. If you do get involved with them, only invest what you can afford to lose. And if you have a loss, don't pledge any more security.

If in the past you've gained through taking risks, then continue along these lines; however, if the reverse holds true, stay away from this because you are expressing the Capricorn traits on their negative side and are likely to get a repeat performance. And a Capricorn, of all signs, does not like to lose once, let alone twice!

Too much thought is given to your investments. Often your lack of confidence makes you hold back so long that by the time you get in, it's really too late to make any gains. If you'd listen to some financial wizards in the investment-counseling field, and learn to trust their judgment instead of yours, you'd fare a lot better, that is if you've been a loser most of your life.

If you decide to purchase contemporary prints, make sure that the gallery dealer guarantees the authenticity of his/her prints in writing. Never buy purely for investment. If you buy what you really like, you should be prepared to make mistakes, but there's no reason why you shouldn't as least keep pace with rising costs. Read books on the subject, or join a print club. If you know what you're doing, you can buy a print for a small amount of money that can keep you ahead of increased living costs.

When you are investing in non-income producing assets such as real estate that is not producing spendable money, then you should also strive to accumulate an equal amount in liquid assets. This liquidity can be in the form of cash, bonds, stocks, Swiss currency, traveler's checks, gold, silver, cash-value life insurance, or even a pension.

You alone must live with the investments you make. Because you tend to worry and get depressed, you should make decisions you can be comfortable with.

If you can't live at peace with securities, don't own them. However, you are the type that has to invest your money so it's working for you. Keep aware of world conditions so you can be in and out of investments according to the interest rate.

Are you a winner or loser? It not only depends upon your Sun sign and how you use it, but also on the influence of Jupiter and Saturn. Jupiter attracts a gain, whereas Saturn attracts a loss. Everyone has these planets in his/her horoscope. (In fact, Saturn rules the sign Capricorn.) But their influence depends upon whether their harmonious or inharmonious side is expressed at the moment a decision is made.

Under the influence of the positive side of Saturn, you are practical, conservative, cautious, serious, contemplative, and make a move only when you are sure the time is ripe. Long-range investments are favored. You use sound judgment, and thus can buy to advantage.

Under the influence of the negative side of Saturn you are pessimistic and cry poverty; you worry, gripe, complain, and have the blues. You are slow because you are afraid of making the wrong move, and thus can attract losses. You lack confidence and chances are if you purchase anything, it could be a real downer.

Whenever you are depressed and feel the Saturn negative traits, avoid investing in anything, because your Saturn is being stimulated in your horoscope at that moment (this could last an hour, a day, a week, a month, a year, or more). If you do invest when this inharmonious energy is being expressed, you are likely to attract a loss.

Under the influence of the positive side of Jupiter you are confident, optimistic, cheerful, easygoing, honest, understanding, happy, and generous. Speculation is favored and brings success. You use sound judgment and can sell to an advantage, take options, buy on margin, and do well all around.

Under the influence of the negative side of Jupiter you are overly confident, too optimistic, wasteful, ostentatious, extravagant, and refuse to take into account prices, expenditures, or the views of others. You are in the mood to do everything to excess. At a party you'd be on center stage making everyone laugh. If you sell an investment when you are in this frame of mind you won't get the price it's worth; your judgment will be off.

Whenever you discover you are using the negative side of Jupiter, don't take a chance with the stock market or any other form of investment. Lie low and wait until the positive side of Jupiter is being expressed, then sell. It'll be worth the wait.

In astrology *buying* is ruled by Saturn and *selling* by Jupiter. Every time you buy under a harmonious Saturn aspect your purchase will be a bargain, a good deal, or investment. Every time you sell under a harmonious Jupiter aspect your sale will be a considerable gain. The moment these planets are activated in your horoscope are determined by your time, place, day, month, and year of birth. But you don't need a horoscope to know when you are in a depressed state or happy mood. By being aware of your frame of mind, you'll know how to invest wisely. The moment the negative side of Jupiter, Saturn, or Capricorn is expressed, that's the time to watch out for losses; the reverse if true when their positive side is expressed.

Now that you are armed with this information you can invest wisely and be ready for whatever the world economy brings. However, you are one step further ahead than the majority of people because by using this positive energy you can improve your chances to be wealthy.

CHAPTER ELEVEN

Aquarius - Money and Investments

Those born from January 20 through February 18 have the Sun in the sign Aquarius. Every sign of the zodiac corresponds to a particular type of prosperity; it's what you do and how you use it that determines whether you'll be successful or not.

Do your erratic spending habits put you behind the eight ball? Instead, wouldn't it be better if you could prevent losses, shortages, and hardships? By knowing your faults and how to correct them you can enjoy life more, save money, and, be in tip-top shape. And that's worth doing something about it, isn't it?

YOUR MONEY

Because you lack a fixed or certain course, you are known as the "Erratic Spender of the Zodiac." You go to extremes, either being tight and not letting loose of a dime, or suddenly squandering every penny you have on God only knows what.

You're the type who watched the first moon landing in awe, and immediately called an airline and reserved your ticket for the first commercial flight to the moon. And it's no joke, it's serious, because you know that someday the public will be allowed to take trips there. You've got to be on the passenger list as one of the first. And the cost doesn't matter; you'll put a deposit down and save for it. That is, until something unusual comes along to make you blow the cash.

You do your shopping just as crazily as you live your life. Usually when you go to a store, you know what you want and where to get it. Everything is bought in a flash. If there's a bargain sale, and you're there, you'll take advantage of it. But you don't go out of your way looking for one. Quality is preferred although it's what makes your eyes twinkle that you end up purchasing.

Your taste in clothes can run from reserved to bohemian; it depends upon what strikes your fancy. Money is spent on gadgets, especially for automobiles, or on computers, on electric equipment for home or business use, or pendulums for dowsing, or on miniature pyramids to help you meditate, and provide more shaves from a single razor blade, or help grow unusually large plants. You'll experiment with them all.

Your dollars are spent running from one psychic, astrologer, palmist, or card or tea-leaf reader to another. When you hear about a good phrenologist, you dart off immediately to have the bumps on your head read. But it's the numerologist who ties everything up in a neat package when he/she verifies everything all the others told you.

An Aquarian probably originated the nudist camp; you love to be free as the Air sign you're ruled by, and don't mind shelling out a few bucks to be a member. Probably the first person who ever saw an UFO landing was an Aquarian. Or did you also start space clubs? Or perhaps some of your cash is spent on joining a witch's coven. Or even better yet, like my dear friend Hans Holzer, who is known as the Ghost Hunter, you may have decided to finance your own expedition to hunt ghosts. Happy hunting!

Your ingenious ideas can bring you great wealth. It's important that you have a few greenbacks stashed away so you can come and go as you please. You gals may be like Betty Friedan and be involved with the women's lib movement. This is one of those causes you are delighted to donate time and money to.

You're always surprising everyone with extraordinary gifts. Restaurants are frequented without regard for the price of the meal. It's the conversations that turn you on, not the food. There's a positive and negative side of Aquarius, and if the positive is expressed it's easier to attain the material gains that can give you the freedom desired.

Your Positive Side

Do your modern ideas pay off in substantial financial rewards? Will you experiment with way-out and untried methods? Is money gained as a result? Have you always looked for new ways to make a buck? If so, when found, were they profitable? Can you sense coming trends, and as a result reap financial benefits? If you answered the preceding questions with a "yes" you are using the harmonious traits you are known for, and as a result, prosperity can be more easily attracted.

Do you know that you are ahead of the times? Those dollars are gained by sudden decisions and actions whenever an original idea pops into your head. It's the mental stimulation that gets you "high," not the resultant cash that flows in.

Because you are an Air sign, you tend to be a dreamer and live in the clouds most of the time. But somehow you manage to come down to earth every now and then to make those castles in the sky come true; that's when they are put to practical use in the world of reality. And when they bring in financial dividends, you've got the extra cash with which to float away wherever you're inspired to go.

You are completely stymied when money comes in from left field. But that's the way it's been all your life. It's found in the streets, or comes in the mail as a refund from who knows what. Perhaps you donated a few bucks to improve world conditions and now that same organization wants to make you a part of their salaried group. That letter you wrote impressed them so much that they want you to do some special work in their behalf; therefore they've enclosed a check to secure your future services. However, you don't want the money, you'll do it for nothing because the spiritual rewards gained are payment enough. However, you cash the check and send the money to a poor starving family you've read about.

Those dollars may come flowing in through some unusual action of yours such as happened to Aquarian Mia Farrow when she cropped her hair. In true Aquarian fashion it caught on and became an overnight fad that still endures. It also helped Mia's earning power when it brought in more roles in films.

Did you know that your sign rules inventions? Is it any wonder then that

Thomas A. Edison was one of you? Perhaps you may devise some new gadget that may become the new "in" thing; or perhaps it's an unusual type of restaurant you open — that one-of-a-kind that later is franchised as a chain. Whatever it is, you can expect to see favorable monetary results.

Perhaps you capitalize on your eccentric personality as the late Aquarian Tallulah Bankhead did. She was an original from the word go. Her calling everyone "dahling" (because she couldn't remember the names of all the people she met) became classic and is a device still used by many. Tallulah's wild escapades and life-style, typical of your sign, increased her box-office earnings.

You are fascinated by the new and are always seeking a fresh approach to problems. You are an ultra-progressive individual who has your eyes and ears open at all times. Anything that cuts down on time and labor, thus speeding up production, is adopted by you. As a result your company is going to benefit financially — and so will you.

Often money is earned through temporary, part-time, and free-lance work. This gives you the time you need to pursue your hobbies and educational interests. You may go to school on and off for years — and all over the world.

Perhaps you're a registered nurse and want to expand your knowledge to include drugless forms of healing: acupuncture, hypnotism, reflexology, rolfing, shiatsu, or chua k'a massages. Short courses in these off-the-beaten-track subjects are preferred. Eventually you may combine your fields of knowledge and reap enormous sums of money through your modern practices. However, it's not those dollars that appeal to you, it's being able to help your fellow man.

A creative project is likely to capture your interest almost every day of your life. Money is spent impulsively on it, without thought of the outcome. It's the love of the novel, the unique the eccentric that appeals to you. But because your artistic work is so phenomenal, word gets around and the dough starts to pour in.

You are also known as the "Gimmick Sign of the Zodiac." It seems as though you are always getting brainstorms for your boss, pals, and yourself. These flashes are not rare, they are daily occurrences you've learned to live with. In fact they often astound you as much as they do everyone else. Your intuition not only helps others make a buck, but fattens your wallet, too.

Your Negative Side

Do you lose money from your eccentric notions? Are you unpredictable? Does this behavior cause financial setbacks? Do you invest on spur-of-the-moment whims? Later were you sorry you did? Are you careless with dough?

Does your independence cause monetary losses? Have you had mostly financial losses that were sudden, unaccountable, and came from out of the clear blue sky? Are your bucks spent on fads or the latest "in" places? Do you feel the money was wasted? Do you get so wrapped up in theories you lose sight of money making projects? Are greenbacks lost because you cancel appointments? If you answered the preceding questions with a "yes" you are using the inharmonious traits you are known for, and as a result, it's difficult to attract prosperity.

Is your financial condition poor because of all your new-founded enterprises? You are in and out of so many ventures that no one can keep up with you. The moment you realize that a newfangled idea is nothing more than hot air, you dump it, regardless of labor or money spent on it. After getting rid of one project, you may suddenly jump into another one. And there you go all gung-ho again shelling out those greenbacks as if they're play money. It's your game and hopefully you'll win it on this new "baby."

Your desire to do things your own way can cause you to be broke, especially if your self-employed. It's important to you to be free to express your creative talents as desired. Perhaps you're a writer and refuse to change a few things around and, as a result, wind up being your own publisher.

You're a great believer in reform and may donate huge sums to a group to carry on their activities. Often it is throwing money down the drain, because the cause may be unpopular and fold before it gets very far. It may frustrate you that it didn't get off the ground. However, it's forgotten the moment a new group comes along, waving banners; your legal tender isn't far behind. In fact you'll catch up with them and fork over every dime you have.

You can lose a lot of money by being too independent with the public. If you are tied up with a slow-thinking and slow-moving customer, you may be so abrupt that the client leaves in a huff and puff without purchasing anything. It doesn't disturb you because you believe that life is short and that you should be selective as to who you want to be around.

You can't stand going into debt but if you get inspired with a new idea that you want to put into effect immediately, you may neglect your bills, rent, and other necessities just to put every penny into this new project. Your financial responsibilities could increase and pile up with unpaid bills. Or perhaps you get evicted or a foreclosure occurs on your home because you are so far behind with the mortgage payments. You may wind up declaring bankruptcy.

You're always in and out of hot water when it comes to making a living. One day you show up late, another you extend your lunch hour to three hours, all because you wanted to catch a new antique car show that just opened. So it's not a surprise to your co-workers that the boss has fired you. Your finances may suffer while you're in between jobs, but you are accustomed to sudden terminations of work.

Perhaps you are like the late Aquarian King Farouk who spent a fortune on a licentious and profligate life-style. He was known for his wild parties that lasted for days. Or perhaps you don't dissipate quite that much, but instead just lose your weekly salary on riotous living over the weekend.

Most of your money problems may come through other people. You might loan a pal a few bucks, or take a friend out to cure his/her depression; if you can cheer him/her up you'll feel your evening well spent. Or you may see a poor beggar in the street and give the street person every cent you have. Just as you think you have a nice bankroll saved, an emergency comes along and someone needs your assistance. You are always around to lend a helping hand, but it's so very very costly to your pocketbook.

A few of you Aquarians have some weird ideas: You love to go into debt and spend money on the most extravagant purchases imaginable, but only if you can shock a buddy while doing it. So you take a friend to the department store saying you are just going to look around. And then the game starts as you purchase one enormous object after another. The amounts charged may go into the thousands, but you don't care because that's when the fun starts. The disbelief on your pal's face is worth the price paid.

You tend to be completely mesmerized by the latest time-saving devices such as machinery and electronic equipment, such as computers. If you get wind of something new that is going to be made available soon, you'll call and order it sight unseen. You tell yourself that this up-to-date model may be an improvement over the one you purchased last month. And since you are an I-know-it-all Aquarian, an accountant's advice is not needed. Financial setbacks occur and you can't seem to understand why you aren't making larger profits when you've got the best equipment money can buy.

Monetary losses don't faze you. The debts incurred through your extravagance bug you because you dislike obligations; they keep you bound when you seek freedom. However, you never learn from your mistakes. If you had to do it all over again, you'd leap right in. You should learn how to handle money so you won't be in poor circumstances if a recession occurs.

HOW TO HANDLE YOUR MONEY

Have you ever wondered how you could participate in those outlandish notions and yet have money in the bank? Wouldn't you like to avoid those paralyzing moments when you are shocked to learn that you'll be broke until your next paycheck or free-lance job comes through? Do you realize that this situation can be avoided?

Is your money being spent on a variety of things that are only used once? Doesn't it bother the practical side of your nature to lose a pile of dough because you jumped in without looking? If you could find a means to escape the mental imprisonment your debts have caused, wouldn't it be well worth the effort to try?

If you answered "yes" to the preceding questions, these are the areas you've got to work with and change. Because you are stubborn and dislike listening to others, it may be difficult to do. However, it's your belief that nothing's impossible. Therefore give it a try by taking one step at a time.

Don't refuse to think and plan your future before taking action. Instead of spending money you don't have, save the cash until you can afford to buy what you desire. If in doubt, ask an accountant. Be tolerant of the views of others. You may be surprised by what you learn. Avoid being contrary just to be different. Your belief that only *you* know how to handle your finances can keep you in hot water.

Try to live within your means. It's something your serious side can do very easily. But when the eccentric side comes to the fore, you are in deep trouble.

Before you shell out any cash or use a charge card, review your expenditures and ask yourself if you really need the desired item; if so, why? And what will it do for you? Are you getting value for your money?

Instead of shocking people with the enormous sums you can splurge in a few seconds, surprise them with your humanitarian accomplishments and the bucks you can earn from something that is highly unusual. This will give you a greater satisfaction than going practically bankrupt.

Before donating to a cause, have it checked out thoroughly; find out how many people are for it, how long it's been operative. Give of your time rather than spending every nickel you have on it.

Instead of purchasing everything that comes along, hold on longer to a computer or equipment that you already have. If you continue to buy every new electronic item that is available, you'll have difficulties making a profit in business. Keep in mind that because we are in the electronic age, technology is developing too fast for your pocketbook to keep up.

When dealing with the public try to realize that not everyone can size up an object as quickly as you. Use the impersonal friendliness you are known for instead of being tactless. Too much independence can be a fault rather than an asset. If in doubt, just open the cash register and see which action rings up the sales.

Continue to develop all those new ideas that pop in out of the blue. Make them worthwhile and saleable. Some leapfrogging may help rather than hinder if you don't lose sight of your financial objectives. Weigh all the pros and cons before disbursing funds in a project. Once money has been spent, don't let things slide in favor of a new interest; instead, stick with your aims until they've been accomplished.

Theories about how the universe can be saved tend to occupy so much of your time that there's little room left to devote to making a living. If you want to help mankind, instead of talking and dreaming about it, take action. But be practical. Get involved in your spare moments and don't let this interest interfere with a job or keep you broke.

In case you're interested in getting out of debt, why not take on a side job of your very own? Because you are interested in off-the-beaten-track subjects, why not sell miniature pyramid kits or pendulums to your pals and acquaintances? Just think of the fun you'll have when demonstrating them! And the extra cash in you wallet won't hurt, either.

Avoid recklessness. Try to recall past experiences when you got yourself into a jam because you spent every dime you had on some new project that fascinated you. If you've got a house in mind that you are thinking of purchasing, figure out whether you can afford to meet the mortgage payments on it; if not, shop around for a less expensive place. You are the type who generally sticks to legal commitments even at your own expense. If a piece of property binds you so you're a prisoner to your home, you'll be one very unhappy Aquarian.

Set up a goal for money and give yourself a deadline to meet it. Start a financial plan that allows you a few bucks to goof off with. Think of the future rather than the now. Save for those later years when you are older, or retired, and you'll have something to fall back on. Otherwise one of your biggest fears may come true, being dependent upon children and friends to support you.

Write down every cent you spend regardless of whether it's on chewing gum, bus fare, or a small loan to a pal. By keeping a record of your expenditures you'll be amazed to see how those little things you ignored add up to rather large amounts.

Start a budget. Write down your income and out of it allow twenty-five percent for rent, utilities, telephone; twenty percent for food; twenty percent for money owed on loans; ten percent on transportation (car insurance, not car payments); five percent for medical and dental; five percent for clothing; five percent for recreation; seven percent for savings and investments; three percent for miscellaneous — all those little items you can't recall spending cash on.

These percentages are, however, just traditional guidelines. Depending on your circumstances, some percentage units may vary. You might be sharing expenses with a mate or living free with your parents.

Tear up credit cards so you won't be tempted to go on a spree. Pay off credit-card bills as fast as is possible. The interest you save could go for some self-indulgence. To save money you can cut down on clothing, eating out, entertainment, recreation, and gifts bought throughout the year.

Outline in red ink your desires to save money. Look them over *every day,* and when you start to spend do it according to your budget. Don't go overboard with entertainment expenses. Keep your allowance down to a minimum. There are many inexpensive forms of entertainment and recreation. At the top of the list are museums and archaeological and historical sites. Of course those that are at a distance cost more due to the transportation expense and may be indulged in only every so often.

It's easy for you to become enraptured with music, so go to some free concerts. Attend all the different types of antique shows that come to town. Instead of going to the movies several times a week, save some money by getting together with your friends to discuss theories, revolutionary ideas, or the occult and scientific fields. These intellectual conversations may turn into debating sessions — something you get "high" on.

For physical gratification, and to give you that sense of freedom you require, go to a discotheque and dance your heart out. Take up modern or aerobic dancing if you've got the time to spare. Roller disco is another form of recreation and entertainment that pleases you.

Because you're an Air sign, try your hand at parachuting; you'll love the feeling of flying like a bird in the sky. Snow or water skiing gives you renewed energy when the breeze hits your face. For those lazy moments, try some Ping-Pong, go for a walk, or hike in the woods. To keep your ankles trim (ruled by your sign), exercise, or ride a bike. Get on a horse and breathe the fresh air as you go galloping around. And when you want to get within yourself, and in tune with the universe, meditate by doing some yoga. Most of the diversions mentioned are not that costly. Stay within the limits of your budget and you'll be better prepared for economic uncertainties.

YOUR INVESTMENTS

You can benefit by setting aside money now so your future will be secure. Or perhaps you prefer investing in something other than a business. However, before you go leaping into any undertaking, it would be to your advantage to understand your assets and shortcomings, thereby avoiding pitfalls.

Your Positive Side

A "yes" answer to any of the following questions indicates that you are expressing harmonious Aquarius traits, thus enhancing your chances to gain prosperity: Do you make sudden investments in line with someone else's ideas? Does it pay off? Can you sense coming trends and invest accordingly? If so are benefits reaped? Do you invest in areas that do not tie you down to long-term commitments? Will you invest in an unpopular stock, or other area, just to be different? If so, have you profited by it? Have you attracted sudden windfalls with warrants? Do you keep up to date on the latest rising costs and interest rates?

Are you aware that you're an investor who goes to the extremes of conservativeness and speculativeness? You can patiently wait for those long-term maturation dates until, suddenly, the urge strikes and you want quick returns for every dime invested. But luckily, you do as well when you are in and out of the market because you are smart enough to combine your intuitiveness with the facts and use the going interest rates as a gauge.

If it's announced that an old part of the city is going to have millions of dollars poured into modernizing it, you'll be the first one to take an active part in the program. The dough it costs, and eventually makes, is not as important to you as the desire to rebuild the old and dilapidated structures into new and beautiful ones. Generally you profit from this type of transaction, especially if it is thoroughly thought out beforehand.

Often you attend an auction just to get an idea of how the market is swinging at the moment. You figure this pre-education may pay off later. However, due to your erratic nature, you wind up with an antiquity you couldn't resist. Fortunately your expertise in this department enables you to get a good buy.

Your real thrill comes when you go to the flea market and, accidentally, notice a rare coin on a charm bracelet. Because the owner has it lying in a pile with some actual junk jewelry, you know that he/she is not aware of its true value. But if you let him/her know about it, you won't be able to purchase it. So you engage in one of your favorite pastimes — bargaining. When you leave this person's stall, you can't believe that you've hit it big with this coin that might be worth a thousand dollars. Later you have it appraised and are happy to learn your judgment was exact almost to the penny.

Your vital interest in bettering conditions for mankind is satisfied when you invest in municipal bonds. But you don't just stop there. You get all of your friends together and expound at great lengths upon why these new housing and other projects are needed. Your audience is magnetized by your oratorical delivery and agree to invest in the tax-exempt municipals. They look to you as a leader who is involved in a humanitarian cause that also brings financial benefits for everyone concerned.

Your Negative Side

A "yes" answer to the following questions indicates that you are expressing the inharmonious Aquarius traits, thus, lessening your chances to gain prosperity: Do you invest on a whim? Later are you sorry you did? Have you lost money on investments because you were too impatient? Will you invest in an unpopular item just to be different? Are you surprised when it turns out to be a loser?

Has your I-know-it-all attitude caused losses with investments because you failed to listen to a broker's advice? Are you unpredictable? If so, has this caused financial setbacks? Are you careless with the way you invest? Did you sink money into something because you were unduly influenced by a fascinating person? If so, did it cause a loss?

Are you aware that many of your financial nightmares are because you were too carried away with your eccentric notions? You get so wrapped up in anything that is off the beaten track that you lose sight of whether you will profit by it. Risks are taken for the sheer novelty of making an oddity turn into an overnight fad.

Perhaps you got all hopped up with a chain of UFO flying saucer restaurants that would whisk the diners away to nearby sites while they were eating and return them to their place of origin by the end of the meal. If latecomers arrived, they'd have to wait for the flying saucer restaurant to return for the second dinner seating. Of course, the project proved to be too expensive and impractical. You came out of it with an empty pocketbook but mentally you still believe it's a winner, don't you?

Contracts on interest rates futures can be costly when you don't devote enough time to keeping up with the latest developments in the government. Magazines, newspapers, and the Internet are too quickly scanned; important details are overlooked. That, combined with your hectic lifestyle — is it any wonder you got wiped out with that last margin call?

When someone comes along with something unusual and you're bored, or in a rut, you are vulnerable for jumping in and investing every cent you have on the project, such as that time you sank a huge sum of money into a graphology research and service firm. They were to offer their services to corporations for a nominal fee, to analyze the handwriting of potential employees. However, it never got off the ground because the corporations failed to respond to the advertising. So there went your money down the drain.

The new issues on the stock exchange interest you because they are companies in embryo. True to your Aquarian nature you want to help them, especially if it's something close to your heart such as conservation of natural resources. After the corporation goes bankrupt, you're still in a daze and can't understand what went wrong. The loss of your money isn't as serious a thing to you as the loss of what that company stood for. Of course, this attitude doesn't help you beat rising prices.

WHAT SHOULD YOU INVEST IN?

If you want to profit try to stay out of too many novel and off-the-beaten-track investment areas. Of course to keep you happy you will have to invest in something that is unusual, but first check it out thoroughly and, second, ask an accountant or investment counselor for advice. Avoid being an I-know-it-all; that can be your ruination.

Stay in short-, intermediate-, and long-term maturation periods with bonds. If you diversify you may be content with the variety offered, and thus not be tempted to chase after way-out ventures and take foolish chances.

Anything which involves the government (ruled by your sign) may appeal to you, such as Series E, U.S. Savings Bonds. If you like, purchase the Series E bonds and when you've accumulated enough, convert them into H bonds. For tax purposes hold on to the Series E bonds for as many years as you can because they are not taxable until they are cashed in. If they are converted into H bonds there is no tax on your Series E bonds.

Another area that is safe and sure are government funds which are bought or traded. They pay high interest rates and are issued by different agencies of the government. Because you like to help people, just think of how you'd be helping the farmer when the government loans him money. These government bills and notes are short term, usually for six or nine months.

Treasury bills and notes also appeal to your sign. There are some which are for twenty-six weeks, ninety days, and longer.

In the futures market you may be interested in speculating on Treasury bills and notes (very risky), dollar and foreign-currency futures. If in the past you've gained through speculation, then continue along these lines. However, if the reverse holds true, stay away from this because you are expressing the Aquarius traits on their negative side and are likely to get a repeat performance. Abide by this rule with margin accounts or any area that is known to be speculative.

Because you love theories, try index funds. They are funds designed to move along with the market indicators like Standard & Poor's 500 stock index. They are based on the theory that matching the market averages will produce better long-run performance than the efforts of money managers. Do you agree with their theory?

The no-load (no sales fees) bear and bull fund may appeal to you because you are encouraged to switch assets back and forth at no extra charge. That may keep you mentally active and pepped up. Convertible bonds may intrigue you because they pay fixed (and you're a fixed sign) interest instead of variable dividends and their yields are more predictable than those on stocks. Options can be risky, but substantial gains may give you extra money to go fight some cause.

Anything that is foreign usually appeals to the Aquarian nature. So why not try Eurodollars, or open an overseas bank account or invest in foreign currencies such as that of Costa Rica (ruled by Aquarius)? Foreign traveler's checks, especially the Swiss ones, will stir that traveling bug that hits you more often than it does most people. These checks have no time limit on redemption and when the dollar goes down, you make money.

Buy long-term durables, tools, raw materials, replacement parts, etc., if you can, in case you need to use them to barter with in times of financial crisis or recession. For the art lover in you, invest in an art mutual fund on the Geneva or Amsterdam exchange.

You are a true collector and just about anything in the collectible market attracts you: stamps, coins, rare and first editions and comic books, historical documents, autographs of celebrities, shells, woodcuts in the contemporary print line, graphic posters, antique cars, odd gadgets, or anything else that is out of the ordinary.

Also you collect fine art and may lean to abstract, cubism, and impressionism, because they allow freedom for the artist to express his/her individuality, moods, feelings, and ideas. Reproductions go against your grain; originals are a must. Oriental rugs, tapestries, antiques, and sculpture appeal to your interest in the past. You may prefer collecting miniatures such as figurines and statuettes. Antiquities is your real "bag," especially Polynesian, African, Oriental, and pre-Columbian.

Perhaps you'd like to invest in the gem your sign rules — the blue sapphire. Or what about your sign's stones — black pearl and obsidian? Buy shares in them, purchase your own mine, or go into them as a business.

In the foreign-bond market your sign is attracted to the Aquarius-ruled country of Costa Rica. Perhaps you want to invest in the foreign currency of Costa Rica.

To offset your chances of being in a poor position as prices rise, and due to your erratic nature, you need to invest in a financial program designed to provide future security. Perhaps a fixed-income refund annuity or deferred Swiss franc annuity may appeal to you.

When you keep abreast of world affairs you are one step ahead when it comes to investing wisely. If you want to seek the advice of a broker (which you may not want to do, but should consider doing), perhaps one who thinks along the same lines as you would be desirable. Therefore, deal with another Aquarian (who will out talk whom?), Aries, Gemini, Leo, Sagittarius, or Pisces.

These signs will encourage those calculated risks that you enjoy now and then, but must beware of. They, like you, take chances. So from a strictly financial standpoint, they may not be the best signs for you to listen to or be involved with. Scorpio also falls into this category; however, the two of you may lock horns with a round of stubbornness. You really need a broker who is practical and able to provide the balance you so sorely need. Therefore, consider Capricorn, Taurus, and Virgo. They are the best suited for safe and sound investments. Taurus may be too fixed, like you, so disagreements could occur. They all may be too slow for you in speech and action. Cancer and Libra are not bad choices although they can be almost as erratic as you. So confusion may reign.

If you are lucky you might find a broker who is another Aquarius, or an Aries, Gemini, Leo, Sagittarius, or Pisces Sun sign, and this individual *may also have* Taurus, Virgo, or Capricorn as a *dominant* sign in his/her horoscope. If this occurs you'll have the best of two worlds: one who is inclined to speculate but who uses sound judgment.

Astrology can guide you in the type of bonds your sign should consider investing in. The Aquarius/Uranus-ruled bonds are those that deal with electricity, power plants, public projects, pollution control, county improvement, and urban development.

Because everything in life has an astrological correspondence, each type of corporate bond or stock has a sign/planet that rules it. Therefore, under the Aquarius/Uranus influence, invest in manufacturing corporations that produce computerized equipment (including desktop-size computers), computer memory circuits, cell phones, semi-conductors, silicon, automobiles, air-pollution control devices, air filters, air conditioners, gadgets, or inventions.

Other Aquarius/Uranus-ruled companies are those that deal with electricity (appliances, electrical products, electric utility stocks or bonds) wiring, telephone wires, microphones, loudspeakers, technology, digital equipment, Web Sites, energy, uranium (ore, mining company or source of power), radium, electronics (including game companies, medical devices, data systems), electrons, laser beams, the Internet, and computer time-sharing services to businesses.

If those don't capture your interest, perhaps these will: corporations that deal with scientific devices, space programs, space exploration labs, air-control towers, aerodynamic research, psychiatric centers, research projects which aid mankind or the universe, modern mechanical devices, innovations, novelties, interior decorating, and all those companies involved with a new process, plant, equipment, or product.

HOW TO HANDLE YOUR INVESTMENTS

Be leery of eccentric areas that are too far ahead of the times unless they've been thoroughly checked as to their durability and usefulness. Safe and sure areas should be sought, although to keep your spirits up, you need to invest in some risky and unusual ventures.

Your sign is intuitive and if you've gained in the past through intuition, continue to do so. Never leap into an investment just because you're in the mood to do something crazy to shock a friend. Stop, think, and analyze the pros and cons of every step you wish to take. You alone must live with the investments you make. It's your money, so make decisions you can be comfortable with. If securities make you too high strung or depressed, don't own them.

Find out how much you can afford to lose. An accountant can guide you in this matter. Listen to the advice of a broker, investment counselor, or accountant instead of making yourself the sole expert. It may amaze you what you can learn.

Try to stay clear of margin accounts. Put up for collateral only that which you can afford to be without. Curb impulsiveness in all investment areas. If you wish to reap profits, strive for consistent effort. Don't get lost in a maze of experimental and untested ideas or theories. Be suspicious of unheard-of plans or projects; investigate everyone connected with them.

This is the age of changes; something your sign is familiar with. Anticipate changes when investing. Usually you are not doing what others are and may profit by that. You value the theory of contrary opinion and may come out ahead of others; just don't overshoot your mark.

Perhaps you'd like to diversify with twenty-five percent of your savings in a savings account; twenty-five percent in stocks and bonds; ten percent in a gambling fund for your off-the-beaten-track investments; ten percent in collectibles; five percent in foreign currency; twenty-five percent in real estate. Or you could divide it a little differently, and knowing you — you will.

When you are investing in non-income producing assets like real estate that is not producing spendable money, then you should also strive to accumulate an equal amount in liquid assets. This liquidity can be in the form of cash, bonds, stocks, foreign currencies or traveler's checks, cash-value life insurance, or even a pension. You may throw in some gold. Stay away from silver as it's too volatile.

Are you a winner or loser? It not only depends upon your Sun sign and how you use it, but also on the influence of Jupiter and Saturn. Jupiter attracts a gain, whereas Saturn attracts a loss. Everyone has these planets in his/her horoscope. But their influence depends upon whether their harmonious or inharmonious side is expressed at the moment a decision is made.

Under the influence of the positive side of Saturn, you are practical, conservative, cautious, serious, contemplative, and make a move only when you are sure the time is ripe. Long-range investments are favored. You use sound judgment, and thus can buy to advantage.

Under the influence of the negative side of Saturn you are pessimistic and cry poverty; you worry, gripe, complain, and have the blues. You are slow because you are afraid of making the wrong move, and thus can attract losses. You lack confidence and chances are if you purchase anything, it could be a real downer.

Whenever you are depressed and feel the Saturn negative traits, avoid investing in anything, because your Saturn is being stimulated in your horoscope at that moment (this could last an hour, a day, a week, a month, a year, or more). If you do invest when this inharmonious energy is being expressed, you are likely to attract a loss.

Under the influence of the positive side of Jupiter you are confident, optimistic, cheerful, easygoing, honest, understanding, happy, and generous. Speculation is favored and brings success. You use sound judgment and can sell to an advantage, write options, buy on margin, and do well all around.

Under the influence of the negative side of Jupiter you are overly confident, too optimistic, wasteful, ostentatious, extravagant, and refuse to take into account prices, expenditures, or the views of others. You are in the mood to do everything to excess. At a party you'd be on center stage making everyone laugh. If you sell an investment when you are in this frame of mind you won't get the price it's worth; your judgment will be off.

Whenever you discover you are using the negative side of Jupiter, don't take a chance with the stock market or any other form of investment. Lie low and wait until the positive side of Jupiter is being expressed, then sell. It'll be worth the wait.

In astrology *buying* is ruled by Saturn and *selling* by Jupiter. Every time you buy under a harmonious Saturn aspect your purchase will be a bargain, a good deal, or investment. Every time you sell under a harmonious Jupiter aspect your sale will be a considerable gain. The moment these planets are activated in your horoscope are determined by your time, place, day, month, and year of birth. But you don't need a horoscope to know when you are in a depressed state or happy mood. By being aware of your frame of mind, you'll know how to invest wisely. The moment the negative side of Jupiter, Saturn, or Aquarius is expressed, that's the time to watch out for losses; the reverse is true when their positive side is expressed.

Now that you are armed with this information you can invest wisely and be ready for whatever the world economy brings. However, you are one step further ahead than the majority of people because by using this positive energy you can improve your chances to be wealthy.

CHAPTER TWELVE

Pisces — Money and Investments

Those born from February 19 through March 20 have the Sun in the sign Pisces. Every sign of the zodiac corresponds to a particular type of prosperity; it's what you do and how you use it that determines whether you'll be successful or not.

Do you want to wind up in a mess because of your impractical spending habits? Instead, wouldn't it be better if you could prevent losses, shortages, and banish worrisome thoughts from your mind? By knowing your faults and how to correct them you can enjoy life more, save money, and, be in tip-top shape. And that's worth changing a few bad habits for, isn't it?

YOUR MONEY

There are two peas in a pod; you and inflation. Anyway, that's the way it appears. You are a dreamer with the greatest imagination of all. While your mind drifts to the billions of dollars that are on their way flying to you, your pocketbook is being emptied — but it's not a thief who puts his hand in it, it's you. Later you can't recall where your money disappeared to so fast.

Your constant money binges are equal to your emotional ones: heavy. Purchases are made for all your friends and loved ones. You buy something for yourself last. And if you had to, you'd give the shirt off your back to someone in need — even a stranger. You donate your last quarter to a church or a street person. Your contributions to charity are enormous when you have the cash to spare; when you don't have much, you give what you can.

Elaborate sums are spent on your hobbies. If the photography bug hits you, it'll be a long time before your pocketbook gets cured from that large outlay of cash that went for the "works." Those vacations you spend by the water (you sign's natural habitat) are costly, but you do love to relax and enjoy the beauties of nature. Boating is your favorite form of recreation and is expensive with that boat or yacht docked at the harbor. And what about your sailboat tied up over yonder?

To be surrounded by your friends and loved ones is so delightful. Fine wines, liqueurs, and gourmet food are indulged in: The price of the meal isn't important as long as the restaurant is romantic with soft lights, candles, and dreamy music in the background. It's too much work to cook at home, and as long as you have a buck, why not take your pals out? And what about your weight? You'll do like Pisces Elizabeth Taylor did and go on a diet.

Does money mean anything to you? Why, no, of course not. It's only so you can indulge in an easy life of pleasure, love, fun, and have time to grow spiritually. The physical earth isn't as important as those galaxies beyond our own. Anyway, that's what you tell yourself while in your world of tomorrow. But when you come down off that cloud and wipe the stardust out of your eyes, you are the biggest wheeler-dealer alive.

The fortune you make, once you go the financial route, is so stupendous that most people get dizzy just hearing about it. Pisces Gloria Vanderbilt was born into wealth, but she is to be admired for working hard and becoming opulent on her own merits and talents in the design field — ruled by her sign.

There are two types of Pisceans: one who goes after dough and the other who is dependent upon someone else's bankroll. You guys can just as easily sponge off a woman as you lazy, indolent gals can cling to a man and his cash. However, there's a positive side and negative side of Pisces, and if the positive side is expressed, you have a better chance of winding up as the goose who lays the golden egg.

Your Positive Side

Do you get involved in huge money-making projects? If so, do they pay off? Are you a giver? Does it come back to you double? Do you follow your hunches with monetary deals? If so, have they proven correct? Are you able to perceive when someone is trying to con you out of a buck? Have you made dough through get-rich-quick schemes? If you answered the preceding questions with a "yes," you are using the harmonious traits you are known for and as a result you will attract prosperity more easily.

Do you know that you have the capacity to promote anything? Money is gained through being able to stir someone's imagination to such a point that the person will buy whatever you are selling. And while you are doing your "thing" you really believe every word you say.

Your ideas for riches are enormous. They spiral upward so high that it seems as if they are too far beyond anything we can fathom. But when they are given practicality, Lady Luck smiles at you happily as she hands you riches.

You have the power to take an emotion and dramatize it with such feeling that it appears as if it's coming from within your very soul. And it probably is. This talent can make you famous and affluent. In the creative field you've seen it expressed so many times, by so many great Pisceans: Joanne Woodward through acting; Renoir through painting; Rudolf Nureyev through the dance form; Elizabeth Barrett Browning through her immortal poetry that stirs your being just as much as it moved her to write it.

You are fond of the material things that money can buy. To avoid being without them, you may devote hours of your time to thinking about how you can get involved in some large-scale operation without too much physical effort on your part!

Once you've tuned in and discovered the means to get that dough, contacts are made with all the influential people you know. Then you are on your way to the realization of those dreams. It's amazing the areas you may get involved in: anything from getting a treasure hunt financed in the depths of the ocean to selling whiskey to the Eskimos.

Those dollars may be gained through taking a risk. There's never a stake that's too high for you. Your psychic abilities have been proven many times. For instance, at the race track when you experience a vision in your mind's eye of a particular horse winning a race, it's a long shot, but you don't care. Every dime you have is bet on it. When you go to collect your winnings, you happily smile while giving thanks for being so wondrously endowed with ESP.

Your talent for creating an illusion may earn you money through the world of photography, as it did Piscean Lord Snowden, who was a court photographer at the time he met the princess whom he later married in true fairy-tale fashion. Pisces dreams do come true, don't they?

Or perhaps, like those of you who are in the advertising field, you earn a lot of dough by promoting illusion. The public is swayed by those ideas you gave birth to — they are seen as TV commercials. Who else but a Piscean could envision such mouth-watering food scenes, or other such eye-appealing ads?

Those dollars may be gained through fanciful notions put into reality while you're socializing. You can charm anyone with your warmth, kindness, and sympathy. A person can bend your ear with his/her problems. You are understanding and take them on as if they were your very own. Later you benefit financially by getting the individual's business. However, the help was from your heart, you had no thought of recompense.

You are idealistic and can earn money by being so. Perhaps, like Piscean Ralph Nader, you want to help the populace so they aren't cheated, or to strive for better conditions for mankind. So you devise a means to get this across. It's just another form of Piscean promotion with a difference: It helps the consumer but doesn't cost Pisces a dime.

You'll spend every cent you have on something you believe in. You look up and see the rainbow in the sky. The road to the pot of gold is followed to the very end as you bring your product to the world. Nothing is done on a small scale because your thinking is grand. Ballyhoo is the name of the game while the cash register rings in all those dollars and cents you knew were out there waiting for you. You are glad that you listened to your sixth sense and took a chance on huge expenditures.

Your Negative Side

Do you prefer making a buck the easy way, even if it's dishonest? Have you been taken by falling for a sob story? Do you continually get involved in get-rich-quick schemes? Are losses incurred?

Would you spend every cent you had on something you did not investigate, but believed in? Are you readily bamboozled? Would you donate almost everything you have to a spiritual cause and live off welfare? Have you been accused of being unrealistic toward money? Do investments fizzle or fail to yield what is anticipated? Are you a foolish and impractical spender? If you answered the preceding questions with a "yes," you are using the inharmonious traits you are known for, and as a result it's difficult to attract prosperity.

Are you aware that you're generous to a fault? You give and give and give. If ever there was a Santa Claus — it's you! The sacrifices you make for a pal, loved one, or relative are nothing compared to how wonderful it makes you feel to do a good deed — to buy gifts, pick up restaurant tabs, give away theater tickets, and loan cash when it's needed. But you don't call it a loan because you never expect to get it back. You are a real believer in keeping money in circulation.

A lot of dough has been lost through listening to the advice of everyone you meet. When someone comes on strong with financial know-how, your eyes get big and you really believe you know what the person's talking about. Then after you've shelled out a few bucks on the project, you realize that you shouldn't have done it. You tell yourself that you're not going to pay any more attention to anyone's suggestions — you'll go by your own judgment next time. But you don't always keep your promise to yourself.

Those dollars disappear fast every time you go to a bar and make bets on the baseball game with everyone in the place. Because you are always in the corner for the underdog, that's the team you wager on. Of course, when they lose, your heart goes out to them. It doesn't even enter your mind that you've lost a big wad of dough.

However, while sitting around and chatting with a new drinking buddy, you are told about a fantastic real estate offer in the Midwest. You are given an inside tip that no one else knows: There's oil on this particular piece of land. If you invest immediately, before the word gets around that it's a hot deal, you'll be in the chips and make an overnight fortune. Of course it is all too good to be true, you tell yourself, because you've been looking for this type of windfall for some time now.

The next day you draw out a large sum of money and deposit it in your new pal's account. The papers are signed and you are on your way to becoming that millionaire you always knew you'd be. A few weeks later you decide to take a trip to see your property and lo and behold, it doesn't exist! The person who sold it to you has flown the coop and you're penniless. And you wonder, how many more times are you going to be involved in fraudulent deals?

It isn't long afterwards that your best friend propositions you to start into a partnership that can't fail. Well, you've saved a few bucks since that last phony deal, so why not give this one a chance? At least it's with a pal, not a stranger. So you are now in the mail-order business part time. According to the figures given by the company from whom you buy the merchandise, you're supposed to make a few thousand dollars a week. But with the price of the catalogues and the labor involved, your profit isn't anywhere near that figure. After a year you abandon the business and are stuck with a load of goods that you wind up giving to the church bazaar. You tell yourself that at the rate you've been going, you are reaching the point where you don't trust yourself, or anyone else, with business propositions. But somehow that point seems to always be just over the blue horizon, doesn't it?

Are you the type of Pisces who loses money because you lied or conned someone and later got caught? Perhaps your spiel over the telephone to a stranger went something like this: "Hello, I'm in real trouble because by mistake my employees printed 'Lyn' on a ball point pen. They didn't finish it because Lynton Industries canceled the order. So, do you want your name printed on it? You could give it away to customers. I'm in a real jam, can't you help me? This is Saturday, as you know, and I'm paying my help overtime, but I need your okay to finish the order."

You believe in putting on a front to attract clients. As a result enormous sums are spent on a swank office and all the finest equipment money can buy. Your expense account for entertainment is unbelievable. You feel more deals are made at luncheons and dinners than anywhere else: Feed a man, give him some booze, get him a girl, and you've got it made. However, not all transactions are culminated. Many fall by the wayside.

You are a big worrier and your concern over your debts start to mount daily. It seems like you can never get ahead, that there's always some bill to be paid. The cash that comes in seems to drift through your fingers like sand. You throw good money after bad on all those new ventures. Your spending sprees should be curbed. In fact, you should learn how to handle your dough so you don't get into worse messes than you do, especially if a recession occurs.

HOW TO HANDLE YOUR MONEY

Wouldn't you like to stop worrying so much about your bills? Have you ever wondered how you can live it up and yet have money in the bank? Doesn't it bother you that you are so gullible that you fall for all those phony money-making deals? Have you been living high on the hog?

Wouldn't it be nice to avoid financial pinches so you wouldn't have to ask a pal for a loan to tide you over? Is your expense account so high that you have very little money for anything else? Is your cash going out to help a buddy who later turns on you? Have you ever thought all of these circumstances could be avoided?

If you answered "yes" to the preceding questions, these are the areas you've got to work with and change. It's difficult to break habits, but not impossible. If you want to stay out of financial disasters and wind up ahead of the game, it's best you start now instead of putting it off to some future date.

Don't jump into any money-making scheme without having first asked an accountant or lawyer to investigate the background of the person who propositioned you and also have the entire deal checked thoroughly. Don't ask friends, ask only professional experts. Anytime it sounds too good to be true, it could be a con. Think, "If this is so fantastic, why am I being offered this project? Why doesn't the person invest in it himself or herself?" Think logically about what is or is not practical based upon your past experience. Don't believe so much in the flowery words of others, and don't believe that you are going to make such stupendous amounts of money. It's possible, but not always probable. Your sign's keyword is *"I believe"* and that's your downfall because you believe in and trust others entirely too much.

Never bet your entire savings or paycheck on anything. Gamble only what you can afford to lose. If you want to wager on the underdog, choose a strong team you think might actually win the game as well as beat the spread (if you're a "point spread" bettor — and you probably are). Consider your gambling expenses as some form of recreation or entertainment, never bet more than you might spend on some other form of recreation such as going boating for the weekend. One of your problems is that you are always thinking about the fantastic sums you'd like to win, and when you don't, you get disappointed. Instead, keep in mind, "What can I afford to lose?"

Avoid being overly generous. You won't forfeit anyone's love if you tighten your purse strings a little. I know it gives you such pleasure to see the light sparkle in your sweetheart's eyes as you had her/him a gift, but don't do it on a daily basis. She'll/He'll appreciate you more if she's/he's not spoiled and can be surprised every now and then. In fact her/his eyes will dance for joy and that's much better than just a tiny spark of light, isn't it?

Cut down on some of that outlay of cash that goes for expensive jewelry. If you have the dough to spare, go ahead, but why not buy simulated diamonds or other jewelry? Unless a person's got a magnifying glass, he/she won't know the difference. However, if you are investing in it for yourself as a hedge against inflation, that's an entirely different matter. Then, naturally, the genuine article is desired, not a bauble.

If you are in the market to buy a house, watch going overboard on the most spacious and plush place you see. Shop around; make sure the mortgage rates are low and that the purchase won't put you into such a financial bind that your fun has to be curtailed. That alone would be such a downer for you because the pleasures of living are more important than just existing in an unexciting and dull environment.

It's good to put on a front and impress potential clients, but you tend to go to unnecessary excess. If you want all those ornate furnishings, try to get them wholesale. Just because a computer or office machinery has a fancy price, it doesn't mean it's going to give you the service that other cheaper models may give. Be practical and first get an accountant's opinion.

How would you like to make some extra money in your spare time to pay for some of those expensive tastes you have? Your sign rules poetry, so if you feel you're talented in that department, try sending your poems to the various magazines; it's not the big-paying market that you may desire, but you might find it spiritually rewarding.

Try your hand at oil portraits made from photography. Coloring photos can be done from the home with little outlay of legal tender. Sell photo stamps, money, or posters; see if your pals would be interested. Or take photographs on weekends; perhaps a shopping center or department store would let you do your thing as a promotional gimmick for the store. Or make candles in your basement and sell them to stores or friends or peddle them from house to house.

Or perhaps you know a lot of people and through social contacts can get a finder's fee for discovering new businesses, new products, new inventions, new patents, etc. This is a typical Pisces occupation that could bring in some of that big bundle you're looking for. Or if you've found you are extremely psychic, cash in on this gift; give readings to people. If you're accurate, word of mouth can keep you in the chips. And besides, you like helping people.

Be leery of any high-pressure salespeople. The moment anyone talks fast, doesn't let you ask questions, and doesn't give you good answers, investigate the person and his/her claims. If you say you'd like time to think about it, that he/she should call you in a week — you'll probably never hear from the individual again. That's one tip-off that he's/she's just cruising through the area as the tonic seller did in years gone by.

Start a financial plan that will let you enjoy yourself now and, when you are older, or retired, still leave you something to fall back on. Start with a budget: It's a must. Write down your income, how much you need for basic necessities (rent, utilities, telephone), as well as food, medical and dental expenses, life insurance, and transportation to and from work (include car insurance, but not the car payments). Figure out how much is spent on clothing, eating out, entertainment, recreation, and gifts bought throughout the year, including Christmas — these are the areas you can cut down on in order to save money and/or invest it wisely.

Now what about the dough you shell out in loans, credit cards, or charge accounts? List them and pay them off as fast as you can. Cut up and throw out your credit cards; save on interest. Pay cash in the future. However, if it's a business expense account, make sure it's paid on time so you can avoid finance charges.

A traditional and broad guideline you may wish to follow in relation to your take-home pay is: twenty-five percent for housing (telephone, utilities, rent); twenty percent each for loan repayments and food (groceries and food away from home); ten percent for transportation; five percent for dental and medical; and ten percent for clothing and recreation; two percent for life insurance; one percent for miscellaneous; seven percent savings and/or investment. Your gambling money should come out of entertainment or recreation. Never touch your savings.

Don't blow everything on entertainment expense. Keep your allowance down to a minimum. Attend anything that is free: concerts, shows, school plays, sporting events. Or if it is not possible due to the area where you live, go to inexpensive movies, theaters, etc. Go to museums, art galleries, and to hobby, craft, and other exhibits.

Don't splurge on that boat you want; rent if possible. Figure out whether you rent it often enough in a year to justify your purchasing a boat of your own, or whether renting is the cheapest route. Don't overspend on some new hobby that strikes your fancy and that could be given up when you tire of it.

Some Pisces fun areas that are not too costly involve: floating on water, shooting the rapids, water-rafting, swimming, surfing, scuba diving, water skiing, ice- and roller-skating. The skateboard just might be exciting enough for you. Or go dancing: Your sign rules the feet and Pisceans are, generally, great dancers. How about tap, ballet, disco, and ballroom? For those quiet moments, to seek that inner peace that is such a necessity for you, try some yoga. Or do some daydreaming about Utopia, but don't forget to come back to reality to make that "killing" so a recession won't faze you.

YOUR INVESTMENTS

You can benefit by setting aside money now so your future will be secure. Or perhaps you prefer investing in something other than a business. Before you go leaping into any undertaking, though, it would be to your advantage to understand your assets and shortcomings, thereby avoiding pitfalls.

Your Positive Side

A "yes" answer to the following questions indicates that you are expressing harmonious Pisces traits, thus enhancing your chances to gain prosperity: Do you follow your hunches with investments? Did you do extremely well as a result? Have you made many sacrifices in order to save your money and invest in the stock market? If so, were they worth it? Did you make profitable investments by listening to other people's advice? Are you able to perceive when someone is trying to con you into a shady deal? Have you done well by taking risks? Do you live solely off your investments?

Are you aware that you're a speculator from the day one? You've probably been taking chances all your life. It's the thought of that bundle that will allow you to retire to Shangri-La that spurs you on. You are a natural when it comes to taking a risk. Quick profit is your cup of tea. In fact you'd like to make those dollars overnight instead of waiting for thirty days or more.

You are delighted to be a Broadway "angel," aren't you? Or how about that last theatrical production you backed in your hometown? The film industry fascinates you, so you may splurge in this area. When you invest in it, you feel that you have your own little part in the world of make-believe where you can pretend and be whatever you want to be, your dream come true. Generally show business is lucky for you. Why shouldn't it be? Dramatics and theatrics are ruled by your sign!

And options, warrants, and futures were made just especially for you, weren't they? The greater the risk, the larger the return. You use short selling to profit from a falling market. If the stock falls in price, you buy it again at the lower price and return it to the broker you borrowed it from, thereby leaving you with a nice fat profit.

Real estate near the water is difficult for you to turn down. If it's with a view of an ocean, lake or river, you are so enchanted with owning it that you'll buy it at any price. Luckily your ESP guides you correctly. This type of property is good for soothing your emotions and calming you down. Staring at the water seems to transport you to never-never land.

Do you know that the stock market, in general, is ruled by your sign? No wonder you've always been attracted to it. You are a player from the word go. Overnight gains with huge returns are your baby. You manage to wheel and deal with those new-issue and over-the-counter stocks. The small and new corporations give you a spiritual feeling because they are the underdogs you're trying to help. Of course, the quick gains they may bring, at a cheap price, brighten your day even more. You've been fortunate that you've got a good broker who gives you some hot tips.

Your Negative Side

A "yes" answer to the following questions indicates that you're expressing the inharmonious Pisces traits, thus lessening your chances to gain prosperity. Do investments fizzle or fail to yield the returns anticipated? Have you ever invested blindly in real estate? Did you later wish you hadn't? Would you buy an oil well sight unseen? Did you buy enormous shares of stock through a friend's tip? If so, did you lose everything because the company went bankrupt?

Are you easily influenced by the possibilities of quick gains through speculation? Does the reverse usually happen? Did you ever have a stock market broker that embezzled from you as well as from others? If so, did the person escape to another country with the funds? Would you spend every dime you have on something without reading the prospectus carefully? Did you buy a painting at an auction that later turned out to be a fake?

Is it the story of your life to fall hook, line, and sinker for an investment that promises overnight riches? Are you aware that you never learn from your past errors? The gambler in you lives in the world of the imagination. In this fantasy land bygone days are erased and the present is put aside temporarily. And tomorrow is beckoning with promises of gold-paved streets, billowy clouds made of dollar bills, and your own special magic carpet to ride around on as you reach over and touch all this wealth which belongs to you — and you will gladly share it with those in need.

When you wake up all starry eyed and see that you are back in the world of today, you are so disappointed that you shell out every cent you have to take a chance and make those rapturous dreams come true. But when they don't, you retreat once again into an illusory world which is more real than the one you physically exist in.

Sufficient thought is *not* given to the practicality of the areas you invest in; in fact, your sign is known for being a foolish and impractical investor. Therefore you attract losses. Some of your follies result from your penchant for wish fulfillments and your disinclination to concentrate on facts, statistics, reports, and sound judgment.

A margin account allows you the break you need to really make that fortune without much investment on your part. You can speculate on futures contracts for a small deposit, usually about fifteen percent, and take full advantage of the price swings. If you predict correctly you can make a profit on all of the funds invested for only the small down payment. However, when your ESP method of predicting fails, you are wiped out completely.

Next time you have a little cash saved, you decide to try another margin account, only this time you are going to speculate in the oil futures market. You just have a hunch that the price of oil is going to move down by a specific date so you'll sell it short and repurchase it later when it is, hopefully, much lower. However, you haven't been keeping up with world events so you weren't aware of the latest OPEC meeting where prices of crude oil were changed. So by the date of your margin call, the stock has soared to an unbelievable price and you can't meet it. So again you take a beating that wipes you out.

WHAT SHOULD YOU INVEST IN?

"Risky ventures" are the name of your game; but if you want to be a winner more often than a loser, you should stay clear of taking too many chances. To compensate and keep you in constant anticipation of a quick return, your best bet is to follow a diversified policy: short-, intermediate-, and long-term maturation dates with bonds; speculative stocks and blue chips; and roll-over ninety-day Treasury bills and notes.

The thirty-day commercial paper put out by major corporations who want to raise money is something that appeals to you. However, it's not guaranteed, and is consequently risky. You could lose everything from it if the company doesn't have the money to pay off its debt.

Certificates of deposit are short-term debt instruments which can provide very high interest income on short-term investments. They are issued by the bank and are safe — just what you should consider investing in.

High yield bonds offer speculative appreciation potential if the fortunes of the company improve and the bond rises in price to reflect this better outlook. They are a class of mutual fund and the high yields they offer will keep you in a bed of roses. They are risky because some of them are low-rated or even unrated corporate bonds often called "junk bonds." Think twice before investing.

The oil and gas company (ruled by your sign) mutual funds might be worth considering. There is some safety in them. Or perhaps you'd be interested in a no-load (no sales fees) bear and bull fund. You'd be busy with this because you'd be encouraged to switch assets back and forth between the bear and bull fund. In your sign's symbol there are two fish going in opposite directions — one wants to swim upstream and the other downstream — so this bull and bear fund could remind you that you get wishy-washy and want to go in two opposite directions. It will offer some excitement, pep your life up and perhaps your pocketbook, too!

For a safe and secure feeling, perhaps you'd be interested in the money market funds which invest in large-denomination bank certificates of deposit, corporations' short-term debts, and government securities. When prices are rising money market funds are appropriate for the cyclical strategy. They are know as "liquidity funds."

Other safe areas are government funds, which are six- and nine-month bills and notes that are backed up by the government; they pay more interest than certificates of deposit. Investment notes, also called thrift certificates are risky, so think twice with them. Their high yield may attract you. Money market option investments are rather risky, but may also reap above-average gains.

Common and preferred stocks are typical Pisces investments. So are new issues and over-the-counter stocks, options, commodity futures, and any other futures contracts. You find them appealing because of the quick and enormous profits to be made from them — like six thousand dollars a day in the futures market!

Or perhaps you'd want to invest in a stock-and-bond fund. It is aggressive, emphasizes capital gains, and may be risky. These "beta" funds are high and can move up or down more than the general market.

In the collectibles, you're a great fan of Oriental rugs, antiquities, antiques, sculpture, paintings, and contemporary prints such as silk-screens or serigraphs. Perhaps you'd like to invest in the gems your sign rules — pearl and peridot. Or the stones — coral, gravel, pumice, and sand. Buy shares in them, purchase your own mine, dive for pearls, or go into these areas as a business.

A tax shelter with a write-off involving oil and gas drilling or jet-plane leasing would appeal to you. If they are not on the up and up, you'll be audited by the IRS, so check this out carefully with an accountant. Other tax shelter areas are U.S. savings bonds, tax-exempt mutual funds, and deferred annuities. To offset your chances of being in a poor position if a recession occurs, and due to your extremely speculative nature, you need to invest in a financial program designed to provide future security. Perhaps one of these tax shelters is what you are seeking. They are not quite the Utopia you long for, but may help bring you that much closer.

In the foreign-bond market your sign is attracted to the Pisces-ruled country of the Netherlands (Holland) of the city of Toronto (Canada). Perhaps in the foreign-currency market the Canadian dollar appeals to you.

You don't always keep abreast of the trends and of what's happening in the world; therefore you are *not* one step ahead when it comes to investing wisely. Perhaps the advice of an expert could prove beneficial. Or you could start reading the financial newspapers and magazines more often or scan the Internet.

A broker who thinks along the same lines as you may be desirable. Therefore deal with another Pisces, Aries, Gemini, Leo, Scorpio, Sagittarius, or Aquarius. These signs will encourage those calculated risks that you must beware of, but not necessarily follow. They, like you, take chances. So from a strictly financial standpoint they may not be the best signs for you to listen to or be involved with.

You really need a broker who is practical and able to provide the balance you so sorely need. Therefore, consider Capricorn, Taurus, and Virgo. They are the best suited for safe and sound investments. However, you may find Virgo too full of details and statistics. These signs may be too slow to action although you yourself are not always that fast, depending upon where your mind is at the moment; here on earth or wandering.

Cancer and Libra are indecisive and so can you be. But you'll like Cancer's sympathy with and desire for change, and Libra's weighing the pros and cons may be good for you.

If you are lucky you might find a broker who is another Pisces or Aries, Gemini, Leo, Scorpio, Sagittarius or Aquarius Sun sign and this individual *may also have* Taurus, Virgo, or Capricorn as a *dominant* sign in his horoscope. If this occurs you'll have the best of two worlds: one inclined to speculate but using sound judgment.

Astrology can guide you as to the type of bonds your sign should consider investing in. Therefore be on the alert for the Pisces/Neptune-ruled municipal-bonds tax-exempt revenue from hospitals, airports, and port facilities.

Because everything in life has an astrological correspondence, each type of corporate bond, stock, or commodity has a sign/planet that rules it. Therefore, under the Pisces/Neptune influence, invest in manufacturing corporations that produce DDT and other insecticides, poisons, tobacco, drugs, pills, pharmaceutical drugs, patent medicines, rubber, foam rubber, silicone (sealants and greases made from them), artificial products, plastics, paint, turpentine, and tires.

If these areas don't capture your interest, perhaps other Pisces/Neptune rulerships will, so try companies that produce glass, contact lenses, shoes, aerosol sprays (perfume, cleaner, or for the hair), synthetic products (nylon, rayon), submarines, boats, water products (including waterbeds), aquariums, beverages, liquids, soft drinks, air-conditioning, film, water companies (spring, mineral, distilled, soda, carbonated, sparkling), soup (frozen, canned, packaged), gas, oil, or petroleum.

Other Pisces/Neptune-ruled firms on the stock exchange or in corporate bonds may involve neptunium, undersea plants, drug-yielding plants, beneath-the-ocean research, ocean farming laboratories, oceanographic equipment, seaplanes, jets, space capsules, airplanes, aviation, balloons, parachutes, jet leasing firms, the fishing industry, recreational centers, amusement and recreation parks such as Disneyland and Walt Disney World, or other places which deal with fantasy, the circus, motion pictures, the theater, music, or photography.

Other Pisces/Neptune areas are oil-fired utility company stocks or stocks and bonds involving hospitals, scientific laboratories, medical-drug companies, tire retreaders, oil-drilling equipment, oil-producing industry and equipment manufacturing, airborne navigation, barge-fleet operations, helicopters, offshore drilling companies, oil-well equipment supplies, brokerage firms, and any business that deals with promotions and sales as its chief objective.

In the commodity futures market the Pisces/Neptune rulerships are tobacco, nicotine, pharmaceuticals, rubber, orange juice, and petroleum (crude, gasoline, fuel oil).

HOW TO HANDLE YOUR INVESTMENTS

Try to be as conservative as you can with only a few risky ventures. Be leery of new projects and some of those new issues on the stock exchange. Have everything thoroughly checked by an accountant or lawyer and don't be too busy daydreaming to look at the details by studying the company records and statistics.

Because you dislike discipline and nine-to-five hours, you prefer making a buck the easy way without having to work hard for it. Therefore you are vulnerable to all those phony schemes that fall right into your lap. The ideal life for you is to live off of your investments and continue to wheel and deal in them all. However, you should take care that they are all safe and sound.

Beware of land deals in the middle of nowhere that are extremely cheap. These lots may have nothing installed on them but unpaved roads. If you're thinking of buying property in a so-called "sportsman's dream" it could be a waist-deep swamp with no access roads. View the land and have an attorney conduct a title search. Then decide whether you'll shell out any money.

Also, be leery of "London options" as they can be frauds. Options and futures definitely are up your alley as far as the profits are concerned, but they can keep you in the hole if you go overboard with them; and you are the type to do just that. If in the past you've gained through speculation, then continue along these lines; however, if the reverse is true, stay away from this because you are expressing the Pisces traits on their negative side and are likely to get a repeat performance. Abide by this rule with margin accounts or any other area that is known to be risky.

You are psychic, although if you use mostly the negative side of Pisces, you could be off with your psychic impressions. No one is one hundred percent accurate all the time. Keep this in mind when using it to invest by. It's best to stop, think, and analyze the pros and cons of every step you wish to take and seek expert advice.

When you are investing in non-income producing assets, like real estate that is not producing spendable money, then you should also strive to accumulate an equal amount in liquid assets. This liquidity can be bonds, stocks, cash, gold, cash-value life insurance, or even a pension. Perhaps you'd like twenty-five percent of your savings in a savings account, twenty-five percent each in stocks and bonds (especially mutuals), and twenty-five percent for your gambling-fling fund.

Are you a winner or loser? It not only depends upon your Sun sign and how you use it, but also on the influence of Jupiter and Saturn. Jupiter attracts a gain, whereas Saturn attracts a loss. Everyone has these planets in his/her horoscope. But their influence depends upon whether their harmonious or inharmonious side is expressed at the moment a decision is made.

Under the influence of the positive side of Saturn, you are practical, conservative, cautious, serious, contemplative, and make a move only when you are sure the time is ripe. Long-range investments are favored. You use sound judgment, and thus can buy to advantage.

Under the influence of the negative side of Saturn you are pessimistic and cry poverty; you worry, gripe, complain, and have the blues. You are slow because you are afraid of making the wrong move, and thus can attract losses. You lack confidence and chances are if you purchase anything, it could be a real downer.

Whenever you are depressed and feel the Saturn negative traits, avoid investing in anything, because your Saturn is being stimulated in your horoscope at that moment (this could last an hour, a day, a week, a month, a year, or more). If you do invest when this inharmonious energy is being expressed, you are likely to attract a loss.

Under the influence of the positive side of Jupiter you are confident, optimistic, cheerful, easygoing, honest, understanding, happy, and generous. Speculation is favored and brings success. You use sound judgment and can sell to an advantage, write options, buy on margin, and do well all around.

Under the influence of the negative side of Jupiter you are overly confident, too optimistic, wasteful, ostentatious, extravagant, and refuse to take into account prices, expenditures, or the views of others. You are in the mood to do everything to excess. At a party you'd be on center stage making everyone laugh. If you sell an investment when you are in this frame of mind you won't get the price it's worth; your judgment will be off.

Whenever you discover you are using the negative side of Jupiter, don't take a chance with the stock market or any other form of investment. Lie low and wait until the positive side of Jupiter is being expressed, then sell. It'll be worth the wait.

In astrology *buying* is ruled by Saturn and *selling* by Jupiter. Every time you buy under a harmonious Saturn aspect your purchase will be a bargain, a good deal, or investment. Every time you sell under a harmonious Jupiter aspect your sale will be considerable gain. The moment these planets are activated in your horoscope are determined by your time, place, day, month, and year of birth. But you don't need a horoscope to know when you are in a depressed state or happy mood. By being aware of your frame of mind, you'll know how to invest wisely. The moment the negative side of Jupiter, Saturn, or Pisces is expressed, that's the time to watch out for losses; the reverse if true when their positive side is expressed.

Now that you are armed with this information you can invest wisely and be ready for whatever the world economy brings. However, you are one step further ahead than the majority of people because by using this positive energy you can improve your chances to be wealthy.

www.ingramcontent.com/pod-product-compliance
Lightning Source LLC
Chambersburg PA
CBHW051208200326
41519CB00025B/7043